PC Recording Studios

Studios

FOR

DUMMIES®

PC Recording Studios

FOR

DUMMIES®

by Jeff Strong

Wiley Publishing, Inc.

621.3893
STR

PC Recording Studios For Dummies®

Published by
Wiley Publishing, Inc.
111 River Street
Hoboken, NJ 07030-5774

www.wiley.com

Copyright © 2005 by Wiley Publishing, Inc., Indianapolis, Indiana

Published by Wiley Publishing, Inc., Indianapolis, Indiana

Published simultaneously in Canada

For general information on our other products and services, please contact our Customer Care Department within the U.S. at 800-762-2974, outside the U.S. at 317-572-3993, or fax 317-572-4002.

For technical support, please visit www.wiley.com/techsupport.

Wiley also publishes its books in a variety of electronic formats. Some content that appears in print may not be available in electronic books.

Library of Congress Control Number Is Available from the Publisher.

ISBN: 0-7645-7707-7

Manufactured in the United States of America

10 9 8 7 6 5 4 3 2 1

1O/RY/QT/QV/IN

WILEY

About the Author

Jeff Strong is the author of *Home Recording for Musicians For Dummies* as well as *Pro Tools All-in-One Desk Reference For Dummies* and is President of the REI Institute, a MusicMedicine research organization and therapy provider. Jeff graduated from the Percussion Institute of Technology at the Musician's Institute in Los Angeles in 1983, and has either worked in or owned a recording studio since 1985. Every week, he records dozens of custom-client CDs by using the kinds of audio recording software covered in these pages. He has also released eight commercially available CDs, four of which can be found at www.reiinstitute.com.

Author's Acknowledgments

This book wouldn't have happened without the inspiration and vision of Senior Acquisitions Editor Steve Hayes. This is my third book with Steve; this one was just as much fun to do as the first. A hearty thanks to my agent Carol Susan Roth for making sure I get what's coming to me.

Books, by nature, are a team effort — and this book is the result of an extremely talented and dedicated team of professionals: Project Editor Paul Levesque (my partner in crime for the third time), who reminded me what a great editor can do for a writer; Technical Editor Erik Scull, who kept me on the straight and narrow; and Copy Editor Virginia Sanders, whose dry sense of humor put a smile on my face more than once during this process.

I am especially grateful for the love and support of my wife Beth and my daughter Tovah, who never cease to amaze me in their capacity to endure non-stop recording talk.

Publisher's Acknowledgments

We're proud of this book; please send us your comments through our online registration form located at www.dummies.com/register.

Some of the people who helped bring this book to market include the following:

Acquisitions, Editorial, and Media Development

Senior Project Editor: Paul Levesque

Acquisitions Editor: Steve Hayes

Copy Editor: Virginia Sanders

Technical Editor: Erik Scull

Editorial Manager: Leah Cameron

Permissions Editor: Laura Moss

Media Development Manager: Laura VanWinkle

Media Development Supervisor: Richard Graves

Editorial Assistant: Amanda Fox

Cartoons: Rich Tennant (www.the5thwave.com)

Composition Services

Project Coordinator: Adrienne Martinez

Layout and Graphics: Carl Byers, Lauren Goddard, Heather Ryan, Julie Trippetti

Proofreaders: Leeann Harney, Jessica Kramer, Joe Niesen, Carl Pierce, TECHBOOKS Production Services

Indexer: TECHBOOKS Production Services

Publishing and Editorial for Technology Dummies

    Richard Swadley, Vice President and Executive Group Publisher

    Andy Cummings, Vice President and Publisher

  Mary Bednarek, Executive Acquisitions Director

    Mary C. Corder, Editorial Director

Publishing for Consumer Dummies

    Diane Graves Steele, Vice President and Publisher

    Joyce Pepple, Acquisitions Director

Composition Services

    Gerry Fahey, Vice President of Production Services

    Debbie Stailey, Director of Composition Services

Contents at a Glance

Table of Contents

Introduction

*A*s computers have gotten more powerful, they've become the standard tools for recording, editing, and mixing audio. More and more professional studios are using them because of their power — and more and more amateurs are using them because they're also relatively inexpensive and easy to use.

For many people — especially any technophobic musicians out there (you know who you are) — the thought of recording on a computer is daunting. You have to deal with hardware issue (what kind of computer do I get?) and software issue (how do I work this #@*% thing?). Add to this the sometimes-complicated workings of the non-audio computer software and you get a deer-in-the-headlights look from otherwise intelligent, articulate people.

Well, I hear ya. I don't consider myself a techy (although I fear I might be turning into one), and getting up-to-speed when it came to recording into a computer left me scratching my head a few times. Luckily for you, I've stopped scratching my head and have managed to make some semblance of sense out of the whole thing.

About This Book

PC Recording Studios For Dummies is an introduction into the world of computer-based audio recording. This book takes the mystery (and frustration) out of recording into a computer. You discover tips to help you make the process of recording music easy and the final product sound as good as possible.

PC Recording Studios For Dummies gets you going quickly so that you can spend your valuable time recording music — not tweaking your computer settings.

Here's a quick rundown of what you can find in this book:

- ✔ You discover the basic components of a computer-based recording studio.
- ✔ You find out what hardware and software you need.

✔ You get hands-on steps guiding you through the computer-based recording process.

✔ You explore the many powerful add-ons that you can use to take basic tracks and turn them into the music you hear in your head.

✔ You discover free (or really cheap) software that you can use to create your next masterpiece.

The best thing about this book is that you get all this information without the brain-numbing technical jargon and posturing that you find in so many computer-related books. After all, the computer should be a tool that you use to create your art, not an obstacle to it.

Not-So-Foolish Assumptions

As much as I hate to admit this, I made some assumptions about you, the reader, when I wrote this book. Actually, I think you'll be glad I did. First, I assumed you want to record audio into a computer (hence the title: *PC Recording Studios For Dummies*) and I assumed that you aren't a techy but you know the basics about using a computer, such as how to use a mouse, load software, and other rudimentary skills. I also assumed that you have some basic idea of how music is recorded. (If you don't have any idea about what the music-recording process entails, you might want to check out one of my other recording books: *Home Recording For Musicians For Dummies* — that is, if you haven't already read it.)

Aside from these very basic assumptions, I don't assume that you've ever used a computer to record music before or that you even play any musical instrument. If you're a musician, I don't assume that you make a specific type of music. Whether you're making music from the sounds of whales mating or you're composing the next top-ten smash hit, the info in this book is equally relevant. I also assume that when I say "electric bass" you know I'm not referring to a plastic fish singing "Take Me to the River."

How This Book Is Organized

PC Recording Studios For Dummies is organized so that you can find the information that you want quickly and easily. Each part contains chapters that cover a specific aspect of the computer recording process.

Part I: Computer Recording Basics

Part I covers the basics of computer-based recording. Chapter 1 introduces you to the individual components of a computer studio and explains what everything is for. Chapter 2 shows you how to set up a system so that it is easy to work with and sounds good. You also look into how you can set up your studio to sound as good as possible without having to spend a fortune on acoustical treatments.

Part II: Choosing and Installing Computer Hardware

Part II gets into gear talk. Here I focus on the hardware you need to have around if you want to record into your computer. Chapter 3 explores the core of your system: the computer itself. This chapter covers both Mac and Windows systems and shows you what to look for when buying or upgrading your computer. Chapter 4 examines the audio-based hardware you need, such as the audio and MIDI interface and other components that get the sound in and out of the digital domain. Chapter 5 walks you through the process of getting all this hardware hooked up and running properly.

Part III: Choosing and Installing Recording Software

Part III digs into the software that you need if you want to record audio inside your computer. Chapter 6 explains the different functions of audio and MIDI recording programs so you can decide what features you need for your system. Chapter 7 gives you a look into some of the most popular programs used for recording, editing, and mixing your music. Chapter 8 guides you through the process of installing your software into your computer. I cover both Windows XP and Mac OS X. This chapter gives you the settings you need to get you up and running, and you find tips to keep your system stable.

Part IV: Revving Up the Recording Process

Part IV kicks your recording process into high gear. Chapter 9 covers the basics of getting a decent sound from the source and making sure that it stays decent as it enters your computer. Chapter 10 focuses on the specifics of recording and editing audio, and Chapter 11 keys into this same process with recording and editing MIDI (Musical Instrument Digital Interface). Chapter 12 looks at working with loops (short musical snippets that you can use to compose your songs), and Chapter 13 digs into recording with software instruments called soft-synths. Chapter 14 gives you information on mixing and mastering all your tracks within your computer.

Part V: Playing with Plug-Ins

Part V explores the role of plug-ins (software processors that you "plug in" to your instrument tracks) in computer-based recording. Plug-ins are one of the most versatile tools for recording in a computer, and you need to understand them so that you can use them effectively. So, Chapter 15 introduces you to these powerful tools and shows you the basics of using them in your songs. Chapter 16 looks at equalizer plug-ins, which you can use to sculpt the frequencies of your tracks. Chapter 17 examines the process of adding effects — such as reverb and delay — to your recordings. Chapter 18 demystifies dynamics processors and shows you how to use them to add that certain *je ne sais quoi* to the sound of your music.

Part VI: The Part of Tens

A staple of every *For Dummies* book, this Part of Tens contains some chapters to help you along the way. This section contains three chapters: Chapter 19 offers tips to improve the performance of your system and keep it running smoothly. Chapter 20 points you to some Internet resources that I've found to be helpful for rounding out my computer recording knowledge. Chapter 21 lists free (or really cheap) software that you can use when you record.

Icons Used in This Book

As with all *For Dummies* books, I use a few icons to highlight certain information that I feel is especially valuable.

Certain techniques are very important or can come in handy on a regular basis. This icon gives you gentle nudges to put these foremost in your mind.

Throughout the book, I include technical background on certain subjects that isn't necessary but can be useful if you like to know the techier side of things. This icon shows up so that you know to shift mental gears for some dense information.

This icon highlights expert advice and ideas that can help you to produce better recordings.

This icon lets you know when making a wrong move could damage your equipment, your ears, or your song.

Where to Go from Here

I set up this book so that you can either read it cover to cover or jump around and read only those parts that interest you at the time. For instance, if you're getting ready to buy a computer to record on, check out Chapter 3. If you already have a computer and want to know what software to buy, jump to Chapters 6 and 7. If you've set up your hardware and software and you want to see how to add effects to your song, go to Chapter 18.

For the most part, starting at Chapter 1 gets you up to speed on this whole computer-based audio thing and helps you understand where to start down this road.

Part I

Computer Recording Basics

"I laid down a general shuffling sound, over dubbed with periodic coughing, some muted talking files, and an awesome ringing cell phone loop."

In this part . . .

Part I gets you started by introducing you to the basics of computer-based recording. Chapter 1 explores the individual components of a computer studio and shows you what everything is designed to be used for. Chapter 2 helps you set up the physical space in your studio so that you can get the best sound from it.

Chapter 1

Discovering What You Need

In This Chapter

▶ Understanding the components of a computer-based studio

▶ Discovering how each component contributes to the final sound

Whether you use a Windows or Macintosh computer for your home recording studio, your system of choice employs much of the same basic technology. In fact, your simple computer-based studio consists of the same basic components as a typical million-dollar professional studio complex — they're just in a different physical format. For example, instead of the huge mixing board that you see in a commercial studio, you're going to be working with a piece of software in your computer. It might not look as imposing, but it performs the same functions (and then some).

In this chapter, you discover the purpose of each individual component of a computer-based recording studio — and you also discover how each of these components relates to the quality of sound that you ultimately get from your studio. This knowledge will definitely help you when it comes to spending the right amount of money on the right stuff. (See Chapters 3, 4, and 8 for more on purchasing gear.)

 I use the term component pretty broadly in this chapter and include everything you may use in your studio from preamps and microphones that you need to capture the sound to the software you use for editing to the blank CDs you use to store your musical data on.

Looking at the Larger Picture

At first glance, trying to figure out what you need to record your music with a computer can be confusing. Taking a quick look through this chapter will probably reinforce this perspective — at least initially. Before you get a brain cramp trying to figure out the more arcane jargon, here's a short list of what a typical computer-based home studio consists of:

✔ **Audio interface:** The audio interface is a piece of hardware that allows you to get sound from the outside world into your computer. Most audio interfaces contain everything you need to accomplish this task, including preamps, direct boxes, AD and DA converters, and a sound card. Confused by all these components? You won't be for long — as you read this chapter, all these items will start making sense to you. Many types of interfaces are available, each with different features. At least one option will surely meet your particular needs.

✔ **Computer:** This is an obvious one, but it's an item that confuses a lot of people. Of course you know you need a computer to make music with a computer, but the question that always comes up is, "What kind of computer?" I describe the basics of an audio-recording computer later in this chapter and even dedicate an entire chapter to this seemingly innocent question (see Chapter 3).

✔ **Input device:** Input devices include instruments, mics, and any other device that lets you input sound into your computer.

✔ **Mastering media:** The mastering media is where you put your finished music. This can be CDs, or it can be in the form of computer files such as MP3, WAV, AIFF, and others.

✔ **Monitors:** Monitors consist of speakers or headphones. These are important because you need to hear what you're recording or mixing.

✔ **Software:** Music software can vary considerably. You can find simple programs that let you assemble pieces of pre-recorded music (called loops) such as Apple's GarageBand or basic recording programs such as Guitar Tracks Pro by Cakewalk. You can also find more sophisticated programs such as MOTU's Digital Performer or Steinberg's Cubase — ones that allow you to record and mix hundreds of audio and MIDI (Musical Instrument Digital Interface) tracks, software synthesizers, and limitless effects.

Software can also exist in the form of synthesizers, samplers, and digital signal processors (DSPs) such as effect plug-ins.

As you're probably aware, a recording studio can have lots of gear — from a locker full of microphones and roomful of instruments to a pile of electronic gear such as preamps, compressors, mixers, and speakers. All this equipment is seductive, and you could spend all your time fussing with gear and not get any recording done. (In fact, this happens a lot.) Try not to focus too much on the equipment. Instead, put your energy into making music.

As you get more and more involved in recording, you'll find that you can add almost any of the individual components that I describe in this chapter to your existing system to expand and enhance what you can do. For example, even if your audio interface comes with a preamp (or two, or four, or more), you might want to get hold of a dedicated external preamp to improve the sound or create a specific effect from your microphones.

Interpreting Input Devices

All your expensive recording gear is useless if you have nothing to plug in to it. This is where the input device comes into play. An *input device* is, simply, any instrument, microphone, or sound module that produces or delivers a sound to the recorder.

Instruments

Your electric guitar, bass, synthesizer, and drum machines are typical of the instruments that plug in to the interface and represent most of the input devices that you use in your studio. The synthesizer and drum machine can plug directly into the Line In inputs of your interface, whereas your electric guitar and bass need a direct box (or its equivalent) to plug in to first. (Most audio interfaces allow you to plug directly into one of the preamps, so you don't need a separate direct box.)

A *direct box* is an intermediary device that allows you to plug your guitar directly into the mixer without going through your amp first. (For more on direct boxes, see the upcoming section "Deciphering direct boxes.") Check out Figure 1-1 for an example of an instrument-input device.

Figure 1-1: An instrument-input device, which you can plug right into your audio interface.

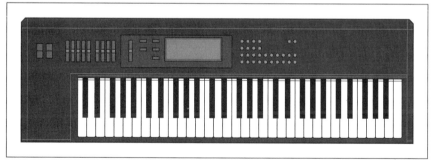

Microphone

A microphone (abbreviated *mic*) enables you to record the sound of a voice or an acoustic instrument — sound sources that, last time I checked, couldn't be plugged directly into the interface. A mic (shown in Figure 1-2) converts sound waves into electrical energy that can be amplified by the preamp and understood by the interface. As you find out in Chapter 3, a lot of different types of mics are available, and choosing the best one for a particular application is like choosing the color of paint to put on a canvas.

Figure 1-2:
A mic.
Use a mic
when your
instrument
can't plug
directly into
your audio
interface.

Sound modules and soft-synths

Sound modules are special kinds of synthesizers and/or drum machines. What makes a sound module different from a regular synthesizer or drum machine is that these contain no triggers or keys that you can play. Instead, sound modules are controlled externally by another synthesizer's keyboard or by a Musical Instrument Digital Interface (MIDI) controller (a specialized box designed to control MIDI instruments). Sound modules have MIDI ports (MIDI jacks) to enable you to connect them to other equipment.

Often sound modules are *rack-mountable,* meaning they have screw holes and mounting ears so that you can put them into an audio component rack. Some controllers, however, are not rack-mountable. Figure 1-3, for example, shows a drum module that rests on a stand or tabletop.

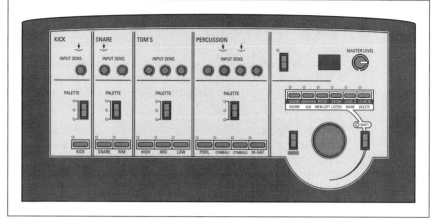

Figure 1-3:
The sound module can be plugged right into the mixer but has to be played by another source.

Soft-synths are software versions of sound modules, housed in your computer as programs. These software programs have no need of external MIDI connections because they're *virtual* sound modules — they live on your computer's hard drive. You just insert them into your recording program as plug-ins.

Examining the Audio Interface

In order to record into a computer, you need a device called an *audio interface*. The audio interface is a piece of hardware that acts as an intermediary between the analog world of your mics and instruments and the digital world of your computer. Traditionally (if there can be traditions in such a new technology), you needed the following pieces of gear:

- ✔ **Sound card:** This card — also called a *PCI card* because it fits in the Peripheral Component Interface (PCI) slot in your computer — allows your computer to read and understand the digital information coming from and going to the converters. Without a sound card, your computer doesn't know what to do with the musical data that it receives (or that your hard drive stores).

- ✔ **Analog-to-digital (AD) and digital-to-analog (DA) converters:** These converters allow you to get the sound from your instrument, direct box, or preamp to the sound card (the AD converter's job) and from your computer back out to your monitors (the DA converter's job).

Nowadays, both the sound card and converters are usually part of the audio interface, so you don't have to buy them separately.

An audio interface also generally contains everything else you need to get your instruments and mic signals into your computer properly. These components include:

- ✔ **Direct box:** A direct box (technically called a Direct Induction Box or DI box for short) lets you plug your guitar directly into your recording device (in this case your computer) without having to go through your amp first.

- ✔ **Microphone preamp:** This is a requirement if you want to plug your mic into your recording device. The preamp amplifies the signal coming from your mic so that it can be recorded.

Audio interfaces have different ways of handling both these components. Some contain preamps that can act as both a microphone preamp and a direct box, but others also have instrument inputs that function like a direct box and allow you to plug guitars directly into them. Most audio interfaces have at least two and as many as eight inputs with preamps. (Chapter 3 shares more on instrument inputs and preamps.)

Audio interfaces come in many varieties — varieties that use one of the three following ways to connect to your computer:

- ✔ **Through a PCI card connected to your computer's PCI slot:** This method is the old standard for getting audio in and out of a computer. PCI-based interfaces come in several varieties, which include the following:

    - Separate sound cards with no analog inputs and outputs.

    - Analog inputs and outputs within the card.

    - Analog inputs and outputs housed in a separate box (called a *break-out box*).

If you want to go the PCI route, make sure that your computer has PCI slots that are compatible with the PCI interface that you're considering. (Not all are; the Digidesign 001, for example, doesn't work in Mac G5 computers.)

- ✔ **Through an interface connected to the USB port:** This method is handy because most computers have at least one USB port. The only problem with USB for recording audio is the relatively slow transfer speed. USB 1.1 generally limits you to two inputs (although you can find some interfaces with as many as six inputs) and two outputs. It also introduces more *latency* — the delay from the audio going in and coming back out of your computer — than the PCI or Firewire (see the next bullet) options. (Dealing with latency definitely adds some steps to the recording process; I spell out the steps for overcoming this problem in Chapter 10.)

USB 2.0–compatible interfaces are just beginning to hit the market. USB 2.0 offers a much faster transfer rate than USB 1.1, so the limited input and latency issues won't be a problem in the not-too-distant future (assuming you have both a computer and USB audio interface that function with USB 2.0).

✔ **Through your FireWire port:** FireWire is preferable to USB because the transfer speed is fast enough to keep latency down to a minimum. FireWire ports are inexpensive and available on laptop computers as well as desktop ones, which makes Firewire interfaces more versatile than PCI-based systems.

Because you have so many audio interface options to choose from, I detail what to look for in Chapter 3.

Singling out a sound card

A sound card is necessary for your computer to be able to record or playback digital audio data. All computers come with a basic sound card, but for recording music you most likely need to get a better one. Keep in mind, though, that buying a soundcard separately isn't your best option because you'll still need to get the AD and DA converters and other components that are included in an audio interface. And all audio interfaces come with a (usually pretty good) soundcard so a separate sound card isn't necessary.

Examining AD and DA converters

When you play your instrument or sing into a mic, the *signal* that you're producing is an analog one. It consists of electrical impulses representing sound waves. In order for you to record, store, or playback these impulses in your computer, you need to convert these impulses into and out of digital bits. (You know, 1s and 0s.) You do this with AD and DA converters.

The quality of the sound of your recordings is hugely influenced by the quality of your sound card and converters. Because this is such an important part of the recording puzzle, I explain the intricacies of digital audio conversion, recording, and playback in Chapter 3. (I make it easy to understand, I promise.) Before you go out and buy an audio interface, I highly recommend that you read Chapter 3.

Deciphering direct boxes

A direct box (or DI box, short for *Direct Induction*) is traditionally used to connect your guitar or bass directly into the mixer without having to run it through your amp first. A direct box's purpose is twofold: to change the guitar's impedance level (a guitar has a high impedance, and a mixer has a low impedance) so it matches your mixer to create the best sound possible, and to change the nature of the cord connection from unbalanced (quarter-inch) to balanced (XLR) so you can use a long cord without creating noise. (For more on cord types and balanced signals versus unbalanced signals, go to Chapter 5.)

Because you're unlikely to need a long run of cords from your guitar to your mixer (the main reason for going from an unbalanced to a balanced connection), your main purpose in using a direct box is to act as an impedance transformer (it changes your guitar's signal from high to low impedance). Without a direct box changing your impedance levels, your guitar signal might sound thin or have excess noise.

Depending on how many mics and guitars you want to plug in to your audio interface (and depending on which interface you have), you might not need to buy a separate direct box. Most audio interfaces have inputs that can handle any and all impedance-transforming chores associated with the signal from your guitar or bass. These are usually the inputs with the preamps already built in. (See the next section.)

Perusing the preamp

Microphones produce a lower signal level than do line-level devices (synthesizers, for example); thus they need to have their signal level increased. For this purpose, you need a *preamp,* a device that boosts a mic's output. Preamps can be internal or external, meaning they could reside within your audio interface or exist as a separate unit that you plug in between your mic and audio interface.

The preamp is one of the most crucial elements of a recording system. It can affect your instrument's sound significantly. Most professional recording studios have a variety of preamps to choose from, and engineers use a particular preamp based on the type of sound they're trying to capture.

The three basic types of preamps available are solid-state, tube, and hybrid.

Solid-state

Solid-state preamps use transistors to boost the level of the mic or instrument. Top-quality (expensive) solid-state preamps are generally designed to produce a sound that's clear and accurate (GML and Crane Song brands, for instance). Solid-state preamps can also be designed to add a pleasing distortion to the music (Neve, API, and Neve-clone preamps, for example). Many recording professionals prefer the clear and accurate sound of a solid-state preamp for acoustic or classical music or any situation when capturing a very natural sound is important. The preamps in your audio interface are solid-state — though certainly not as high a quality as many of the more expensive external preamps — and are usually designed to more on the "clean sound" side of the spectrum, rather than the "pleasingly distorted" side.

Tube

Since the beginning of the digital recording revolution, professionals have been complaining about the harshness of digital recording. As a result, many digital-recording pros prefer classic *tube* preamps because they can add warmth to the recording. This warmth is actually a distortion, albeit a pleasing one. All-tube preamps are generally very expensive, but they're highly sought after among digital recording aficionados because of their sound. Tube preamps work well with music when you want to add color to the sound (for example, adding some distortion to your sound source or enhancing certain pleasing tones in your instrument). No wonder they show up a lot in rock and blues — and they're great for recording drums. You can also find tube preamps that are clean and open, such as those made by Manley Labs.

Hybrid

A *hybrid* preamp contains both solid-state and tube components. Most of the inexpensive tube preamps that you find in the marketplace are actually hybrids. (These are also called *starved-plate* designs, because the tubes don't run the same level of voltage as expensive tube designs.) These types of preamps are usually designed to add the classic tube warmth to your instrument's sound. How much the sound is colored by the tubes — and how pleasing that colored sound is to the listener's ears — depends on the quality of the preamp. Most hybrid preamps allow you to dial in the amount of *character* (pleasing distortion) that you want. You won't find a hybrid preamp that sounds as good as a great (or even pretty decent) solid-state or tube preamp, but you might find one that works well enough for your needs.

Your audio interface comes with a limited number of solid-state preamps (usually two to four, but sometimes as many as eight). If you want to plug in more mics than the number of preamps you have or if you want to be able to produce different sounds from your preamps, you need to buy one or more external preamps, such as the one shown in Figure 1-4.

Figure 1-4: An external preamp.

Clueing In to the Computer

No matter which platform of computer you choose, Mac or PC, the stuff you find inside your computer plays a major role in determining how smoothly (or how less-than-smoothly) your computer recording system runs. (Chapter 3 details the best computer setups for audio.)

To set up a computer to record audio properly, you need several things:

- ✔ **A computer** (Preferably with a speedy processor.)
- ✔ **Bunches (BIG bunches) of memory** (The words *too much* don't apply.)
- ✔ **Dual hard drives** (One just won't cut it.)
- ✔ **An audio interface** (See the "Examining the Audio Interface" section earlier in this chapter and also see Chapter 4.)
- ✔ **The software** (See the "Signing On to Software" section later in this chapter and also see Chapter 3.)

The following list clues you in on the various pieces of hardware that you find in your computer:

- ✔ **The CPU:** The CPU (processor) is the heart of your computer studio. The speed of your CPU ultimately dictates just how well any program runs on it. As a general rule, for audio, get the fastest processor that you can afford. For most audio software, you need *at least* a Pentium III for the PC or a G3 for Mac. If you can afford it, get a *dedicated* computer — one that you have specifically set aside for recording audio — because running other types of applications (such as home finance, word processors, or video games) can cause problems with your audio applications and reduce the stability of your system.

- ✔ **Memory:** Computer-based audio programs and all their associated plug-ins are RAM (random access memory) hogs. My advice: Get a lot of RAM. Okay, that's not very specific, but how much you really need depends on your recording style. If you do a lot of audio tracks and want reverb or some effect on each track, you need more RAM (and a faster processor).

Many recording software programs recommend a minimum of 384MB of RAM, but you should really get a lot more. And I mean a *lot* more. At least a gigabyte, but you can never have too much. Also, don't skimp on the quality of the RAM you use. Cheap RAM is worse than no RAM at all, so I recommend that you buy name brand RAM.

Regardless of the platform you choose (PC or Mac), keep in mind that you can never have too fast a processor or too much memory.

✔ **Hard drives:** To record audio, be sure you get the right type of hard drives. Notice how I said hard *drives* (plural). Yep, you should get more than one if you want to record more than a few tracks of audio. You want one hard drive to hold all the software and the operating system — and *another* drive just for the audio data. Having two greatly increases the likelihood that your system remains stable and doesn't crash on you, especially if you try to run 16 or more tracks.

As for the size of the hard drive, bigger is better, at least in the audio drive where you store your music. For the core system drive, you can get by with a 10GB (gigabyte) drive; for the audio, 20GB is still pretty conservative because audio data can take up a ton of space. For example, a 5-minute song that has 16 audio tracks recorded at a 24-bit resolution and 44.1-kHz bandwidth would take up about 600MB of hard drive space (that's about 7.5MB per track minute).

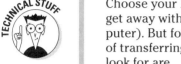

Choose your hard drives wisely. For the software hard drive, you can get away with a stock drive (usually the one that comes with your computer). But for the audio, you need a drive that can handle the demands of transferring audio data at high speed. The main things you want to look for are

- **Spindle speed:** Also called *rotational speed,* this is the rate at which the hard drive spins. For the most part, a 7,200 rpm (rotations per minute) drive works well for recording and playing back audio.

- **Seek time:** This is the amount of time the drive takes to find the data stored on it. You want an average seek time under 10 ms (milliseconds).

- **Buffer size:** Often called *cache buffers,* these memory units store data as it's being transferred. You want a buffer size of at least 2MB.

The track count that your system can handle is directly related to the speed of your hard drive — the faster the drive, the more tracks you can record and play back at once. (Of course, the type of drive you get determines how large a role your processor plays.) My current choice for a drive is a Maxtor 7,200 rpm ATA IDE drive with an 8.5 ms seek time and 2MB cache buffer. A 100GB drive currently costs around $100.

Signing On to Software

One thing I guarantee is that you won't have a hard time finding a piece of software that meets your musical needs. Heck, I'll even go so far as to guarantee that choosing the best software among the plethora of options won't be easy. I'm sorry if this bursts your bubble, but someone had to say it. Yep, the options for audio are endless. (Well, almost endless.) Even though I explore audio software in detail in Chapters 7 and 8, here's a quick rundown on the basic components of audio recording software:

- ✔ **The mixer:** The mixer lets you adjust the level (volume) of your instruments, route your signals where you want them, and add effects or other digital signal processing to your tracks. The mixer is one of the most important pieces of gear in a recording studio — even a computer-based one. All audio recording software contains a mixer.

- ✔ **The arranger:** The arranger is where you can organize your musical ideas. All audio recording software has some sort of arrange function.

- ✔ **The editor:** One of the best things about computer-based recording is that you can generally do sophisticated editing of the audio data. The editing capabilities of the many software programs vary considerably. Some — such as Pro Tools — have very powerful audio editing while others — can you say "Logic Pro" — have very powerful MIDI editing.

- ✔ **MIDI sequencer:** MIDI (short for Musical Instrument Digital Interface — a communication protocol for musical instruments) is often part of audio recording software and — like editing capabilities — the MIDI capabilities in the different programs vary. Pro Tools, for example, is known for having rudimentary MIDI capabilities, whereas SONAR and Logic Pro have powerful MIDI features.

- ✔ **Digital signal processor:** Digital signal processing (DSP) is anything you do to the sound of your audio data other than adjust the volume. This includes equalization, dynamics processing, and effects processing (and many other kinds of tweaks).

Meeting the mixer

The mixer is the heart of any recording system. Although the mixer might seem daunting with all its knobs, buttons, sliders, and jacks — take a look at Figure 1-5 to see what I mean — it's really one of the most interesting and versatile pieces of equipment in your studio. With the mixer, you can control the volume level of the incoming signal, adjust the tonal quality of an instrument, blend the signals of two or more instruments together, and a host of other things. And don't worry; as you read through this book, you get the hang of all those knobs in no time.

For the computer-based home recordist (that's you), the mixer is incorporated into your computer software. (Of course, you can always use an external hardware mixer if you want, but it's not necessary.)

The mixer in all the audio recording software programs does the job well enough that you don't need an external mixer, although some people prefer having physical faders and knobs to mess with. If you're a knob-turner and like to physically touch the instrument you're playing (or, for that matter, the gadget you're tweaking), I heartily recommend that you get a dedicated computer-control surface, such as the Mackie Control (shown in Figure 1-6). A *computer-control surface* is a unit that lets you get your knobs and faders while still using the internal mixer in your recording software. This can be an advantage because it eliminates the need for lots of analog-to-digital conversions (ADCs) and digital-to-analog conversions (DACs). (And that's not counting the actual converters, which can cost a lot of money.) On the other hand, if you prefer clicking a mouse or typing on a keyboard (the kind with letters on the keys), choose a software version.

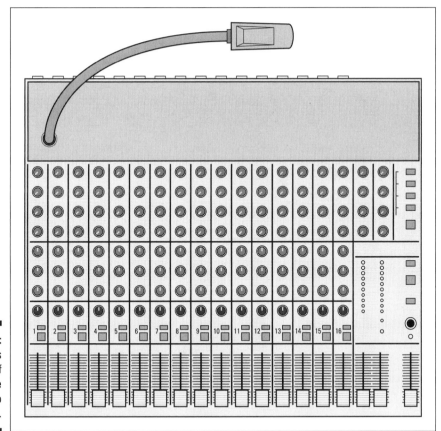

Figure 1-5:
The mixer is the heart of your home studio system.

Figure 1-6:
A computer-control surface offers you real knobs and faders and still uses the mixer that's part of your software.

Accessing the arranger

Audio software makes arranging your musical ideas very easy. Usually with just a click-drag of your mouse you can move sections of data around. Figure 1-7 shows a screen shot of a typical arrangement window. From this window you can perform any number of functions, including trying alternate arrangements for your song; taking the best parts of your performances and placing them exactly where you want them; and countless others.

Exploring the editor

Being able to make miniscule edits to your recorded performances is one of the reasons many people want to record on a computer. Between the usually large video monitor that most people have and the functions of most audio recording programs, editing is a breeze. Check out Figure 1-8 for a look at the editing window for a popular brand of software. From this window you can improve the quality of your music dramatically with the help of a few editing tricks — getting rid of unwanted noise (those darned chair squeaks, for example) or fixing the occasional bad note in an otherwise inspiring performance, to name a few. Of course the downside is editing too much and sucking the life out of a performance, but you wouldn't do that (would you?). Chapter 6 talks about editing capabilities in some of the more popular brands of software, and Chapter 11 explores how to use these capabilities with your music.

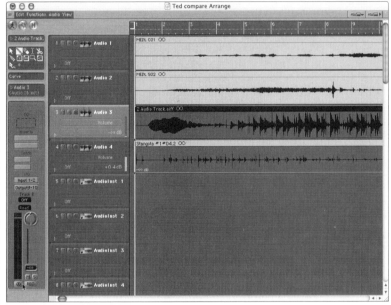

Figure 1-7:
An arrangement window in audio software programs lets you perform many useful functions.

Figure 1-8:
Editing in audio software programs makes it easy to fix problems with your performances.

Managing the MIDI sequencer

A MIDI sequencer is where you can record MIDI performance data into your computer for playback and editing. MIDI sequencing allows you to record your performance and choose the sound that accompanies it later on. The MIDI data that you record is simply performance information, such as when a note is played, the velocity (volume) of the note, and when the note was released, to name a few.

MIDI (Music Instrument Digital Interface) is a protocol that musical instrument manufacturers (in a rare moment of cooperation) developed to allow one digital instrument to communicate with another. MIDI uses binary digital data, in the form of 1s and 0s, to tell an instrument to play or release a note, to change sounds, and a host of other messages. Chapter 4 explains more about the other gear you need to do MIDI in your studio, and Chapter 11 lays out how to use MIDI for your musical ideas.

Most audio recording software contains some sort of MIDI sequencing capabilities. Some are fairly simple and let you record, playback, and edit the data, but others offer much more advanced features that let you work with the data in intricate ways. Check out Figure 1-9 to see a couple MIDI windows in a MIDI powerhouse program.

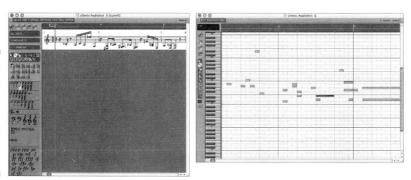

Figure 1-9:
MIDI is easy
to use in
most audio-
recording
software
programs.

Digging into digital signal processors (DSPs)

Part of the recording process involves making adjustments to a sound either before or after it's been recorded. This is the job of the *signal processor.* Signal processors come in three varieties — equalizers, dynamic processors, and effects processors. They can be incorporated into the system or work as separate, standalone units. For most home recordists, the signal processors of choice are integrated into the software as plug-ins, although you can also use external processors by sending the audio out of your computer and back in again.

Equalization (EQ)

Equalizers enable you to adjust the frequencies of a sound in a variety of ways. In effect, you tell the frequencies to

- ✔ **Go away:** You can get rid of unwanted noise or an annoying ringing by reducing select frequencies.

- ✔ **Come hither:** Add *life* or *presence* to an instrument by bringing the best characteristics of that instrument forward.

- ✔ **Scoot over:** You can make room within the frequency spectrum for each of the instruments in your mix by selectively boosting or cutting certain frequencies.

You can find out more about EQ (and discover some great EQ tips and tricks) in Chapter 16. The three main types of EQ are graphic, shelf, and parametric. Here's the rundown:

Graphic EQ

Use *graphic equalizers* to choose a specific frequency to increase or decrease by a certain amount, generally up to 6 or 12 decibels (dB). Doing so enables you to eliminate an offending frequency from the signal or make other adjustments to the tonal quality of the source signal. The graphic EQ will have a certain number of frequency bands that you can adjust. You're limited to only those frequency bands that your EQ has available. Figure 1-10 shows a typical graphic EQ.

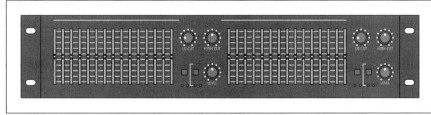

Figure 1-10:
A graphic
equalizer.

Shelf EQ

A *shelf equalizer* affects a range of frequencies above or below the target frequency. Shelf EQs are generally used to *roll off* the top or bottom end of the frequency spectrum. For example, you can set a shelf EQ to roll off the frequencies below 250 Hz (hertz) to reduce the amount of *rumble* (low-frequency noise) in a recording. You can see how this looks in Figure 1-11. Notice how the shelf EQ gradually reduces the amount of energy (sound) below the set point and then levels off: hence, the *shelf* in its name.

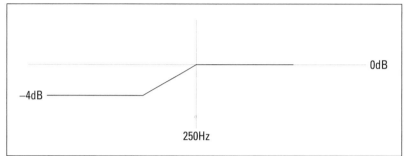

Figure 1-11:
A shelf equalizer works this way.

Parametric EQ

The *parametric equalizer* enables you to choose the specific frequency that you want to affect, as well as the range of frequencies to put around that frequency. With a parametric EQ, you dial in the frequency that you want to change, and then you set the range (referred to as the Q) — that is, the number of octaves that the EQ will affect. Check out Figure 1-12: The two diagrams show how the Q relates to the range of frequencies affected. (The higher the Q setting, the narrower the band of frequencies affected.)

The beauty of a parametric EQ is that you can take a small band (range) of frequencies and add or cut them. Doing this allows you to get the various instruments in a mix to fit in with one another (called *carving out frequencies*). For example, a lot of times the bass guitar gets lost behind the booming frequencies of the kick drum (200–500 Hz). By setting the Q to cover this frequency range and setting the level at about –6dB (reducing by 6 decibels), you effectively make room for the bass guitar to be heard in the mix.

You'll find that the parametric EQ is one of your most useful tools when mixing all your individual tracks into a stereo pair (part of the mixing process covered in Chapter 14). I describe this tool in detail in Chapter 16.

Dynamic processors

Dynamic processors are devices that regulate the amount of sound (energy) that passes through them. This amount is defined as the *dynamic range* — the range between the softest sound and the loudest sound. Dynamic processors come in three varieties: *compressors/limiters, gates,* and *expanders.* I explain each variety in the following sections.

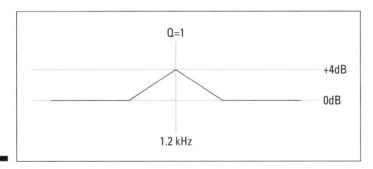

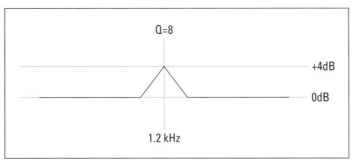

Figure 1-12:
A parametric
equalizer
in a digital
system. Top:
Using a
small Q.
Bottom:
Using a
large Q.

Dynamic processors are useful in a variety of ways. Use them to

✔ Control the signal going into the mixer and recorder.

✔ Tame the levels and correct the effects of an erratic musical performance when mixing.

✔ Optimize the levels of the finished stereo tracks when mastering — the final step in making your music. (Chapter 14 covers mastering in greater detail.)

Dynamic processors are some of the most useful tools that you have in your home studio. See Chapter 18 for more on dynamic processors.

Compressors/limiters

The compressor's job is to compress the dynamic range of the sound being affected. The purpose of the compressor is to eliminate *transients* (unusually loud notes) that can create *clipping* (digital distortion). The compressor limits not only how loud a note can be, but it also reduces the difference between the loudest and softest note (compressing the dynamic range).

Compressors are used extensively on vocals; the device keeps transients at bay by gently reducing the highest level that goes through it. Compressors are also used in mastering to raise the overall volume of a song without creating distortion. The device does this by reducing the overall dynamic range, and as a result, a compressor effectively raises the volume of the softer notes without allowing the louder notes to be too loud and distorting.

A *limiter* works much like the compressor, except that it severely limits the highest level of a sound source. The limiter is basically a compressor on steroids: It gives you beefed-up control over volume. Any signal above a certain level, called the *threshold,* gets chopped off rather than compressed (as with the compressor). A limiter is a good choice in extreme situations, such as when you want a really in-your-face snare drum sound. In this instance, the limiter essentially eliminates any dynamic variation from the drummer's snare drum hits and makes them all as loud as possible.

Gates

A *gate* is basically the opposite of the limiter. Rather than limiting how loud a note can get, the gate limits how *soft* a note can get. The gate filters out any sound below a certain setting (the threshold) while allowing any note above that threshold to be heard.

Recordists often use gates on drums to keep unwanted sounds from the cymbals from bleeding through to the tom-tom or snare drum mics, or on guitars by refusing to allow the noise generated by guitar effects to be heard when the instrument isn't playing.

Expander

The *expander* is basically the opposite of a compressor — instead of *attenuating* (reducing the volume of) the loudest notes in a performance, an expander attenuates the softest notes. For example, if you have a singer whose breath you can hear in the mic and you want to get rid of that particular blemish, just set the expander to go on at a level just above the annoying breath sounds, and it will subtly drop out the offending noise.

Effects processors

Effects are historically used to mimic real-world situations. As a home recordist, you'll likely discover a great affinity toward your effects processors because they enable you to create sonic environments without having to rent some great recording room. For example, imagine dragging your drums and all your recording equipment into a large cathedral, setting them up, and spending several hours getting the mics placed just right. Sounds like a lot of work, right? (I get tired just thinking about it.) Well, how about recording your drums in your modest home studio and simply choosing the "cathedral hall reverb" patch instead? Now that's much easier.

I can practically guarantee that you'll use effects processors all the time in your studio. Scope out Chapter 17 for how to use them effectively.

In the world of effects processors, you have many choices, and many more show up every year. The most common effects processors are (in no particular order) reverb, delay, chorus, flanger, and pitch correction. Read on for the lowdown on each type.

Reverb

Reverb is undoubtedly the most commonly used effects processor. With reverb, you can make any instrument sound as if it were recorded in almost any environment. Reverb, a natural part of every sound, is the result of the sound bouncing around inside a room. The larger the room, the more pronounced the reverb. The purpose of a reverb in audio production is to make an instrument sound more natural (especially because most instruments are recorded in small, non-reverberant rooms) or to add a special effect. Reverb can make almost any recorded instrument sound better — if used correctly.

Delay

Think of delays as the recording studio's version of an echo. The delay can be set to happen immediately after the original sound or be delayed much longer. Delay can sound natural or be used as a spacey special effect. You can have a single echo or multiple delays (very common with the snare drum in reggae music, for instance). Delays are commonly used on vocals and guitar, although you can hear them on just about any instrument, depending on the style of music.

Chorus

A chorus effect can make one instrument sound like several. Chorus effects add very-slightly-off-tune versions of the unaffected sound, which results in a fuller sound. You find chorus effects used on vocals, guitars, and lots of other melodic instruments.

Flanger

A flanger (pronounced *flanj*-er) effect is similar to a chorus effect in sound except that the flanger gets its sound from *delaying* part of the affected sound in relation to the original, rather than altering its pitch. Recordists sometimes use flangers on background vocals and solo instruments to add an interesting texture. This is a unique sound that you recognize almost immediately upon hearing it.

The flanger effect comes from the early days in recording. You create the flanger effect the old-fashioned way by using a two-track recorder to record a duplicate track of the track that you want to flange. You then play the two identical parts back at the same time and gently press against the edge of the two-track tape (the one with the duplicate part) while it's running. This delays certain parts of the sound slightly and drastically changes the character of the instrument.

Nowadays, you can just choose the flanger patch (sound) on your effects processor to get this sound. Isn't technology great?

Pitch correction

Pitch correction, like its name suggests, is used to correct an out-of-tune note. You can use this effect to help a singer or an instrument player sound better by fixing those notes that are slightly out of tune. Pitch correction (also called *auto-tune*) has gotten a bad rap lately (mainly from its overuse and potential for abuse with a singer who can't sing in key). When used sparingly and appropriately, pitch correction can make an otherwise decent vocal performance really shine. It can also be used to create some interesting effects, such as that robotic vocal sound that you hear on so many of the pop songs on the radio nowadays. An easily distinguished example would be the lead vocal on Cher's "Believe."

Monitors

To record and mix music, you need to be able to hear it. (Hey, obvious facts need love, too.) Monitors make this happen. You can use headphones or speakers as monitors; most home studios use both. Monitors are an essential part of a recording studio because you need to get what you're recording and mixing into your ears for you to make sure that it sounds good.

Without good speakers, you won't know what your mixes are going to sound like on other speakers. (Find out more about mixing in Chapter 14.)

Headphones

Chances are that your first home studio will be in a spare bedroom or a corner of your garage or basement. All your recording, monitoring, and mixing will be done in this room. If that's the case, you'll find that a set of headphones is indispensable. When you use headphones, you can turn off your speakers and still hear what's being (or has been) recorded. When you go to record a guitar with a mic in front of the guitar amp, you want to hear only the guitar — not the guitar amp *and* the guitar amp coming back through your monitors. A good pair of headphones will allow you to do this. (See Figure 1-13.)

Figure 1-13:
Studio
headphones.

Speakers

For most home recordists, the first set of monitors consist of the home stereo system, but sooner or later you're gonna want a real set of monitors. Studio monitors come in many varieties, but the home recordist's best bet is a set of near-field monitors. *Near-field monitors* are designed to be positioned close to you (which is often the case anyway because most home recordists have very little room in which to work).

Near-field monitors come with or without an amplifier. The amplified monitors are called *active monitors,* and the non-amplified monitors are referred to as *passive monitors.* Which type of monitor you choose depends on your budget and whether you like the idea of the amp coming with the speakers or prefer to purchase the amp separately. Figure 1-14 has a picture of an active near-field monitor. The amplifier is located inside the speaker cabinet.

Figure 1-14:
An active
near-field
monitor: The
amplifier is
located
inside the
speaker
cabinet.

If you end up getting passive monitors, you need to buy an amplifier to send power to the speakers. The amplifier connects to the outputs of the mixer and boosts the signal to the speakers. A good power amp should be matched in power to work well with whatever speakers you have.

Mastering Media

After you mix your music, you need to put your final music on something. The two most common media for home recordists are CDs and raw computer files. Which medium you choose depends on what your goals are. For instance, if you intend to send your finished mix out to a mastering house, you're better off saving it as raw audio data in a computer file. On the other hand, if you master your music yourself and just want to have it duplicated (or you want to give copies for your friends to play), you would want to use a CD.

CD

With the cost of CD-R (write) and CD-RW (rewrite) drives plummeting, CD mastering is the only choice for most home recordists. With CDs, you can back up large amounts of data at a very low cost and burn audio CDs that can play in any CD player. You can even send out your mastered CD to be duplicated and packaged for retail sale. (Chapter 14 explains the process for burning CDs.)

Computer files

Sometimes you won't want to master your music directly to CD. You might decide to have a professional mastering house do it, or maybe you want to put your music on the Internet. In those situations, store your recordings as computer files. The following sections describe the most commonly used file formats for storing recorded music.

WAV and AIFF

WAV and AIFF (*A*udio *I*nterchange *F*ile *F*ormat) files are the formats for audio files found with most professional audio software. The advantage to saving your music to WAV or AIFF is that when you hand over a CD containing your WAV and/or AIFF files to a mastering house, the recorded sound is actually in a higher-quality format than that of the finished CD (provided your recorder records in 20 or 24 bit, which most do). You can also take your music files to any other studio that supports these file formats and work with them there.

MIDI

A MIDI file isn't an audio file; rather, it's a data file that contains MIDI information that can be transferred from one computer to another. An advantage to MIDI files is that they take up less room than an audio file. The disadvantage is that they contain only the MIDI information and no sound. To play a MIDI file, you have to have a sound module. And the sound you get from the file depends entirely on what sound source you use, such as the particular keyboard or soft-synth.

MP3

MP3 is a file format that has become quite popular on the Internet. Its advantage over audio CDs and other computer files is that it takes up less room. Its disadvantage is that the data is compressed, and the sound quality isn't nearly as good as that of commercial CDs (contrary to what MP3 proponents claim).

Chapter 2

Setting Up Your Recording Space

In This Chapter

▶ Creating an efficient space in which to work

▶ Making your room sound good

Making great-sounding recordings requires many things: good music and musicians, decent gear, solid engineering skills, and a room that sounds good. Let me repeat that last one because this is the most overlooked aspect of making great-sounding music for home recordists — a decent-sounding room. Although most professional studios spend tons of money on making their rooms sound great, you don't have to (as if you could). With a little elbow grease, some rudimentary carpentry skills, and the tips contained in this very chapter, you can make whatever room you set up as your recording space sound pretty decent. In fact, the ideas and strategies I offer here can make your room sound as good as a professionally-designed studio (well, almost). Because it's unlikely that your room is perfect for all your recording needs, I also offer some ideas to get great sounds without the big budget found in professional circles.

Professional studios also take great care to create an environment that is conducive to working efficiently. Most home recordists, on the other hand, put their computer in the corner of a bedroom, hook up a mic or instrument, and call it a studio.

The "pile it up in a corner and call it a studio" approach isn't the only way to go. In this chapter, I help you set up your space so that it has the ergonomic feel that's needed to get a lot done (and get a lot done quicker). Regardless of whether you set up in your bedroom, in your basement, or in the corner of your living room, you'll be able to work as efficiently as possible.

Preparing Your Room

Whether your studio is in the corner of your bedroom, in a spare room, a basement, or a garage, getting it set up so that you can work there efficiently will save you tons of time and aggravation down the road. This section offers some tips for getting the most out of the limited space that you have available. (I'm assuming your space is limited. I know mine is — it seems that no matter how much I have I still don't have enough.)

Creating an efficient working environment

I hope you'll spend a great number of hours in your studio creating some excellent music (possibly to the dismay of the rest of your family). One important thing to keep in mind is that you need to be comfortable.

Setting up your workstation

First, get a good chair and set up your workstation to be as easy to get around as possible. Figure 2-1 shows a classic *L* setup. Notice that everything you need is within arm's reach. If you have enough room, you might want to consider a U-shaped setup instead. You can see that in Figure 2-2.

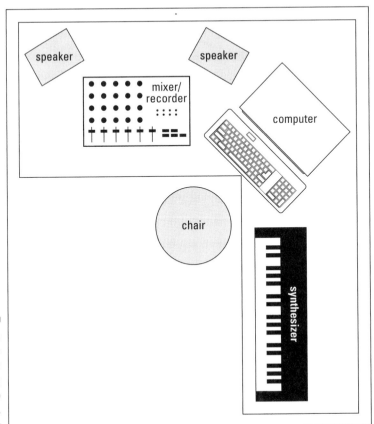

Figure 2-1:
A classic
L setup:
Everything
is easy to
reach.

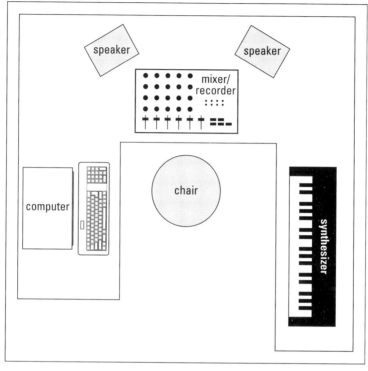

Figure 2-2:
The U-
shaped
setup works
great if you
have the
room for it.

Monitoring your monitor placement

If you have a set of *near-field monitors* — the kind that are designed to be placed close to you — set them up so that they're the same distance from each other *and* from you, at a height that puts them level with your ears. Figure 2-3 illustrates the best placement for your monitors. Placing your monitors this way ensures that you hear the best possible sound from them and can accurately hear the stereo field. (For more on the stereo field, see Chapter 14.)

Working efficiently

Aside from creating a basic equipment layout that works for you, here are some additional things to consider when setting up your studio (and working in it):

 ✔ **Get organized.** Spend some time finding (or creating) places for all your gear and put the gear in those places. Make labels for items like mic and instrument cords (colored tape or tags work well).

✔ **Eliminate distractions.** Turn off the phone, get off the Internet, close the door, and don't answer if anyone knocks. These are a few of the many things you can do to get rid of distractions that will inevitably pop up when you try to do some work in your studio.

✔ **Keep essential gear handy.** For example, I record a lot of drums (and I mean a *lot*), and they need to be miked properly to get the best sound. Because I'm also composing as I work, I keep several mics up on stands and plugged in so that if I'm inspired to lay down a bodhran part all I have to do is grab the drum off a rack, get in front of the right mic, make a minor adjustment to the preamp level (and turn on phantom power to power up the mic if it's not already on), and play. Compare this sequence with having to dig around for the right mic, locate a cord, plug it in to the mic, find a stand and attach the mic to it, connect the cord to the preamp, dial in the preamp level, adjust the mic placement, readjust the preamp level, and so on.

✔ **Distinguish between the producing, engineering, and creating tasks.** Because most home recordists take on all these roles in their studios, you need to be diligent in keeping tabs on which one you perform at a given time. For example, on some days you want to work out ideas for your next song. On these days, take off your engineering hat and stop tweaking knobs. If you don't, before you know it the time you set aside for working out ideas has been spent, and all you have to show for it is a perfectly dialed-in preamp.

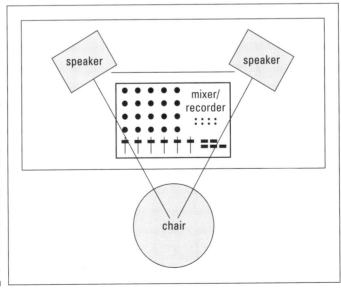

Figure 2-3:
Your
monitors
sound best
when
placed at
equal
distances
from each
other and
you.

Inspiring creativity

It's easy to forget in the midst of all this recording-gear talk that making music is a creative endeavor. It's also easy to forget that creative juices need to flow in order to actually get anything done. As any artist worth his or her salt will tell you, the muse is fickle, and accessing inspiration can be tough. The last thing you need is to create an environment or approach to recording that saps your creativity.

I can't tell you how many home studios I walk into that are about as inspiring to work in as a prison cell (not that I know anything about the aesthetic of prison cells, mind you). Anyway, I highly recommend that you spend some time and money creating a place that you want to go into, a place that helps get you in touch with your muse. For some people, it's candles, incense, and lava lamps. For someone else, it might be stark white walls and angular metal furniture. Get in touch with your own inner interior designer and get creative in making a special place that says, "Creativity happens here." This way you'll want to go to your studio and you'll feel inspired when you get there.

Taming heat and dust

The number-one enemy of electronic equipment is heat. Dust is a close second. Try to set up your studio in a room that you can keep cool and fairly dust-free. Air conditioning is a must for most studios. Be careful with a window air conditioner, though; it can make a lot of noise, requiring you to shut it off when you record. Depending on where you live, this could heat up your room really fast. To deal with dust, try to cover up your equipment when you're not using it, especially your mics. A plastic bag placed over the top of a mic on a stand works well.

Quieting your computer

Unless you work on a laptop that doesn't have a fan, you're going to find that your computer makes quite a bit of noise. In fact, why don't you go give it a listen right now. I'll wait. . . .

It's noisy isn't it? This is a problem because most people are used to putting their computer's CPU unit either on or under their desks. If you record with a microphone in your room, all the computer noise is going to end up on your track. This can cause problems even if you don't use mics when you record. The constant whirring of the fans and hard drives will make it difficult for you to properly hear what's coming out of your monitors. This can result in you recording tracks that don't sound right or mixing your music less than optimally.

You can reduce the sound from your computer in three basic ways:

- ✔ **Put the computer's CPU unit in another room.** If you have a closet or an adjoining room that you can put your CPU unit in, this is the easiest and safest solution. For most computers, all you have to do is get extension cords for your video monitor(s), keyboard, and mouse and run the cords through a hole in the wall. The cords cost only a few dollars. (I have a Mac tower with an LCD screen — the most expensive configuration for extending video cables — and it cost me under $100 to run two video monitors an extra 8 feet.)

- ✔ **Put the main CPU unit in an isolation box.** You can create a box (much like the amp isolator box that I describe later in this chapter) to put your computer into. This approach isn't quite as simple as putting an amp in a box because you need to make sure that computer gets cool air to keep it from overheating. This requires insulated ducts and fans that are sized properly for your computer. It can and has been done, so if you don't have the option of putting your CPU in another room, you can use this approach. Just make sure that you don't let your computer overheat — otherwise, you might fry the internal components such as hard drives, motherboard, or CPU board. You can find some links to articles about boxing a computer on my Web site at www.jeffstrong.com.

- ✔ **Liquid cool it.** For many hardcore users, liquid cooling is preferable to boxing the computer. (Using a separate room is still the preferred option if it's at all possible.) Liquid cooling means eliminating the fans in your computer and replacing them with components that allow you to run cool water over your computer's critical components such as hard drives, motherboards, and processor chips. For some computers, that process is relatively easy because the parts are readily available. For others — computers such as the Mac G4 or G5 towers — finding the parts can be a hassle. You can expect to spend a few more dollars on liquid cooling than you would spend on running longer cords and drilling small holes into an adjoining room. For some links to resources on liquid cooling, go to my Web site at www.jeffstrong.com.

Whichever option you choose, you'll benefit because your music will sound better, so I encourage you to adopt one of these three approaches.

Optimizing Sounds in Your Room

Chances are that your studio occupies a corner in your living room, a spare bedroom, or a section of your basement or garage. All these spaces are less-than-ideal recording environments. Even if you intend to record mostly by plugging your instrument or sound module directly into the mixer, how your room sounds will have a big effect on how good your music turns out to be.

As a home recordist, you're unlikely to have easy access to the resources that create a top-notch sound room. Commercial studios spend serious cash — up to seven figures — to make their rooms sound, well, *professional*. You don't need to spend near that amount of money (you mean you don't *want* to sell off your private jet?) to get great-sounding recordings. All it takes is a little understanding of the way sound travels, some ingenuity, and a little bit of work.

Keeping the sound in or out of your room

One of the concerns that you (and your neighbors) are probably going to have when you start recording in your home is the amount of sound that gets in and out of your room. Sound waves are nasty little boogers. They get through almost any surface, and there's not a lot you can do to stop it from happening.

You've probably noticed this phenomenon when somebody with a massive subwoofer in his car drives by blasting some obnoxious music. (Ever notice how someone else's music is obnoxious whereas your music never is, no matter how loud you play it? Amazing.) Your windows rattle, your walls shake, and your favorite mug flies off the shelf and breaks into a thousand pieces. Well, this is one of the problems with sound: It's physical energy.

The best (and classic) way to isolate your studio room from everything around it is to build a room within a room. This essentially involves building a six-sided box just inside the floor, ceiling, and walls of your existing room. The trick with this approach is that the box you build in your room has to be isolated from the structure of the room itself. If it's not, the vibration simply travels from your inner room to the outer one — or vice versa. Most pros use rubber membranes to create this isolation. The process can get pretty involved, so I don't go into detail here, but you can go to my Web site (www.jeffstrong.com) to find some links to resources to get you started.

For the purpose of most home recordists — folks who usually don't have the money or space to build a room within a room — the best thing you can do is to try to understand what noises are getting in and getting out and deal with those. For example, if you live in a house or apartment with neighbors close by, don't record live drums at night. You could also consider using a drum machine or electronic drum set (plugged directly into the recorder) instead.

Another idea is to try to choose a room in your house or apartment that is farthest away from outside noise (an interior room, for instance). Basements also work well because they're underground, and most of the sound gets absorbed by the surrounding dirt and earthworms. Installing a little fiberglass batting insulation in the ceiling — typical house insulation that you can find at your local home center — can isolate you pretty well from anyone above the basement. Detached garages are generally farther away from other buildings, so sound has a chance to dissipate before it reaches your neighbors (or before your neighbors' noise reaches your garage).

Also keep these things in mind when trying to isolate your studio:

- ✔ **Dead air and mass are your friends.** The whole concept of a room within a room is to create mass and still air space so that the invading or escaping sound gets trapped there. When you work on isolating your room, try to design in some space that can trap air (creating *dead air*) — such as a suspended ceiling or big, upholstered furniture — or use double layers of drywall on your walls (creating *mass*).

- ✔ **Don't expect acoustical foam or carpet to reduce the noise.** Using these can help reduce the amount of sound that bounces around inside the room, but it doesn't do much to keep sound in (or out of) the room.

- ✔ **Isolate the instrument instead of the room.** Isolating the sound of your guitar amp can be much less expensive than trying to soundproof your whole room. Most commercial studios have one or more *isolation booths* for recording vocals and other acoustic instruments. You can use that concept to create your own mini-isolation booths.

One idea for a truly *mini*-isolation booth is to make an insulated box for your guitar (or bass) amp. If you just *have* to crank your amp to get the sound you want, you can place it inside the insulated box to reduce the amount of noise that escapes to the outside world. Check out Figure 2-4 to see what I mean.

You can also create an isolated space in a closet by insulating it and closing the door when you record (I've known people who've put a window in the door and used the insulated closet for a vocal booth), or you can put your guitar amp (or drums) in another room and run a long cord from there to your recorder. If you do this, remember that for long cord runs you need to use balanced cords rather than unbalanced ones (see Chapter 5); otherwise, you might get a bunch of noise, and your signal might be too low to record very well.

Getting the sound in your room under control

After you create a room that's as isolated from the outside world as possible, you need to deal with the way sound acts *within* your room.

Sound travels through the air in the form of waves. These waves bounce around the room and cause *reflections* (reverberations or echoes). One problem with most home studios is that they're small — and sound travels very fast (1,130 feet per second, to be exact). When you sit at your monitors and listen, inevitably you hear the reflected sound as well as the original sound that comes out of your speakers. With big rooms, you can hear the original sound and reflections as separate sounds, meaning that the reflections themselves become less of a problem. For a good home studio, you have to tame these reflections so they don't interfere with your ability to clearly hear what's coming from the speakers.

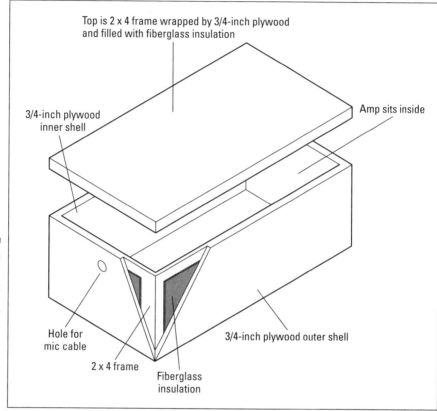

Top is 2 x 4 frame wrapped by 3/4-inch plywood and filled with fiberglass insulation

Amp sits inside

3/4-inch plywood inner shell

Hole for mic cable

2 x 4 frame

Fiberglass insulation

3/4-inch plywood outer shell

Figure 2-4:
An amp-isolator box reduces the amount of noise you hear from your amp, even when it's cranked.

How all these reflections bounce around your room can get pretty compli-cated. Read up on acoustics (the way sound behaves) to discover more about different room modes: *axial* (one dimension), *tangential* (two dimen-sions), and *oblique* (three dimensions). Each relates to the way sound waves interact as they bounce around a room. Knowing your room's modes can help you come up with an acoustical treatment strategy, but some very com-plicated formulas exist for figuring out your room's modes, especially those dastardly tangential and oblique modes.

You can find out more on room modes and find some room mode calculators on the Internet by using your favorite search engine and entering **room modes** as a search term. Go to the Web site matches, and you'll see quite a few places to start looking. (One great resource is Ethan Winer's forum at www.music player.com/cgi-bin/ultimatebb.cgi?ubb=forum;f=26;DaysPrune=30.) I recommend that you research room modes; this topic alone could fill an entire book.

So, at the risk of offending the professional acoustical engineers in the world, I'm going to share some tricks that I've been using in my studios. My main goal has been to create a room with a sound I like and that gives me some measure of control over the reflections within the room. Because I record and mix in one room (as do most home recordists), I find it helpful to be able to make minor adjustments to the sound to accommodate what I'm trying to accomplish.

Sound control plays a major role in two aspects of recording: tracking and mixing. Each requires different approaches for you to get the best possible sound out of your recordings. I cover both these aspects in this section.

Sound control during tracking

Tracking is what you're doing when you're actually recording. Two things can make a tracking room a bad environment for tracking: not enough sound reflection and too much sound reflection. The goal when tracking is to have a room that's not so dead (in terms of sound reflection) that it sucks the life out of your instrument and not so live that it colors the sound too much. The determining factor in how much reflection you want in your room is based on the instrument that you record and the way it sounds in the room.

If your room is too dead (*not enough* sound reflection), try adding some reflective surfaces to liven things up (the room, that is). On the other hand, if your room is too live (*too much* sound reflection), you need to add some absorptive materials to tame those reflections.

You could go out and buy a bunch of foam panels to catch the reflections, or maybe put in a wood floor or attach some paneling to the walls to add some life, but you'd be stuck with the room sounding only one way. It might end up sounding good for recording drums or acoustic guitar, but then it would probably be too live for getting a great vocal sound — which requires a deader space. One solution that I've found to work well is to get (or make) some portable panels that can either absorb or reflect the sound.

Figure 2-5 shows an absorber/reflector that I've used and have found to work quite well. (Go to my Web site, www.jeffstrong.com, for plans to build your own.) One side has an absorptive material (dense fiberglass insulation) and the other a reflective surface (wood). They're put together in an attractive frame and designed to stack easily when you want them out of the way. Even with very little woodworking experience, you can crank out a set of them in a weekend for very little money (about $30 per panel). I guarantee that if you make them (or hire someone to make them for you), you'll find dozens of uses for them around your studio.

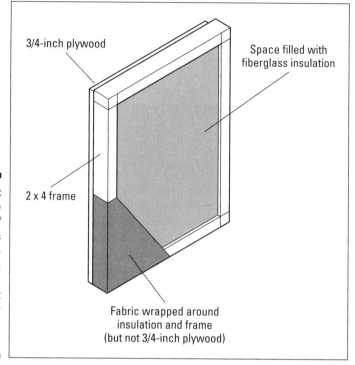

3/4-inch plywood

Space filled with
fiberglass insulation

2 x 4 frame

Fabric wrapped around
insulation and frame
(but not 3/4-inch plywood)

Figure 2-5:
Portable
absorbers/
reflectors
make
changing
the sound
characterist
ics of your
room quick
and easy.

Sound control during mixing

Your first step in getting control of the sound of your (probably less-than-perfect) room during mixing is to get a good pair of near-field monitors. Near-field monitors are designed to be listened to up close (hence the *near* in their name), and they lessen the effects that the rest of the room has on your ability to hear them accurately and get a good mix.

The next step to mixing in an imperfect room is to mix at low volumes. I know; that takes the fun out of it, right? Well, as fun as it might be to mix at high volumes, it rarely translates into a great mix. Great mixing engineers often listen to their mixer at *very low levels.* Yes, they occasionally use high levels, but only after the mixing is pretty much done — and then only for very short periods of time. After all, if you damage your ears, you blow your career as a sound engineer. (Hey, that rhymes! Or is there an echo in here?) I don't want to sound like your mother, but try to resist the temptation to crank it up. Your ears last longer, and your mixes sound better.

Even with these two things (near-field monitors and low mixing levels), you still need to do one more thing to your room to make it work better for you. The secret to a good mixing room is to tame the reflections of the sound coming out of your speakers.

Dealing with high- and mid-range frequencies is pretty easy — just put up some foam panels or the absorptive side of the panels you see in Figure 2-5. (See? I told you that you'd have a use for those panels.) Start by hanging two from the ceiling (or putting them on a stand or table) so they're level with your speakers on the wall behind you. Also put one on each side wall right where the speakers are pointed, as shown in Figure 2-6. This positioning gets rid of the higher frequencies and eliminates much of the echo.

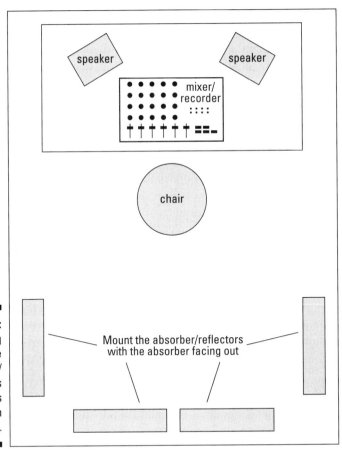

Figure 2-6:
Positioning the absorber/reflectors like this helps with mixing.

You might also need to put something on your ceiling right above your head, especially if you have a low (8 feet or less) or textured ceiling. (You know, one with that popcorny stuff sprayed on.) You might not want to mount one of the absorption panels over your head because they're fairly heavy. (And accidents do happen.) Try wrapping up a couple of 2-x-4-foot panels made of dense fiberglass (the same ones used in the absorber/reflectors) in fabric and hang those instead; they would work just about perfectly. In fact, you can make some overhead *diffusers* like the ones shown in Figure 2-7 very easily. (The plans for these are also on my Web site at `www.jeffstrong.com`.)

You can also place a set of these overhead panels in the corners of your room behind the speakers. Just hang them at the same height of your speakers so that they cut off the corner of the room. If you don't have enough room to fit the panels at an angle in the corner, you can eliminate the backing from the fiberglass and bend the fabric-covered panel to fit right in the corner. Either approach absorbs any sound that bounces around behind the speakers.

Figure 2-7:
Use overhead panels to get rid of reflections off the ceiling.

Another thing that you need to consider when you're mixing is *standing waves*. Standing waves are created when bass tones begin reflecting around your room and bounce into each other. Standing waves have a weird effect on mix quality. They can over-emphasize the bass from your speakers (resulting in mixes that are *short* on bass) or cancel out some — or all — of the bass coming out of your speakers (resulting in mixes with *too much* bass). One of the problems with standing waves is that they can really mess up your mixes, and you might not even be aware that they're there until you listen to your mix in another room and the bass is either too loud or too soft.

To find out whether you have a problem with standing waves in your studio, sit in front of your monitors and put on one of your favorite CDs. Now listen carefully. Okay, now lean forward and backward a little bit. Does the amount of bass that you hear change as you move? Next, get up and walk around the room. Listen for places within the room where the bass seems to be louder or softer. You might find places where the bass drops out almost completely. If either inspection gives you a variable experience of the bass, you're the proud owner of standing waves. Don't worry, though. You can tame that standing-wave monster with a pair of bass traps.

Bass traps absorb the energy in the lower frequencies so they don't bounce all over your room and throw off your mixes. You can buy bass traps made of foam from some music stores or (yep, you guessed it) you can make your own out of wood and insulation. Check out Figure 2-8 for a look at some homemade bass traps. (The plans to make these are — you guessed it — located on my Web site: www.jeffstrong.com.)

The most common placement for bass traps is in the corners behind you when you're sitting at your mixer (as in Figure 2-9). You might also find that putting a set in the other corners of the room helps even more.

After you place the bass traps, do the listening test again. If you notice some areas where the bass seems to get louder or softer, try moving the bass traps around a little. With some trial and error, you'll most likely find a place where they seem to work best.

Try not to get stressed out about the sound of your room. As important as your room's sound is, it has less impact on the quality of your recordings than good, solid engineering practices. I know, I keep saying this, but it's important to remember. So do what you can and then work with what you've got.

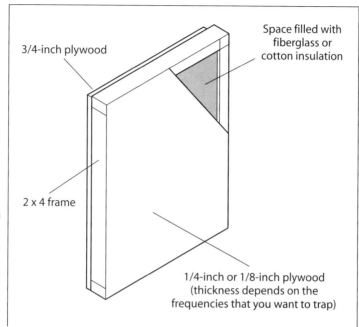

3/4-inch plywood

Space filled with
fiberglass or
cotton insulation

2 x 4 frame

1/4-inch or 1/8-inch plywood
(thickness depends on the
frequencies that you want to trap)

Figure 2-8:
Use bass
traps to
get rid of
standing
waves.

Figure 2-9:
Put bass
traps in the
corners
behind you
to eliminate
standing
waves.

Part II
Choosing and Installing Computer Hardware

The 5th Wave   By Rich Tennant

JERRY AND LYLE ATTEMPT TO LOAD THE NEWEST VERSION OF "TOAST," CD-BURNING SOFTWARE

OK, I got the Sunbeam firewired to the iMac. Try putting the CD in the slot again.

In this part . . .

Part II discusses your hardware needs and helps you set up your computer to record. Chapter 3 shows you what to look for in an audio-recording computer. Whether you use a Mac or a Windows system, you find out what the best system is for your needs. Chapter 4 digs into audio components and helps you find the best audio and MIDI interface along with all the other pieces of gear that you need. Chapter 5 helps you hook everything up and gets you ready to install your software.

Chapter 3

Choosing Computer Components

*C*hances are you already have a computer, and you plan on using it for recording your music. Before you do that, remember that the computer you choose to use for recording your music is one of the most important purchases you'll ever make when it comes to capturing a CD-worthy performance. Recording, editing, and mixing audio are processor-intensive, and with all the different types of software and recording hardware available, having the right computer for your needs is very important.

In this chapter, I guide you through the main considerations you need to make when purchasing a computer for recording your music. I examine the core components of both Windows and Mac-based machines and help you find the best solution for your needs.

An almost infinite variety of computer components are available for each part of your system. Add to this fact the many options for audio recording hardware and software, and it becomes nearly impossible for me to tell you exactly what components will work with the software and hardware you choose. Given this fact, here are some suggestions:

✔ If you're starting from scratch and you're planning on buying a computer for running your audio, choose your software first and build the rest of your system around that choice.

✔ If you already have a computer that you want to use for recording audio, check with the different software and audio interface makers to see whether your current system will work for you. If you discover that your system isn't up to par for recording audio, upgrade your system before you spend your money on the recording gear.

✔ Visit Web sites for each of the audio recording software makers (Chapter 7 lists many of them) to see what hardware they recommend for their systems.

✔ Check one of the many Internet forums out there for recommendations from people who are using the software or audio interface you want to use. You can generally find a forum for each of the popular recording programs on the manufacturer's Web site or by doing a Web search with the software name and *forum* as your keywords.

✔ Go to the Digidesign User's Conference (DUC) for help finding the best hardware and operating system (OS) for your needs. This forum has a topic dedicated to building a recording PC. Although this particular forum topic focuses on computers that work with Pro Tools — a Digidesign product — most of the information provided applies to any recording system. The topic is located at

```
http://duc.digidesign.com/showflat.php?Cat=&Board=UBB32&N
     umber=360675&page=0&view=collapsed&sb=5&o=7&fpart
     =1
```

Selecting a Windows PC

Getting set up with a PC is a little more complicated than it is with a Mac (see the "Choosing a Mac" section later in this chapter), simply because you have to deal with a lot more hardware variables. But as long as you keep the basic system requirements in mind, you can set yourself up with a very powerful system. In this section, I offer several options for getting a Windows PC for recording audio.

Understanding minimum requirements

Windows PC system requirements differ slightly depending on the software and audio interface that you use. Although every audio recording program differs in the minimum system requirements, here's a list that covers the basic minimums for a system that records both audio and MIDI and offers typical editing and plug-in capabilities:

✔ **Processor:** Most manufacturers recommend a Pentium 4 or AMD Athlon XP. These are both fine, but I say get the fastest speed you can afford — a single processor would be good, but a double processor would be even better.

✔ **Operating system:** Current audio recording programs require Windows XP. This is the first really stable OS that Microsoft has made. As far as I'm concerned, this is a no-brainer — even if your choice of software lets you use an earlier version.

✔ **RAM:** Most manufacturers recommend 384 megabytes (MB) of random access memory (RAM). That's is the absolute lowest that I'd get. In fact, I'd double it if you want a system that doesn't get slow and glitchy as you work.

✔ **Hard drives:** Get two — one for the system drive and one for your audio files. I'd recommend 7,200 rpm IDE/ATA drives for at least the audio drive. You can get by with a slower one (such as 5,400 rpm) for your system drive if necessary (in the case of the internal drive in a laptop, for instance).

Note: The rpm doesn't refer to that prehistoric recording storage device known as the vinyl LP (33⅓ rpm) or the single (45 rpm). It refers to the rotations per minute of the drive mechanism.

✔ **Optical drives:** An optical drive is a drive that can read or write from either CDs or DVDs. (They're called optical because the data is written and read by a laser.) My advice to you? Get both a CD-R and a DVD-R drive. A combination drive is fine. It lets you burn CDs of your finished music and make DVD backups of your audio data.

Opting on the operating system

For PC users, Windows XP is the way to go. It is by far the most stable operating system Microsoft has released to date. This difference in stability between Windows XP and the previous version is significant enough that I believe it's worth whatever hassle you need to go through (such as upgrading your PC) to skip the earlier version of Windows.

Both the Home and Professional versions of Windows XP work just fine. The main difference between the two is that the Professional version can run dual-CPU systems. (The *central processing unit,* or CPU, is the main computer brain, so essentially it's a Mutant Computer with Two Brains.) Depending on the software you use, this feature can offer significant performance improvements over a single processor, or it can make no observable difference at all. Check with the manufacturer of the recording software you use to find out whether it supports dual processor computers.

Unless you already own a dual-CPU-equipped computer — or plan to purchase (or build) one in the not-too-distant future, save yourself a few bucks and go with the Windows XP Home edition.

Viewing internal components

When you buy or build a Windows PC for recording, you'd better have a basic understanding of the main components in your system. These components include:

✔ **Central processing unit (CPU):** The CPU is a small chip that is responsible for processing all the data in your computer. It's essentially the computer's brain. Two major CPU manufacturers exist in the PC world — Intel and AMD. Most audio hardware and software support both, and each can work fine as the core of your audio computer. For Intel systems, I recommend going with a Pentium 4, and for AMD systems, the Athlon XP. (If you've got some bucks to spare, you might even go for two of your choice and build a dual-processor machine.)

Avoid the lower-cost (and lower-performance) Intel Celeron and AMD Duron processors.

✔ **Motherboard:** The motherboard is the main circuit board in your computer and holds the CPU, memory, and other peripheral cards. The motherboard you choose depends on whether you're running the Intel or AMD CPU (see the preceding bullet). Each CPU type has its own motherboard requirements, and many choices are available for each, with new motherboards being released all the time. I've had good results over the years with Asus brand motherboards, although other brands can also work well.

When you select a motherboard, your main concerns are that it (a) support the CPU you plan on using and (b) have a *chipset* (a series of chips attached to the motherboard that control data flow) that's compatible with your desired hardware and software.

✔ **Graphics card:** The graphics card is responsible for displaying your software's graphics smoothly. Audio recording programs don't place the same demands on your graphics card that modern game software does, so you don't need the highest end graphics card for your audio computer. A simple 2X or 4X AGP graphics card will work just fine. Make sure, however, that the graphics card you use is compatible with your motherboard. In most cases, the graphics card isn't going to be an issue — but check it out anyway as a hedge against Murphy's Law.

Most audio recording software programs available on the market use two primary workspace windows. Although it's easy enough to switch between the two windows, life can be much easier if you have two monitors so you can see both windows at the same time. Choosing a graphics card that has dual-monitor support can allow you to do switch between windows without hassle. I talk a bit more about the two-monitor option in the "Viewing Video Monitors" section later in this chapter.

Mac or PC: Which one is for you?

It used to be that professional recordists used Macs and only Macs. That isn't the case anymore. Professionals use either platform, Mac or PC (or both, depending on who you talk to). You can find good software and compatible audio hardware for both platforms, so your choice is going to come down to your comfort level and budget. Don't let anyone convince you that you need either a Mac or a Windows PC to record audio. It's just not true. Choose the one you're familiar with or are drawn to. Unless you have a strong bias one way or the other, I recommend that you choose the software first and get the computer that works well with it. If you do prefer a Mac or a Windows PC, your choices for software are narrowed down, but you still have lots of good options for both platforms.

Making your choice

You can get a Windows computer for recording audio in four ways:

✔ **Use the one you already have.** If you already have a computer, this might be your least expensive solution. Depending on the speed and specific components in your system, you might be able to buy an audio interface and a piece of software and get right down to the job of recording . . . or you might need to do some upgrading before you can record.

✔ **Build it from scratch.** This means buying all the parts separately and putting them all together in a computer case. This option often provides the most powerful computer for the least amount of money. The downside is that you have to find the parts, make sure they're compatible, and get your hands dirty. This process isn't very hard, but it does require some skill and confidence. If you're unsure how to build a PC, I recommend checking out Mark L. Chambers' *Building a PC For Dummies,* 4th Edition (Wiley Publishing, Inc.).

If you want to build your own PC from the ground up, I recommend checking out the Web site for the software you intend to use before you start buying anything. Most manufacturers offer some guidelines — some even have specific systems that are approved for use with their products.

The Digidesign Users Conference (DUC), a user forum for fans of all things Digidesign (including Pro Tools), has a forum topic that includes a comprehensive guide to building a PC for the express purpose of audio recording. Although this information applies specifically to Pro Tools systems, these recommendations generally work well for all recording systems. If you really want to go the DIY route, I recommend that you check out this particular forum topic, located at

```
http://duc.digidesign.com/showflat.php?Cat=&Board=UBB32&N
        umber=360675&page=0&view=collapsed&sb=5&o=7&fpart
        =1
```

✔ **Buy an off-the-shelf system.** Many computers that are available at your local computer store can work fine for recording audio. This option represents the easiest way to get a computer. The downside is that you often pay for features you don't need, and the extra features might slow your system down a bit. This is also generally the most expensive option for a recording computer.

✔ **Have one built for you.** If you don't have the skills (or stomach) for building your own computer but you want the most performance out of a computer, having one built by a company that specializes in audio computers might be the best solution. This option costs more than building one yourself, but with it you often get a warranty and are assured of a system that will work for your needs. Having an audio computer built for you from scratch costs about the same as buying an off-the-shelf computer of the same overall quality. Here are a couple of places that build quality audio PCs:

- **Alienware:** This company builds custom Windows PCs for a variety of creative pursuits. You can find it at: `www.alienware.com/Product_Pages/workstation_audio.aspx`.

- **MusicXPC:** You can find some Windows PCs built specifically for audio on its site at: `www.musicxpc.com`.

- **Digital Audio Wave:** These guys make some powerful audio computers, too. Check out: `www.digitalaudiowave.com`.

Choosing a Mac

Choosing a Mac is easy because you don't have nearly as many options to consider and you don't have to worry about the compatibility of the guts of the computer. The downside is that you'll likely end up spending a bit more money compared to building your own Windows PC from scratch. (If you buy an off-the-shelf PC or have one built for you, the cost is going to be similar to that of a comparable Mac.)

Making sense of minimum requirements

All audio hardware and software manufacturers provide a list of minimum system requirements. These requirements are vital to installing and using their products. Here's an example of the typical current minimum requirements that an audio recording software company would require for Macs:

- ✔ **Processor:** Most manufacturers recommend a G4 or G5. For most programs, you can get by with a G4, but a G5 might open the throttle on some programs.

- ✔ **Operating system:** You need OS X. The specific version is negotiable with many manufacturers, but as long as you're going with OS X, get the latest version to be safe.

- ✔ **RAM:** The minimum here is the same as for a Windows system — 384 megabytes (MB). That's is the absolute lowest that you should get. Instead, shoot for the 1-gigabyte (GB) route if you can swing it.

- ✔ **Hard drives:** As with all audio recording systems you need two — one for the system drive and one for your audio files. I'd recommend 7,200 rpm IDE/ATA drives for at least the audio drive. You can get by with a slower one for your system drive if necessary (in the case of the internal drive in a laptop, for instance).

- ✔ **Optical drives:** Optical drives are drives that can read or write from CDs or DVDs. If I were you, I'd get both a CD-R and a DVD-R drive. A combination drive is fine. It lets you burn CDs of your finished music and make DVD backups of your audio data.

For the most part, the minimum is exactly that: the absolute minimum. Don't expect to have a powerhouse system if you settle for just the minimum requirements. To record more than a few tracks or run more than a couple instances of plug-ins, you need as much power as you can get. I recommend that you buy the fastest computer you can afford, especially if you intend to record your entire band or if you want to use a bunch of soft-synths or plug-in effects in your music.

Opting on an operating system

Even though many people still get by using OS 9, OS X is the operating system that you really need to use to get the most out of the newest audio recording software. All new Macs are being shipped with OS X, and some audio hardware and software won't work on OS 9.

If you have an older computer that runs OS 9 and you can't upgrade to X, you're stuck using an older version of an audio recording program because the newer versions aren't being written for OS 9. These options work fine, but I've got to tell you that OS X is a much better operating system than OS 9. In fact, the improvement from OS 9 to OS X is so dramatic that I'd upgrade my entire system if I had to rather than deal with the limitations present in OS 9 (but then I'm hardcore).

Understanding Mac configurations

Macs come complete, so it's much easier to make a decision on which Mac to buy compared to the many variables you have to contend with when using a Windows PC. The main consideration that you have to face is what audio interface technology you use. For example, the iMac (and the eMac, Powerbook or iBook for that matter) doesn't have a PCI slot, so you can't use a PCI-based audio interface with it.

Following is a quick rundown of the basic configurations of the various Apple offerings and how they work for audio:

✔ **Power Mac:** This is the top-of-the-line Apple computer. The Power Mac is a desktop computer that has several PCI slots, room for four drives, an option for two processors, and room for tons of RAM. If you have the means, this is the most powerful solution, and you can expand it as needed. Another advantage is that you can put the main CPU unit in a room away from your monitor, which keeps the noise of the computer out of your recordings.

✔ **iMac:** The iMac is available with quite a bit of power (single processor G5 as of this writing), so it can handle most people's audio needs. It's relatively inexpensive so it fits the budget for many users. It does have some disadvantages (aside from the single processor limit). It lacks PCI slots and doesn't have any room for internal drives beyond the included hard drive (fine for your system drive) and optical drive (get one with both CD-R and DVD-R capabilities). So to use this computer for audio you need to use either a USB or FireWire interface and you need an external FireWire drive. You also really should max out the RAM right away because the machines don't come with very much. One other disadvantage is that the monitor is part of the unit, so your hard drive and fan noise will be in the same room that you record in. This fact might present a noise-bleed problem if you record with microphones, especially when recording quiet instruments.

If you get creative, you can get past the noisy-fan-and-hard-drive deficit. For example, you can use a *control surface* (a unit that lets you control your recording software without using the mouse or keyboard) and put it as far away as possible with a sound-absorbing baffle (a thick blanket hung on a stand works well) between you and the computer when you record.

✔ **eMac:** The eMac has many of the same characteristics as the iMac except it's in a less attractive container. The advantage with the eMac is that it's pretty inexpensive and has all the power of the more expensive iMac. Like with the iMac, if you intend to use an eMac for recording, you need to max out the RAM, add an external FireWire drive, and use a FireWire or USB audio interface.

✔ **PowerBook:** The PowerBook is Apple's best laptop computer. As of this writing, PowerBooks aren't available with a G5 processor, so the best you can do is a G4 — which is fast enough for most users, anyway. Because laptops don't have a PCI slot or room for any extra hard drives, you'll need to get a FireWire-based unit. (You can use a USB audio interface, but I wouldn't recommend getting a USB drive. They just aren't fast enough — even the USB 2 versions.) Also, make sure that you get more RAM than is standard and get at least a CD-R optical drive, if not a DVD-R/CD-R combo drive.

✔ **iBook:** The iBook is a less expensive laptop that usually is a couple steps slower in processor speed than the PowerBook. (The G4 iBooks just became available.) Keep in mind as well that you don't have as many ports or RAM capabilities. Still, a G4 iBook can work for many people. In fact, because the iBook is so quiet, I prefer it over the eMac or iMac for recording. Sure, you'll spend a bit more for the iBook than the eMac or iMac, but you'll end up with a portable recording studio. Remember that, with an iBook, you still need to use a USB or FireWire interface, an external FireWire drive, and maxed-out RAM. You might also need to get a FireWire optical drive to record your CDs and DVD backups.

You don't need the newest, fastest computer ever made to record your music. Get what you can afford (or use what you have) and get to work. When you hit the limits of your system, then consider upgrading. As of this writing, I'm still using a G4 single processor Power Mac and a PowerBook for all my music. I'm not planning on upgrading the main computer units for a while yet because I have yet to feel in any real way limited by them. I regularly upgrade the software and operating system, but the hardware waits until I can't get what I want to get done with what I've got. I usually last about four to five years between major hardware upgrades. Remember that you still need to spend good money on things like microphones and preamps, so don't blow you whole wad on the latest greatest computer hardware.

Making your choice

For the most part, any PowerBook, Power Mac G4 with the AGP graphics card, and of course the Power Mac G5s would do quite nicely. In addition to these models, an iMac, iBook or eMac could work well, but you'll need to check out the compatibility documents for the hardware and recording program you intend to use.

The audio interface you have dictates what type of computer you can use. For example, if you have a Digi 001, you need a computer with an open PCI slot. This eliminates everything except the G4 or G5 because these are the only Macs with PCI slots. Come to think of it, with the Digi 001 you have to take the G5 off the list as well, because it uses a PCI configuration that's incompatible with the Digi 001. Other PCI interfaces, such as the RME or MOTU brands, are compatible with both the G4 and the G5. If you want to use a FireWire interface, such as the MOTU 828, or a USB interface, such as the Mackie Spike, you can use any of the Macs because all new Macs have USB and FireWire ports.

Make sure that you have the necessary connectors (and that they're compatible) in your computer to run the type of interface you want to use.

Getting a Handle on Hard Drives

To record audio effectively, you need to have more than one hard drive. This is pretty much non-negotiable if you intend to do any amount of recording, editing, erasing, and re-recording. You need at a minimum two hard drives in your system: one for your system files and applications and the other for all your audio and MIDI files. Here's a look at how to organize them:

✔ **Drive one: The system drive.** For your system drive, you can use the stock drive that came with your computer — but if you have a choice, I recommend getting one with a *spindle speed* (also known as *rotational speed,* the speed at which the hard drive spins) of 7,200 revolutions per minute (rpm). You'll be much happier, and your audio recording program will be much happier, too. And get a *big* one — hard drive, that is.

There's no need to partition your drive, even if you have other programs such as finance or word-processing software on your computer. In fact, doing so might slow down your system.

✔ **Drive two: The audio drive.** Back in the old days, you needed a good high-speed SCSI drive to record and play back audio reliably, but this isn't the case anymore. You can use both IDE and FireWire drives for storing audio, but make sure that you have a drive with the following (or better) specs:

- **Spindle speed:** Also called rotational speed, this is the rate at which the hard drive spins. For the most part, a 7,200-rpm drive will work well for recording and playing back audio.

- **Seek time:** This is the amount of time that the drive takes to find the data that's stored on it. You want an average seek time under 10 milliseconds (ms). Get as low as you can. (I prefer a seek time of 8 to 9 ms.)

- **Buffer size:** Often called a *cache buffer,* buffers are memory units that store data as it's being transferred. You want a buffer size of at least 512K, but get one as big as you can. I recommend a drive with an 8MB buffer.

- **Chipset:** If you use a FireWire drive, make sure that it comes with at least the Oxford 911 bridge chipset. The chipset is necessary to get the most bandwidth out of the drive and results in more tracks in your session.

A drive with these specs in a good size (100GB or so) will run you about $100, so there's no reason not to spring for the second drive.

If you use a FireWire interface for your system, you're best off using an ATA/IDE drive as your audio drive because a FireWire drive will compete with the interface's FireWire connection for bandwidth. If you want to use a PowerBook or other Mac that doesn't have room for a second internal ATA/IDE drive, you might need to get either a PCI (for desktops) or Cardbus (for laptops) FireWire adapter. Using an adapter will let you record and play back more tracks and essentially make your sessions run smoother.

I don't recommend the older USB drives for your audio drive. The connection speed is too slow to record or play back lots of tracks smoothly. The newer USB 2 drives have a connection speed similar to FireWire, so this might be an option if your computer has a high-speed USB-2 port.

Recognizing Your RAM Needs

Most audio recording programs require at least 384MB of RAM (random access memory), but I say go for broke here. Get as much RAM as your system can hold. And don't buy the cheap stuff — get high-quality RAM.

I recommend getting at least 1GB of RAM for music, more if you want to use software samplers or soft-synths because they use a lot of RAM to run efficiently.

Opting for Optical Drives

An *optical drive* is a drive that can read from or write to CDs or DVDs. These types of drives are important for backing up data and burning a CD of your finished music.

I recommend that you get a combination drive — one that can read and write from both CDs and DVDs. Even though you won't be putting your music on DVD, the capacity of a DVD-ROM disc makes backing up your audio files much easier because you can get a lot of data on one DVD. (How much data? Well, you can cram all the data from six CDs onto just one DVD.)

Viewing Video Monitors

When it comes to choosing a monitor, almost any one will do in a pinch, but I recommend the newer LCD monitors because they don't emit any electro-magnetic fields (EMFs) that some recordists have complained interfere with recording. I personally haven't had any problems with the audio while using a standard cathode ray tube (CRT) monitor, but I do find that my eyes get tired a lot quicker with them than when using an LCD monitor.

One final consideration concerns your choice of graphics cards: You might want to consider a *dual-head* AGP (Accelerated Graphics Port or Advanced Graphics Port) graphics card. These work just like any other graphics card, but support the use of dual monitors. Because many audio recording pro-grams use two main display screens, having a dual-display-capable graphics card allows you to hook up two monitors so that you can see both screens without having to toggle between them. Okay, it's certainly not a require-ment, but many people find that it's a nice convenience.

Chapter 4

Examining Audio Components

* *

* *

*B*ecause of all the hoopla that computer-based recording has been getting in the press over the last couple of years, more people figure that because they have a computer they might as well use it to record. Unfortunately, many of these people go to their local musical instrument superstores or favorite online retailers, buy the cheapest recording doohicky possible (after all, the specs are all the same, right?), get home, install it, and proceed to spend countless hours trying to figure out why they can't record anything with it or find out that what they do manage to record sounds worse than the 20-year-old cassette deck they've been using to put their musical ideas down on.

Well, this chapter is designed to save you the frustration (and expense) of not getting the right bits of hardware you need to successfully record with your computer. In this chapter, I guide you through the overwhelming options in audio interfaces and help you find the right one for your needs (and not the seller's need for a big, fat commission). I also explain the other audio components you might want for your home studio, such as MIDI gear, microphones, and monitors (speakers, to you newbies).

Examining the Audio Interface

The audio interface is the key to being able to record into a computer. The interface takes all your analog sources (this includes all your instruments and mics) and turns them into digital bits that your computer can understand and work with. Without the interface, your instruments and computer are speaking two entirely different languages with no hope of understanding one another.

Understanding the interface

Audio interfaces come in a variety of configurations that might or might not contain the following components:

✔ **A sound card:** A sound card — also called a *PCI card* because it fits in the PCI (Peripheral Component Interface) slot in your computer — allows your computer to read and understand the digital information coming from and going to the converters (see next bullet). Without a sound card, your computer doesn't know what to do with the musical data that it receives (or that your hard drive stores).

✔ **Analog-to-digital (AD) and digital-to-analog (DA) converters:** These converters allow you to get the sound from your instrument, direct box, or preamp to the sound card (the AD converter's job) and from your computer back out to your monitors (the DA converter's job).

The division between sound card and AD and DA converters is very slight. In fact, these two components are often bundled together and collectively called a sound card. However, because you can buy these components separately — if and when you get really hard core about recording audio — I list them separately.

✔ **Analog inputs:** These let you plug your instruments into the interface without needing a mixer or any other gear. The analog inputs include:

• **Microphone preamps:** A microphone preamp is necessary for you to plug your microphone into your recording device. A preamp amplifies the signal coming from your microphone so that it can be recorded. Microphone preamps in most audio interfaces can also accept your guitar or bass without having to go through your amp first — much like a direct box would. (For more on direct boxes, see Chapter 1.)

• **Instrument inputs:** In addition to microphone preamps, most interfaces also have ¼-inch TS or TRS inputs that you can plug your keyboards, drum machines and other instruments into. (Not sure about this TS or TRS business? Chapter 5 has more on these and other types of connectors.) Many interfaces also let you plug your guitars directly into these inputs as well so you don't need a direct box. (Again, Chapter 1 has more on direct boxes.)

✔ **Analog outputs.** Audio interfaces all come with at least two analog outputs as well as a headphone jack. These outputs let you plug in your monitors and headphones so that you can hear your recordings. Many interfaces also have additional outputs that allow you to plug your unmixed tracks into an external mixer if you choose. (Though most home recordists don't bother — they choose to mix inside the computer's software instead. Chapter 14 covers mixing in more detail.)

Even though it's really handy to have all the pieces of equipment making up your audio interface housed together in one unit, there's a downside — such all-in-one audio interfaces aren't going to perform as well as higher quality components that you can buy separately. For example, the preamps that come in most interfaces might be serviceable, but they don't offer the clarity that a well-made external preamp can.

Quality is the price you pay for having everything in one unit and having that unit cost less than the individual components would cost separately. The reason I mention this is that, as you build up your engineering skills, you might find that you hit the limits of your equipment. When this happens, you might want to consider adding separate components to improve the quality of your audio *chain*. (The chain is the line of gear that your signal has to travel to get to the hard drive — your voice to the mic to the preamp to the AD converter to the sound card to the hard drive, for example.)

Exploring digital audio specifications

When you start looking at audio interfaces, you'll notice all the specifications thrown around like beaded necklaces at a Mardi Gras celebration. To keep you from getting confused by all the hype produced by the companies trying to sell their particular interface, here's a quick description of the two specs — bit depth and sample rate — that you need to get your mind around if you want to intelligently compare competing products.

Bit depth

When you start looking at audio interfaces, you'll hear jargon such as *16-bit* (the bit depth of audio CDs), *20-bit, 24-bit,* and so forth. This is the *bit depth,* which is described in terms of bits. (A bit, short for BInary digiT, is the basic unit of information in the binary numbering system used by computers.) The numbers 16, 20, and 24 relate to the amount of digital information that can be contained in each of the sample rates that I describe in the next section. The higher the number, the more *dynamic range* — the difference between the loudest and softest sound you want to record and the level of noise in your recording — you can have. Most professional audio gear now records at a 24-bit resolution, which translates to 144dB of dynamic range. (Theoretically, at any rate. In the real world, this dynamic range is slightly lower, ranging around 112dB or even 106dB). With that higher number, however, the sound is going to take up more of your digital storage space. This usually isn't a big deal, though, considering the low cost of huge hard drives.

Sampling rate

The *sampling rate* refers to the frequency at which the converter samples the incoming and outgoing sound source. When a converter *samples* a sound, it actually takes a small snapshot of the audio signal. Typical sample rates for digital recorders are 44.1 kHz (the sample rate for audio CDs), 48 kHz, 88.2 kHz, and 96 kHz (the sampling rate for DVD audio). The higher the number, the more samples that are taken each second, and the larger the frequency range that's captured.

This is one of the key aspects of using higher sampling rates and is called the *Nyquist frequency.* The Nyquist frequency (named after Harry Nyquist, the guy who discovered this) is the highest frequency that a digital sample can represent — and that frequency works out to be exactly half the sample rate. For instance, a 48-kHz sampling rate (the most common rate for professional audio equipment at the time of this writing) can accurately represent frequencies up to 24 kHz. (Not bad, considering that humans can only hear a maximum of 20 kHz — and for musicians who've played in a loud band for a while, that figure might be as low as 17 kHz.) Any frequencies higher than 24 kHz just aren't audible to us, so they're cut off. This range of frequencies is called the *bandwidth* — 48-kHz sampling rate has a bandwidth of 24 kHz.

If this were the only issue, your sampling rate choice would be a no-brainer: Simply use 44.1-kHz sample rate for audio that you'll eventually put on a CD because CDs use a 44.1-kHz sample rate and humans can't hear beyond about 20 kHz anyway. Unfortunately, the real issue with the sample rate has to do with the way the converter filters the audio above the Nyquist frequency. Cheap converters don't have great filters, so the audible sound (the stuff below 20 kHz) can be distorted by the filter even though the converter can capture music beyond what you can hear. For some people, the workaround for this problem is to record at a higher rate, thus putting the filter higher up into the inaudible range where it can't mess with your audible music, and then converting the sample rate later on before you put your music on a CD. And if you do a lot of DSP (digital signal processing, as I describe in Chapter 1), having a higher sample rate can help reduce any degradation in the sound of your music from all the math your computer has to do to process the audio. (Math is inherently hard work — remember Algebra in high school? — but the math that your computer has to do during audio processing is especially a bear because it often has to deal with very small errors [called *rounding errors*] that can eventually add up.) One other advantage with higher sample rates is that the *latency* — the delay caused by digital conversion of DSP functions — is reduced as the sample rate increases.

To take your analog sound — the signal from your mics, guitars, or keyboards — and turn it into digital information, your AD converter takes small snapshots of the incoming signal (at whatever sampling rate the converter uses) and then applies a number to that sample (based on the bit depth).

For example, suppose that you have a 24-bit converter with a 48-kHz sampling rate. When it senses an auditory signal — a vocal perhaps — the AD converter takes a snapshot (measurement) of that signal 48,000 times per second (48 kHz). Each of these snapshots is given a value between –8,395,008 and +8,395,008 (a 24-bit resolution has 16,790,016 possible levels), which puts the vocal sound somewhere on a chart corresponding to a waveform shape. The recorder in turn reads these numbers, and the DA converter translates these numbers back into an analog waveform again (whew!).

Converting an analog signal into digital data and back again is a highly technical process. You could spend months or even years reading about the intricacies of audio conversion. (Check out *Principles of Digital Audio* by Ken C. Pohlmann, or *The Art of Digital Audio* by John Watkinson if you're into this techy stuff.) The most important thing to remember when considering AD and DA converters is how well you like the sound. Even though the digital information might be treated the same way in different converters, the sound might be different for reasons beyond the scope of this book.

Taking a look at interface types

You can get an interface to connect with your computer by using one of three basic interfaces: PCI, FireWire, or USB. Although I cover these types in Chapter 1, here's a rundown on the differences between the three:

- **PCI:** PCI interfaces are inserted into one of the PCI slots located inside your computer's case.

- **FireWire:** FireWire interfaces connect to one of the FireWire ports in your computer.

- **USB:** USB interfaces connect to your computer — you guessed it — through one of the USB ports in your computer.

PCI interfaces

PCI is the old standard for getting audio in and out of a computer and has an advantage over the other interface types because of the fast transfer speed of PCI technology. This type of interface isn't without its problems, however. First, many computers don't have a PCI slot (laptops, for example, and all Macs except the Power Mac) and second, because PCI technology is changing not all cards fit in all computers. This can make finding the right PCI interface more challenging. (Though finding it certainly isn't impossible — besides, I help you out later in this chapter.)

The advantage with PCI interfaces is that the PCI (the river in which the data flows) is the fastest of the currently available ways to get audio into and out of your computer. This means that there is less delay (called *latency*) between the origin of the sound (when you hit a drum, for example) and when it gets into the computer and then back out again to your monitors. This is why many pros still prefer PCI to FireWire or USB.

This doesn't mean that the delay you can get with FireWire or USB has to be noticeable or can't be dealt with. You can in fact deal with it in a number of ways, as you find out in FireWire and USB sections later in this chapter. The latency issue, therefore, isn't the reason to go with PCI. Your decision is going to come down to what interface you find that you like.

PCI interfaces come in the following varieties:

✔ **Separate sound card with no analog inputs and outputs:** In this case, you need to buy separate preamps, direct boxes, and AD and DA converters. For most home recordists, the separate sound card route isn't the best solution. In fact, even for the pros this isn't the most popular choice — so much so that this option is quickly falling from the marketplace. (See Figure 4-1.)

Figure 4-1: Some PCI sound cards, such as the RME Hammerfall, have only digital inputs and outputs.

✔ **Analog inputs and outputs within the card:** It used to be the case that having the analog connection located in the card caused interference with the other components in the computer's housing (such as fans and hard drives) which caused low-level hums in the recorded audio. (Not a sound you'd want, I can assure you.) This generally isn't the case anymore unless it's a really inexpensive card, but the bad rep led buyers to shy away from this approach, and it has become uncommon as a result. You can find some less expensive audio interfaces configured this way, but the higher end of the market has pretty much abandoned it. (See Figure 4-2.)

✔ **Analog inputs and outputs housed in a separate box, called a *break-out box:*** Because of the low-level hum problems in the early interfaces (see the preceding bullet point), most manufacturers of PCI-based audio interfaces put their analog circuitry in a separate box with a cord attached to the PCI card. One advantage to this — besides eliminating the hum in early models — is that you can tweak the input and output levels without having to go into a software menu. The dials for the levels are placed on the break-out box within easy reach. (See Figure 4-3.)

Figure 4-2:
PCI interfaces like the M-Audio Audiophile 2496 often come with analog connectors.

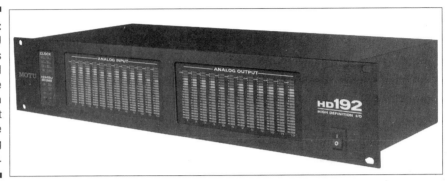

Figure 4-3:
The MOTU
HD192 is
a PCI
interface
with a
break-out
box for the
analog
components.

If you have a laptop and can't go with a PCI-based system and you want the high transfer speed of PCI, some makers of audio interfaces have a card that uses the PCMCIA card-slot. Of course, this works only if you have a laptop equipped with a PCMCIA jack.

If you want to go the PCI route, make sure that your computer has PCI slots that are compatible with the PCI interface that you're considering because not all computers have such slots. For example, the Digidesign 001 doesn't work with the PCI slots that you find in the Mac G5 computers.

Quite a few PCI-based audio interfaces are available on the market, and they range from just a couple hundred dollars up to a couple thousand.

FireWire interfaces

FireWire interfaces connect to the FireWire port in your computer. (Figure 4-4 shows a typical FireWire interface.) FireWire ports are inexpensive and available on laptop computers as well as desktops, which makes FireWire interfaces more versatile than PCI-based systems. For example, you can move the interface from computer to computer easily. If you have a laptop and a desktop computer, using a FireWire interface allows you to switch between the two computers by simply moving the FireWire cable from one to the other. If you want to do some location recording, this is a big plus because you can take your interface and laptop to a great recording room, record the drums or whatever, and then bring it all back home for mixing and editing in your studio.

Even though PCI-based systems have a faster pathway for sending and receiving audio data, FireWire is fast enough for most users. With FireWire, the *latency* that you can expect — the delay between the origin of the sound and when it gets into the computer and then back out again to your monitors — is only marginally more than what you'd get with PCI-based systems.

FireWire interfaces generally come with 8 to 10 inputs and outputs and run from around $500 to $1,500.

The only thing to be aware of when using a FireWire interface — and you want a lot of inputs and/or outputs — is the potential problem that might arise if you also have a FireWire hard drive that you want to record audio to. Basically, having the FireWire interface and the Fire Wire hard drive on the same FireWire bus is asking for trouble because you're sure to hit the limits of the speed of FireWire data transfer. So make sure that the two FireWire devices are on different busses (data channels).

USB interfaces

USB interfaces (see Figure 4-5) are handy because most computers have at least one USB port, so finding a place to plug one in is easy. They also represent a low-cost solution for people needing only a couple inputs and outputs. The only problem with USB for recording audio is the relatively slow transfer speed. This slower transfer speed translates into latencies higher than either FireWire or PCI-based interfaces. The latency is significant enough that you're very likely to hear it when you record.

To get around this deficit, most makers of USB interfaces have incorporated some sort of "no latency monitoring" option. With such an option, you can record without hearing a delay between the tracks that you've already recorded and the one you're currently recording. The problem here is that, with such an option, your newly recorded track gets placed out of synch with the previously recorded tracks. Correcting the synchronization requires you to move your overdubbed tracks within your song file. Admittedly, this process is pretty easy, but it does take time. (I explain how to do this in detail in Chapter 11.) If you don't want the hassle of messing with the latency in USB interface-based systems, your best bet is to go either the PCI, FireWire, or (see the next paragraph, please) the soon-to-be-readily-available USB2 route.

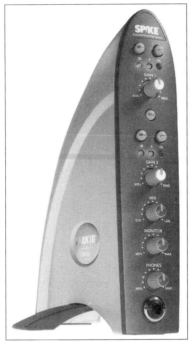

Figure 4-5:
A USB
interface,
like the
Mackie
Spike-XD2,
connects
to your
computer's
USB port.

USB2 interfaces, at the time of this writing, are just becoming available. USB2 has a much higher transfer speed, so the latency issue is, well, a non-issue. As more options appear, you might find that USB2 is the way you want to go.

USB interfaces can be found for under $200, and USB2 interfaces (well, the only one currently available) run about $700.

Controller-based interfaces

Both FireWire and USB interfaces are offered with additional functionality in the form of controllers. These can be keyboard controllers or mixer controllers.

A keyboard controller interface is usually USB-connected and has a couple octaves of keyboard keys as well as two inputs (with preamps) and two outputs. This can be a handy solution if you intend to do a lot of recording with software-based keyboard sounds (called soft-synths — Chapter 13 has more on this) because this type of controller doesn't actually contain any keyboard sounds — the keyboard simply triggers the MIDI sequencer within your recording program. Figure 4-6 shows this type of controller.

Figure 4-6:
A keyboard
controller
interface,
such as the
M-Audio
Ozonic,
offers a
MIDI key-
board and
a couple
audio inputs
and outputs.

Mixer controllers, like the one shown in Figure 4-7, contain multiple audio inputs and outputs along with typical mixer functions — track faders and transport functions, to name just two — that give you the feel of an analog mixer while at the same time allowing you to use your audio recording software program to control the mixer parameters.

Figure 4-7:
The mixer
controller
interface
gives you
the ability to
control your
software
mixer with
physical
controls.

Finding the right interface for you

Over a hundred different audio interfaces are available on the market, with new ones coming out almost daily. As you can imagine, having so many choices out there can make deciding on the perfect one for your studio rather difficult. This section offers some insights based on your needs, the available options, and my ideas about what's important.

Exploring your needs

To help you get clear on your needs and desires — well, at least your audio interface needs and desires — here are some things to consider:

✓ **Budget:** For most people, cost is the primary consideration when looking for a computer interface. Just remember that, when you tote up the price for your new interface, you need to figure in the additional cost of a decent audio recording program. Many people think that the free program that comes with many interfaces is going to be adequate for their needs — and it usually doesn't take long for them to be proven wrong. Most interfaces (aside from the Digidesign ones) come with a basic, entry-level program that you'll likely outgrow very quickly.

✓ **Musical style:** The style of music that you want to record can have an impact on the type of interface that you can use. For example, if you're in a rock band and see yourself recording live — just so you can get the feel of the music to come through in all its in-your-faceness — you might need a lot of inputs and outputs. This pretty much necessitates a PCI or FireWire interface with at least eight analog inputs. On the other hand, if you're into electronic music, a USB keyboard controller interface might be the best solution.

✓ **The computer:** Your choice of computer will play a role in your final decision on an interface. For example, if you have a laptop, you won't be able to go the PCI route, and if you have an older computer without a FireWire port, you obviously can't go that route unless you put one in your computer. In this case, you can use a USB interface, assuming that you have USB ports in your computer or you use one of the very few PCMCIA cards if your laptop has one of these connectors.

✓ **Audio and MIDI capabilities:** Your decision on whether or not you want to do any MIDI recording is going to determine what type of gear you need. Many interfaces come with a single MIDI port. For some people, a single port is just fine, but if you intend to do a lot of MIDIing, you might need more than that. In this case you'll need to budget in a separate MIDI interface.

Examining some options

The following list clues you in on some of the major manufacturers of audio interfaces, and it highlights the flagship products in their lines:

✔ **Aardvark:** (www.aardvarkaudio.com) Aardvark makes several different audio interfaces, most of which are PCI-based. (Okay, they do have one USB interface.) All their interfaces come bundled with the Cubase LE audio recording software program and cost from about $300 to over $1,000. (Cubase LE is the entry-level version of Cubase. Check out Chapter 7 for more information about Cubase software.)

✔ **Digidesign:** (www.digidesign.com) Digidesign is the maker of Pro Tools software. (See Chapter 6 for more on Pro Tools.) Currently, Digidesign makes two FireWire interfaces (the Digi 002 and Digi 002 Rack) and one USB interface (the Mbox). The Digi 002 interface is also a mixer controller. All these interfaces come bundled with Pro Tools LE software (the entry-level version of Pro Tools), and individually they range in price from about $500 to $2,400.

✔ **ECHO:** (www.echoaudio.com) ECHO makes PCI-based interfaces as well as PCMCIA interface cards for laptop computers. Their prices range from under $200 for a PCMCIA 2 input/2 output card to almost $1,000 for an 8 input/8 output system. ECHO interfaces come bundled with Tracktion software.

✔ **Edirol:** (www.edirol.com/products/audio.html) Edirol makes several interfaces, including USB versions, FireWire versions, and the only USB2 interface on the market. Edirol also has some interfaces with effects units built inside them and a keyboard controller interface. As of this writing, Edirol products don't come with any bundled software and run from about $300 to $1,000.

✔ **E-Mu:** (www.emu.com) E-Mu makes a number of PCI-based interfaces, some with analog inputs and outputs in the card itself and others with a separate break-out box for the analog components. A FireWire port is also included with the highest-end model (the 1820M) that lets you plug in a peripheral such as a hard drive. Prices range from under $200 to $600, depending on the number of inputs and outputs you want. Recording software isn't included, but E-Mu includes effects processors that don't rely on the processor power of your computer — the effects use a DSP card in the 1820 model instead.

✔ **Lynx Studio Technology:** (www.lynxstudio.com) Lynx Studio Technology makes high-end PCI cards. These cards consist of 2, 4, or 6 analog inputs and outputs and no preamps. The lack of preamps isn't a problem for most of their users because the kind of folks interested in such high-end cards usually want to use their own converters and analog components (preamps, compressors, and so on) and therefore get these cards to act as the sound card only. All but one of its cards has two digital inputs and outputs. Prices range from around $500 to well over $1,000 depending on your input and output needs. These cards don't come with any software.

✔ **M-Audio:** (www.m-audio.com) M-Audio makes quite a few interfaces, including PCI, FireWire, USB, and keyboard controller options. Prices range from under $200 to around $600. The M-Audio interfaces come bundled with some software — usually Abelton Live Delta, Reason Adapted, and/or others. Check with your dealer to see which software is being offered.

✔ **MOTU (Mark of the Unicorn):** (www.motu.com) MOTU makes both PCI and FireWire interfaces. MOTU is at the higher-end of the complete interface spectrum, which gets reflected in its cost — from about $750 to around $1,800, depending on the number of inputs, outputs, and preamps you want. MOTU interfaces come bundled with the Audio Desk software program, which can be upgraded to Digital Performer for a couple hundred dollars. (Chapter 7 has more on these software programs).

✔ **RME:** (www.rme-audio.com) RME originally made only high-end PCI sound cards that use just digital inputs and outputs. Lately, it has included analog inputs and outputs in some of its products and has added both a PCMCIA card for laptops and a FireWire interface to its line. Prices range from under $300 for the PCMCIA card to over $1,000 for a PCI-based interface with analog input and outputs. RME products don't come with any recording software.

✔ **TASCAM:** (www.tascam.com) TASCAM makes several USB and FireWire interfaces — and many with a mixer controller included. Prices range from about $200 for a simple 2-channel USB interface to around $1,300 for a mixer controller FireWire unit. TASCAM units come with an entry-level version of the Cubasis recording software.

Making your choice

Choosing between all the options out there can be difficult. My advice is pretty simple: Choose the software and get hardware that works with it. The software is where you're going to do your work. The interface is just the way to get the sound to and from the software. If you choose the best software for your long-term needs, you can update and upgrade your hardware as your budget and experience allow.

Check out how your initial decision about what software to use can help you focus on the right interface for you. If you want to work with Pro Tools software, for example, you need to use Digidesign hardware, so right there you've narrowed down the wide world of interface choices to just three models. (Okay, okay, this probably isn't that fair an example because most software is much more forgiving when it comes to the hardware you can use, but it makes a dramatic point, so I use it anyway.) Now if your budget is tight or you need only two inputs at a time, your three choices have suddenly become just one — an Mbox from Digidesign will get you going just fine.

Here's the beauty of it: As your needs grow — say that you decide that you want to record your whole band and need eight inputs — all you have to do is upgrade your hardware to a Digi 002 or Digi 002 Rack. By choosing an interface based on the software, your transition from the two-input USB interface to the eight-input (analog) FireWire interface is as simple as unplugging the Mbox and plugging in the Digi 002 (or Digi 002 Rack). All your existing songs are still accessible to you, and you don't have to learn new software.

On the other hand, if you choose an interface based solely on the hardware features — on the specs, how cool it looks, or what it costs — you might find that the software you want to run doesn't work so well with the interface you bought (or doesn't work at all in the case of Pro Tools). And, as I discuss in Chapter 7, not all software or hardware works well on both computer platforms (Mac and Windows).

Choose the software first. This will dictate, depending on your choice, which computer platform you'll use and will steer you in a direction for an audio interface. The maker of the software lists the types of computers and hardware that will work with its program. Check out the manufacturer's Web site to help you narrow down your choices.

Also, in most cases, the software that's bundled with the audio interface is worth precisely what you paid for it — nothing, or at least close to it. If you plan on recording for months or years to come, you'll find that most of these bundled programs are severely limited, and you'll outgrow them about as fast as you get comfortable using them.

I don't mean to sound negative, but in my experience with helping people set up their studios, I've seen too many people end up spending a lot of time figuring out the free software only to have to start over again with a new program. I suggest that you spend some time going through Chapters 6 and 7 and researching the best software for your needs before you choose the hardware to run it. (This includes computers as well as audio components.)

Making Use of MIDI

Many people who want to record on a computer end up recording MIDI as well as audio. MIDI stands for *M*usical *I*nstrument *D*igital *I*nterface and is a way for you to control one MIDI-equipped instrument from another or from a computer that has MIDI sequencing software. (See Chapter 6.) This lets you record your musical ideas into your computer and edit the data later on. This can be an advantage when the time comes to edit out any performance mistakes you might have committed. Because a MIDI recording is simply performance information — no sound is contained in the files — you can edit any clonkers pretty easily. For example, say you play your part with incredible feeling but you missed a couple notes here and there. With a MIDI recording, you can simply change those incorrect notes into the right ones by dragging them with your mouse. (See Chapter 11 for more details.) If this happens with an audio file, you have to re-record the botched notes by using a punching process, a procedure that I talk about in more detail in Chapter 10. This process takes more time and is more work than fixing a bad MIDI note.

Understanding MIDI

MIDI is a protocol (a set of agreed-upon standards) for issuing commands to MIDI-equipped devices (such as your keyboards and your computer) through a cabled connection and a common digital language. This arrangement allows each MIDI device to understand the other, regardless of manufacturer or instrument. All that's required is an instrument equipped with MIDI ports (jacks).

MIDI data is different from an audio recording because it contains no sound as such; rather, it's limited to *performance information.* This can be information about various performance characteristics, which (for keyboards, at least) includes the following:

- ✔ **Note-on and note-off:** What note is played and when.
- ✔ **Velocity:** How hard someone presses a key.
- ✔ **After-touch:** Whether the key pressure changes after the initial press.
- ✔ **Vibrato and pitch bend:** Whether the pitch changes while a key is pressed.

This information allows the MIDI musician to potentially create a performance that is as rich in texture as those of the world's finest players.

Digital messages sent from one device to another across a cable (called the *MIDI cable,* of course) create MIDI data. The cable connects to MIDI ports on each device, and the messages are sent in the form of binary digits. Each instrument can understand and respond to these messages.

Gearing up

Okay, so this MIDI thing sounds kind of interesting to you, and you want to know just what you're going to need to buy to do some MIDIing yourself. Because you're going to use a computer to record, this can be pretty simple. Here's a list of the basics for a computer-based system:

- ✔ **A sound generator:** This device has locked within it all the wonderful sounds that you want to use to create beautiful music together; it can be a synthesizer, drum machine, sound module, software synthesizer, sampler, or any other MIDI-equipped sound-making device.

- ✔ **A MIDI interface:** You use a MIDI interface to enable your computer to send and receive MIDI data to external MIDI instruments. A number of audio interfaces contain MIDI ports (jacks for connecting MIDI cables; see Chapter 5), but you'll come across some that don't. If the interface has one, it'll generally contain just one input and output. For many people this is enough to get the job done, but for people who want to do a lot of MIDI work, you might need to get a dedicated MIDI interface.

- ✔ **A MIDI controller:** This is the device you use to control the sound generator ("playing" it, essentially) as part of recording your MIDI performance data. This can be a synthesizer, any MIDI-capable keyboard, or one of a number of controllers created specifically to control the soft-synths in your computer.

- ✔ **A sequencer:** This device records and plays the MIDI performances that are programmed into it. The sequencer allows you to program your part into the synthesizer and have it play back automatically (much like the old-time player piano). The sequencer will be part of your audio/MIDI recording software. Check out Chapters 6 and 7 for suggestions on finding the right software for your needs.

In the following sections, I detail each of these basic components so that you have a better sense of what features to look for when you do your MIDI shopping.

Sound generators

The sound generator is the core of the MIDI studio. This is what produces the sounds that you hear. Without it, you might as well skip the rest of the stuff because, of course, you won't hear any of your work.

Sound generators can come in many different shapes and sizes: software synthesizers (soft-synths), the fully functional keyboard synthesizer, the independent drum machine, the standalone sound module, and samplers. Each of these devices has its strengths and weaknesses. (Continue on for the details.)

Soft-synths

If you've chosen a computer-based system to run your home studio on, your DAW (digital audio workstation) software enables you to produce great sounds by using soft-synth plug-ins. Soft-synths are basically software equivalents of standalone synthesizers, sound modules, or samplers. As you can see in Figure 4-8, a soft-synth's GUI — its graphical user interface, the smiling face that the software shows to the world — is often designed to look just like a piece of regular hardware, complete with virtual buttons and knobs.

As in all things, soft-synths have their advantages and disadvantages:

- ✓ **Advantages:** Soft-synths cost less than standalone units because no hardware is involved. In addition, changing sounds or even synthesizer types is quick and easy from within your recording program. Chapters 6 and 7 spell this out in greater detail.

- ✓ **Disadvantages:** Unlike regular synthesizers, soft-synths use up processor power. This can slow down your computer system and prevent you from recording as many audio tracks or applying as many effect patches as you'd like. The way around this is to get an extra hard drive to house all your soft-synth sounds. This keeps them separate from your audio files and often results in you being able to have more playback tracks. (I say *often* because there are a lot variables that come into play here. For the complete scoop on processor demand, see Chapter 3.)

If you don't already own a bunch of synthesizers, I recommend going the soft-synth route. The advantages far outweigh the disadvantages, and the number of options with truly astounding sound is simply staggering (say that fast ten times).

Figure 4-8: Computer-based DAW users can choose soft-synths to create their synthesizer sounds.

Synthesizer

A synthesizer, like the one shown in Figure 4-9, consists of sounds as well as a keyboard for playing those sounds. Synthesizers come in a variety of sizes and configurations. For example, some keyboards come with 61 keys (5 octaves), and others provide as many 88 keys — the same number of keys that you find on an acoustic piano keyboard.

If you're in the market for a synthesizer, you need to consider several things:

✔ **Polyphony:** *Polyphony* is the number of notes that sound at one time. Most decent synthesizers nowadays have at least 16 notes of polyphony, although models that can produce 32 notes at once are not uncommon.

Each manufacturer treats polyphony differently, and the GM standards allow some variations on the effective use of this parameter. (GM stands for General MIDI — a set of sounds common to all MIDI instruments. These sounds let you play a recorded performance on any device and hear the sounds that the composer intended for the piece.) For instance, a synth patch (sound) might use more than one digital sound to create the actual sound you hear. The synth patch that you love so much might, in fact, consist of four different sounds layered on top of one another. In such a case, you just reduced your polyphony by ¾ just by using that one patch. If your synthesizer has 16-note polyphony, it's now down to 4-note polyphony because each of those 4 notes has 4 "sounds" associated with it. If you use this patch, you can play only 4 notes (a simple chord) at a time, not the 16 that you thought you had to work with.

Your best bet is to buy a synthesizer (or sound module) with the highest polyphony you can get (32 notes would be nice), especially if you want to layer one sound on top of another or do multitimbral parts (see next bullet) with your synth.

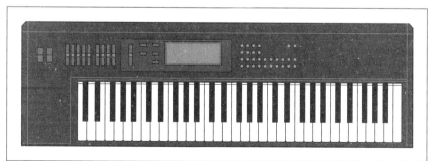

Figure 4-9:
A typical synthesizer contains a keyboard and a variety of sounds.

✔ **Multitimbrality:** Most decent keyboards allow you to play more than one sound patch at a time. This is called *multitimbrality,* which basically allows you to have your keyboard divided up into several groups of sounds. For example, a multitimbral synth can divide a song's chords, melody, bass part, and drum-set sounds into different groups of sounds — and then play all those groups at once.

If you do any sequencing (recording or playing back MIDI data), a multi-timbral synth is a must-have. Otherwise, you would need a separate synthesizer for each type of sound that you want to play. Fortunately, with the GM standards, compatible synthesizers made in the last ten years have the ability to play at least 16 sounds at once.

✔ **Keyboard feel:** Some keyboards have weighted keys and feel like real pianos, but other keyboards have a somewhat spongy action. If you're a trained piano player, a spongy keyboard might feel strange to you. On the other hand, if you have no piano training and don't need weighted keys, you don't necessarily have to pay the extra money for that feature.

✔ **Sound quality:** This is a subjective thing. Choose the synthesizer that has the sounds you think you'll use. I know this seems kind of obvious, but it means that you should buy the synthesizer whose sounds you actually like — even if this means waiting and saving up some more money before you can buy. If you buy a synth based solely on the belief that it was a good deal but don't love the sounds, you've wasted your money because you'll just end up buying the more expensive one later anyway.

✔ **Built-in sequencer:** Many keyboards contain a built-in sequencer, which will allow you to program and play back your performance. Units like these are usually called *keyboard workstations* or *MIDI workstations* because they contain everything you need to create a song. If you're considering one of these complete workstations, take a good, hard look at the sequencer and the user interface — make sure that you like the way these features work for you. Each manufacturer treats the process of sequencing a little differently; you can probably find one that fits your style of working.

Drum machine

A drum machine contains not only the sounds of the drum set and other more exotic drums, but also a sequencer to allow you to program rhythms. Figure 4-10 shows you what a typical drum machine looks like.

Most drum machines contain hundreds of drum sounds, numerous preset rhythm patches, and the ability to program dozens of songs. In addition, all standalone drum machines have pads on which you can play the part. The more advanced drum machines can give your rhythms a more human feel. Effects, such as reverb and delay, are also fairly common on the more advanced drum machines.

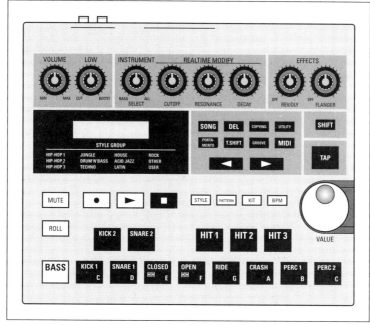

Figure 4-10:
A drum machine has drum sounds and a sequencer to program rhythms.

Sound module

A *sound module* is basically a stripped-down version of a synthesizer or drum machine. Sound modules don't contain triggering devices (such as the keys for the keyboard, hex pickups for the guitar, or pads for the drum machine). What they do contain are a variety of sounds (often hundreds) that a master controller or sequencer can trigger. The advantage to sound modules is that they take up little space and cost considerably less than their fully endowed counterparts (the synths and drum machines, that is).

If you already have a master keyboard, you might find that adding sound modules is a cost- and space-effective way to add more sounds to your system.

Samplers

A *sampler* is a sound module that contains short audio samples of real instruments. Most samplers come with sound libraries containing hundreds of different types of sounds, from acoustic pianos to snare drums to sound effects. These sounds are often much more realistic than those that come in some synthesizers.

The real purpose of a sampler is to allow you to record your own sounds. For example, in the '80s, it was cool to make a drum set out of unusual percussive sounds. A snare drum could be the sound of a flushing toilet (don't laugh, I actually did this) or breaking glass. Tom-toms could be vocal grunts assigned to certain pitches. You'd be amazed at the strange stuff that people have turned into music — all with the help of a sampler.

Another common use of a sampler involves recording short sections of already recorded songs. This can be a melodic or rhythmic phrase, a vocal cue, or a single drum or synth sound. Sampling other songs is common in electronic music, rap, and hip-hop. (Be careful of copyright issues before doing this, however.) If you're into electronic music or hip-hop, you might find a sampler a necessary addition to your studio.

MIDI interface

The MIDI interface allows you to send and receive MIDI information from a computer. Many audio interfaces come standard with a MIDI port, but if you end up doing a lot of MIDI sequencing and use more than one sound module or external controller — or if you lucked out and your audio interface doesn't have a single MIDI port — you need a separate MIDI interface, such as the one shown in Figure 4-11.

MIDI interfaces come in a staggering variety of configurations, so you need to consider several things when you buy a MIDI interface. The following questions can help you to determine your needs:

✔ **What type of computer do you own?** MIDI interfaces are configured to connect to a serial, parallel, or USB port. You determine which one to use by the type of port(s) you have in your computer. For example, new Macs have only a USB port (although you can add a serial port if you remove the internal modem). A PC has either a parallel port or a USB port (sometimes both). PCs also have a joystick port that accepts a special MIDI joystick cable (no MIDI interface is needed).

✔ **How many instruments do you intend to connect?** MIDI interfaces come with a variety of input and output configurations. Models can come with two, four, or even eight ins and outs. There are also thru boxes that have one or more inputs and several outputs. If you have only one or two instruments, you can get by with a smaller interface. (In this case, a 2 x 2 interface — two ins and outs — would work great.) If you have many instruments that you want to connect, you need a larger box.

If you use a keyboard controller such as the M-Audio Oxygen8 shown in Figure 4-12, you don't need a separate MIDI interface because it has one of its own. This type of device connects to your computer's USB port instead of through a MIDI port. This keeps you from having to get a MIDI interface in addition to the keyboard controller. Many controller options use this USB connection.

Figure 4-11:
A MIDI
interface is
necessary if
you want to
connect
your
instrument
to a
computer.

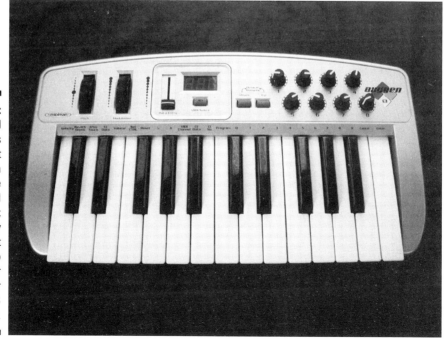

Figure 4-12:
Keyboard
controllers
often don't
need a
separate
MIDI
interface;
they
connect
directly to
your
computer
via a USB
port.

MIDI controller

A MIDI controller is essentially what its name describes — it's a device that can control another MIDI device. MIDI controllers come in many different formats. In fact, a MIDI controller can be anything from a synthesizer to a drum machine, a USB keyboard to a xylophone.

When MIDI first came out, your controller choice was limited to a keyboard, but now you can choose between keyboards, wind controllers (for saxophones or other wind instruments), guitars, or drums. So if you don't play piano, you're not stuck trying to fake your way through a keyboard just so you can use MIDI; you can find a controller that resembles an instrument that you know how to play. Look around, and you might find one (or more) MIDI controllers that allow you to create music your way.

Nowadays you can find MIDI controllers with the following types of connections:

- ✔ **MIDI ports:** All MIDI-compatible instruments, such as a standalone synthesizer, have MIDI ports. To use this type of controller with your computer, you need to have a MIDI or audio interface with MIDI ports in it.

- ✔ **USB:** The trend for many manufacturers is to skip the MIDI ports and to use USB ports instead (Refer to Figure 4-12 for a look at one such controller.) This action allows you to plug your controller directly into your computer without the need for a separate MIDI or MIDI ports in your audio interface.

In addition to controllers with MIDI ports or USB connections, you can also find some MIDI controllers that contain audio interfaces in them. (The M-Audio Ozone, for example, is a MIDI interface, a MIDI controller, and an audio interface all in one.)

Sequencer

Although you can get standalone sequencers as well as sequencers integrated into a synthesizer, you probably want to just use the sequencer in your audio recording software. The reasons for this are many, but the overriding factor is that using the software sequencer lets you keep your MIDI and audio tracks in one place, and most computer MIDI programs offer you more powerful editing capabilities than a sequencer that's contained in a box and that uses a tiny LCD screen.

Not all recording software has MIDI capabilities. Moreover, keep in mind that not all software programs that *do* support MIDI can accomplish the whole MIDI implementation thing equally well. (In fact, you're going to see big differences in quality.) If MIDI is important to you, make sure you get a program that has the functions that you need. (I explain the various recording software programs and where they stand on MIDI in Chapters 6 and 7.)

Adding Microphones to Your Studio

If you're going to want to record any singing or any acoustic instruments, you're going to need at least one microphone. A mic's job is generally to try to capture, as closely as possible, the sound of an instrument. But you can also use a microphone to infuse a specific sound characteristic into a performance.

Making sense of microphone types

This section explores your microphone options and helps you make sense of them.

Construction types

Whether a mic is a $10 cheapie that has a cord permanently attached to it or a $15,000 pro model with gold-plated fittings, all mics convert sound waves to electrical impulses that the preamp or mixer can read and the recorder can store. Each of the three construction types — ribbon, dynamic, and condenser — captures this auditory signal in a different way, and as such, each adds certain characteristics to the sound. Here's how the different mics affect sound:

- **Ribbon:** Adds silkiness to the recorded sound because it rolls off the higher frequencies slightly.
- **Dynamic:** Tends to accent the middle of the frequency spectrum.
- **Condenser:** Tends to have a well-rounded frequency response.

I detail these aspects in the following sections. In most cases, the type of construction dictates the general cost category in which the mics fit.

Condenser microphones

The condenser microphone is, without a doubt, the most popular style of mic used in recording studios (home or commercial). Condenser mics are sensitive and accurate, but they can also be expensive. Recently, however, condenser mics have come down in cost, and you can buy a decent one for around $200. Very good ones start at about $500.

The condenser mic has an extremely thin metal (or metal-coated plastic or Mylar) diaphragm (the part that senses the signal). The diaphragm is suspended in front of a metal plate (called a *backplate*). Polarizing voltage is applied to both the diaphragm and the backplate, creating a static charge in the space between them. When the diaphragm picks up a sound, it vibrates into the field between it and the backplate. This produces a small signal that can then be amplified. Figure 4-13 shows how a condenser mic is constructed.

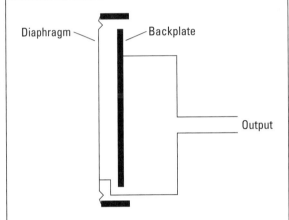

Figure 4-13: A condenser mic consists of a very thin diaphragm suspended parallel to a backplate.

Dynamic microphones

Chances are you've had a chance to use a dynamic mic. Two hugely popular Shure models characterize this type of mic — the SM57 and the SM58, which has a silvery ball of gridded wire at one end and an XLR connector at the other. Dynamic mics have several qualities that make them unique. First, they can handle a lot of volume (technically known as *SPL,* meaning Sound Pressure Level), which makes them perfect for extremely loud signals, such as drums, amplifiers, and some rock vocals. Dynamic mics aren't as transparent as condenser mics (they don't represent high frequencies as accurately), so they often impart a dirty or gritty sound to the signal.

The dynamic mic uses a magnetic field to convert the sound impulse from the diaphragm into electrical energy (as in Figure 4-14). The diaphragm, often made of plastic or Mylar, is located in front of a coil of wire called a *voice coil.* The voice coil is suspended between two magnets. When the diaphragm moves (the result of a sound), the voice coil moves as well. The interaction between the voice coil's movement and the magnets creates the electrical signal.

The sound of a dynamic mic can be described as somewhat boxy, meaning that these mics don't represent the highest or lowest frequencies of your hearing spectrum accurately (not necessarily a bad thing). They're also durable. Rough treatment probably won't damage them much (aside from the diaphragm), and a tough metal screen protects it. Dynamic mics are the type used most often for live shows. They tend to be inexpensive to buy and easy to maintain; you can get a good dynamic mic for around $100.

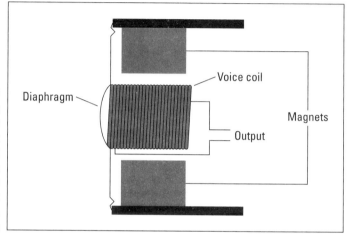

Figure 4-14:
Dynamic mics pick up a signal by using a magnetic field and a voice coil.

Ribbon microphones

A ribbon microphone produces its sound in much the same way as a dynamic mic. The diaphragm is suspended between two magnets (sound familiar?) but this type of mic uses a thin ribbon of aluminum (see Figure 4-15) instead of the plastic or Mylar you'd find in a dynamic mic. Although ribbon mics were very popular from around the 1930s to the 1960s, they've mostly taken a backseat to condenser mics in today's studios. This is mainly because ribbon mics are fragile, expensive, and aren't as transparent as condenser mics. In fact, a gust of wind or a strong breath into the diaphragm is all it takes to break a ribbon mic.

Ribbon mics are experiencing a renaissance because a lot of recording engineers are searching for an old, vintage sound. Ribbon mics have a unique sound that is often described as silky or smooth. This essentially means that the high frequencies tend to *roll off* (gradually reduce) slightly, and the lower frequencies smear together a bit.

Ribbon mics are fairly expensive. You'd be hard pressed to find a new one for much less than $1,000.

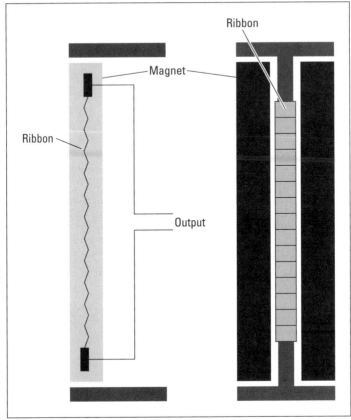

Figure 4-15:
Ribbon mics
use a ribbon
suspended
between two
magnets to
create their
signals.

Polarity patterns

Microphones pick up sounds in different ways, which are known as *polarity patterns*. Here's how the various patterns work:

- ✔ **Omnidirectional** mics can capture sounds all around them.
- ✔ **Cardioid** (or directional) mics pick up sounds just in front of them.
- ✔ **Figure-8** (or bidirectional) mics pick up sounds from both the front and back.

The polarity patterns on mics are represented on a chart that often comes with the mic (or as part of its spec sheet). This chart (often called a *polar graph*) shows how well the mic picks up various frequencies in front of or behind it.

You can say a lot about polarity patterns — in fact, you can find lots that *I've* said about polarity patterns in the second edition of my *Home Recording For Musicians For Dummies* — but I don't have the space in this book to cover *everything.* (Besides, the editors told me to concentrate on the PC stuff.)

Choosing mics

Getting the right mic for the right recording situation is a bit of an art form — an art form I describe in some detail in *Home Recording For Musicians For Dummies.* The following highly condensed version of my What Microphone to Use When spiel sums it all up in just three simple questions:

✔ **What type of music will you record?** If you play rock or pop music, you probably want to start with dynamic mics because they're inexpensive and their limitations in high or low frequencies don't matter as much as they would if (for example) you wanted to record your string quartet. In this case, a pair of condenser mics would do the trick.

✔ **What instruments will you record?** Loud amps, drums, and screaming singers beg to be recorded with dynamic mics, whereas light percussion, vocals, and stand-up basses shine through with large diaphragm condenser mics.

✔ **How many mics will you use at once?** If you need to record your whole band at once, budget constraints might dictate your choice between dynamic and condenser mics or a condenser or ribbon mic for vocals. If you need only a couple mics to record the occasional vocal or instrument, you can invest more in each mic.

Monitors

The last bit of audio component gear you need is some sort of monitor. This can be speakers or headphones. In fact, I recommend that you get both. Headphones allow you to hear yourself while you record, and speakers let you mix more effectively.

Without good monitors, you're mixing in the dark because you don't know what your music is going to sound like on someone else's system. Good monitors let you hear your music clearly enough so that you can create mixes that translate well (meaning they sound good on many playback systems). I discuss this concept in more detail in Chapter 14.

If your budget is really stretched tight and you can't yet afford a decent set of monitor speakers, I recommend that you get a good set of headphones and use them exclusively until you have the bucks for some decent monitors. Another option is to use your stereo speakers as your studio monitors until you can get a real set (still get the good headphones, though).

Headphones

Chances are that your first home studio will be in a spare bedroom or a corner of your garage or basement. All your recording, monitoring, and mixing will be done in this room. If that's the case, you'll find that a set of headphones is indispensable. When you use headphones, you can turn off your speakers and still hear what's being (or has been) recorded. When you go to record a guitar by using a microphone in front of the guitar amp, you want to hear only the guitar — not the guitar amp *and* the guitar amp coming back through your monitors. Headphones allow you to do this.

Headphones can range in price from about $20 up to several hundred, so surely one is within your price range. Before you buy a set of headphones you need to consider one main issue: bleed.

Bleed is the sound from the headphones coming out into the room. This isn't a big deal when you mix or monitor an already recorded track, but it can mess up your music when you record. If you're going to use headphones while you track (record) with a mic, make sure you get headphones with a closed back, such as the AKG 240. Open-back headphones often bleed too much for this purpose. The problem is that you can't always see the difference between open- and closed-back headphones. You need to look at the specs of the headphones to find out.

Monitor speakers

For most home recordists, the first set of monitor speakers (often simply referred to as monitors) consist of the home stereo system, but sooner or later you're gonna want a real set of monitors. Studio monitors come in many varieties, but the home recordist's best bet is a set of near-field monitors. *Near-field monitors* are speakers that are designed to be positioned close to you (which is often the case anyway because most home recordists have very little room in which to work).

Near-field monitors come in two varieties:

✔ **Passive:** Passive monitors are just the speakers themselves, which means that you'll need to buy a separate amplifier to use them. If you go this route, make sure to save some bucks for the amps because they can cost as much as the speakers. Also keep in mind that the kind of amp you get will impact the sound of the speakers — not all amps sound the same.

✔ **Active:** These monitors come with their own amplifiers. Going the active route has a couple advantages: First, the amps are matched to the speakers so you can (theoretically) get a better sound from them, and second, you don't have to buy amplifiers separately. This keeps you from having to make yet another difficult decision when gearing up your studio. (Do you have any idea how many amps are out there? Yep, tons.)

Whatever monitors you get, they only work for mixing your music as well as you can hear them properly. I can't stress enough how important it is to get used to your monitor (see Chapter 14) and to make sure your room sounds as good as possible (see Chapter 2).

Chapter 5

Connecting Your Hardware

In This Chapter

▶ Getting to know the various types of connectors

▶ Plugging in your equipment

▶ Understanding the signal chain

So, you've got a pile of shiny new gear sitting in your recording space and you're ready to start plugging it all in. The problem is that there might be a bunch of cords and jacks that you don't know what to do with. No problem. In this chapter, I help you make sense of all those connectors that you end up using — and help you get them all plugged in properly.

Making Connections

No matter what type of home recording equipment you have, one thing's for sure — you're gonna have to plug in some cords somewhere. Exactly where depends on the particular system you own, so read through this section to make sense of all those different cords and connectors, whether analog or digital.

You probably have a lot of experience with analog connectors and cords, such as the ones on your stereo system. But you might never have come in contact with digital connectors, unless you've plugged in a DVD player to your TV or had a chance to go into a recording studio that uses digital gear.

Analog

No doubt you've had a chance to see and use a variety of analog connectors. If you play an electric guitar or keyboard (synthesizer), for example, you're familiar with a quarter-inch analog plug. And if you've used a variety of different microphones, you've probably come across one with an XLR analog plug.

Keeping the different kinds of analog plugs straight can be a little confusing, however. Why do you have to use one plug for one thing and another for something else? And what's a TRS plug, anyway?

Read on to decipher the secrets of the most common analog connectors: quarter-inch (TS and TRS), XLR, and RCA.

The quarter-inch analog plug

The *quarter-inch plug* is the most common audio connector and one of the most versatile as well. (You see it on cables strung all over the studio to connect instruments, amps, speakers, headphones, and mixers.) Quarter-inch plugs come in two varieties: TS or TRS.

TS

The humble plug at the end of the cord you use for your guitar or synthesizer is an example of a *TS* plug (short for Tip/Sleeve): The *tip* is the very tip of the plug, and the *sleeve* is the rest of the cylindrical metal part. A plastic divider separates the two sections, each of which is connected to a different part of the cable. Check out Figure 5-1 to see this familiar plug.

Figure 5-1:
A typical quarter-inch plug used for guitars and other electric instruments.

TS plugs are used for a variety of purposes — to go from your guitar to your guitar amp, from your synthesizer to your mixer, from your mixer to your power amplifier (amp), and from your power amp to your speakers. You'd expect that one cord could work for all these applications. After all, a TS plug is a TS plug is a TS plug, right? Well, not really. The same plug can be *wired* differently, and it can carry different levels of power. For example, an instrument cord (the one you use for your synthesizer or guitar) contains one wire and a shield — the wire is connected to the tip, and the shield is connected to the sleeve. A speaker cord, on the other hand, contains two wires and no shield — one wire is connected to the tip and the other to the sleeve.

The speaker cord also carries a lot more current (power) than the instrument cable; that's the reason it doesn't have a shield. The high signal level covers up any noise present in the cord. Because there isn't nearly as much current present in an instrument, you don't want to use a speaker cord for your instrument; you need the instrument cable's shield to keep the noise down. If you do use a speaker cord for your instrument, you might end up with some noise — a hiss, buzz, or even a radio broadcast coming out of your amp (or wherever you've plugged in your instrument).

When you buy cords with TS plugs, first be sure to look at (or ask) what purpose the cord is designed for. Then, when you get it home, be sure to make a note of what type of cord it is so that you use it correctly. You can mark your cord a number of ways: You can put colored tape on it (red for speaker or blue for instrument, for example), put a tag or label on it, or, gasp, dot it with nail polish.

You generally don't need to worry about which end of the cord you plug in to your instrument — the signal will travel equally well in either direction. However, currently (so to speak), you can buy cords that are designed to send the current in one direction. (The cord has an arrow on it designating which direction the signal should flow.) I call these *designer cords,* and two of the most common brands are Monster and Planet Waves. The theory behind these cords is that they do a better job of preserving the sound qualities of the instrument for which they're designed. These cords are specifically designed for almost every instrument and application known to humankind.

Instrument cords are often called *unbalanced lines* because of the way they're wired. An unbalanced cord has one wire surrounded by a braided shield; the wire is connected to the tip of the TS plug, and the shield is connected to the sleeve. The signal is sent through the wire, and the shield is used for the ground. (It keeps the noise down.) There are balanced lines as well, which I explain in the upcoming section on TRS plugs.

TRS

A *TRS* (short for Tip/Ring/Sleeve) quarter-inch plug looks like a stereo headphone plug (take a look at Figure 5-2). The *tip* is at the very end of the plug, the *ring* is the small middle section located between the two plastic dividers, and the *sleeve* is the rest of the cylindrical metal part of the plug. A TRS plug can be used several ways: as a stereo cord for headphones, a *balanced cord* or with a *Y cord.*

A *balanced cord* is used on professional audio gear to connect the various pieces of equipment (the mixer to the recorder, for example). The advantage with a balanced cord is that you can have longer cord runs without creating noise.

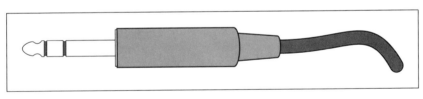

Figure 5-2:
Use a
balanced
(TRS) plug
to connect
professional
audio gear
together.

Why is it that balanced cords are so conveniently noise-free? The balanced cord has two wires and a shield inside, and is wired with the same signal running through both wires. One is 180 degrees out of phase with the other (their waveforms are exactly opposite) — the crest of one wave occurs at exactly the same time as the trough of the other, so they cancel each other out. When they get to the mixer (or wherever they're plugged into), one of the signals is instantly flipped and added to the other. Any noise that was built up in the signal is cancelled out. (Yep, it's wave cancellation from high-school physics. Who knew it also rocks?)

A *Y cord* consists of a TRS plug on one end and two TS plugs on the other, forming — you guessed it — a nice representation of the letter Y. The purpose of this cord is to allow you to insert an effects processor (a compressor or equalizer, for example) into the line-in insert jack of a mixer. The TRS plug both sends and receives a signal. The Y cord is wired so the tip sends the signal and the ring receives it (see Figure 5-3). The sleeve is connected to the shield of each cable.

XLR

The *XLR connector* is used for microphones and some line connections between professional gear. This cable has a female and a male end. (See Figure 5-4.) The cord is wired much like a TRS connector and is balanced to keep the noise down. The XLR microphone cable is also called a *low-Z cable* because it carries a low-impedance signal.

RCA

RCA plugs — named for good old RCA, also called *phono plugs* — are common on home stereo (and some semi-pro) audio gear. (See Figure 5-5.) They function much like a TS plug and aren't very common in professional audio equipment.

Some mixers include them, however, so you can connect a tape deck. They're also used for digital S/PDIF signals. (See the next section for more on these babies.)

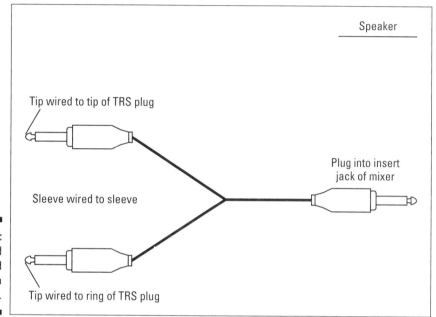

Speaker

Tip wired to tip of TRS plug

Plug into insert jack of mixer

Sleeve wired to sleeve

Figure 5-3:
Use a Y cord to send and receive a signal.

Tip wired to ring of TRS plug

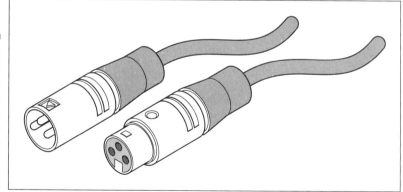

Figure 5-4:
An XLR connector: One end is male (left), and the other is female (right).

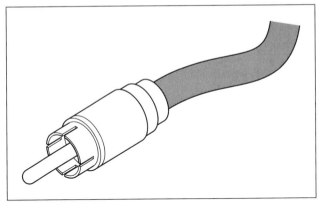

Figure 5-5:
An RCA plug is used mainly on consumer stereo and some semi-pro audio equipment.

Digital

Because you're sure to be using a digital audio interface in combination with your computer when recording, you're going to get comfortable with digital connectors. Digital audio equipment is a recent invention — no one standard has emerged. Because of this lack of standardization, a variety of digital connectors are on the market, only a few (or one) of which might be equipment that you own or intend to purchase. Regardless, knowing about the most common connectors and their purposes will help you decide what equipment is right for you.

MIDI

MIDI, short for Musical Instrument Digital Interface, is a handy communication protocol that allows musical information to pass from one device to another. To allow for the free passage of such information, MIDI jacks are located on a whole host of electronic instruments — synthesizers, drum machines, sound modules, and even some guitars have MIDI jacks. And, in order to connect all these instruments, you need some MIDI cables. The MIDI cable contains five pins (male) that plug in to the female MIDI jack (port) on the instrument or device. (See Figure 5-6.)

Some audio interfaces, such as the Digidesign Digi 002, have MIDI ports in them, but others, such as the MOTU 896, don't. If you want to use MIDI and you have an interface without MIDI ports, you obviously need to buy a separate MIDI interface. Regardless of which audio or MIDI interface you have, you will need to buy the cable for those ports separately.

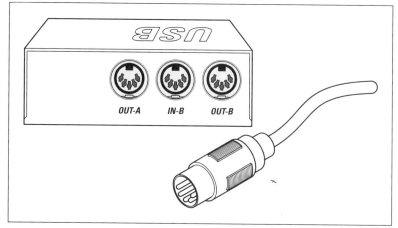

Figure 5-6:
MIDI
connections
have two
male ends.
The device
contains the
female jack.

AES/EBU

AES/EBU (Audio Engineering Society/European Broadcasting Union) cables are much like S/PDIF cables (see the following section). The AES/EBU standards require that these cables transmit two channels of data at a time. They differ from S/PDIF connectors in that they consist of XLR plugs and use balanced cables. (See Figure 5-7.) The AES/EBU standards were developed to be used with professional audio components, hence the use of balanced connections — the kinds used in professional-level equipment.

S/PDIF

S/PDIF (short for Sony/Phillips Digital Interface Format) connectors consist of an unbalanced coaxial cable (one wire and a shield) and RCA plugs. (See Figure 5-7.) They can also be made from fiber-optic cable and a Toslink connector (also called an ADAT optical connector; see Figure 5-8). The S/PDIF format can transmit two channels of digital data at once. S/PDIF protocols are very similar to AES/EBU standards, except S/PDIF was originally designed for the consumer rather than the professional market — which explains why unbalanced cords are used. Even so, you can find S/PDIF connectors on a lot of pro recording gear along with (or instead of) AES/EBU.

If you want to use cords longer than about 3 or 4 feet when you're using a S/PDIF connection — or about 15 feet for AES/EBU connections — your best bet is to use video or digital audio cables. Regular audio cables degrade the sound at longer distances because they can't transmit the type of signal that digital equipment produces without affecting the quality of the sound. If you use regular audio cables for longer distances, the sound loses some definition, becoming what some people describe as grainy.

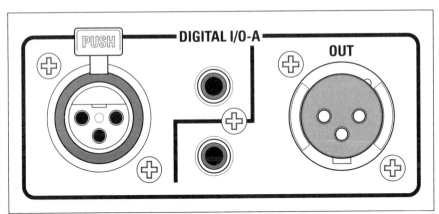

Figure 5-7: S/PDIF and AES/EBU connectors look the same as RCA and XLR connectors, respectively, but are marked as digital.

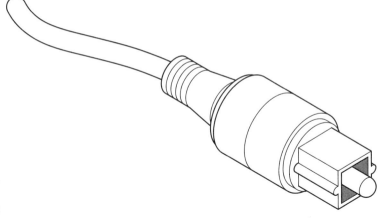

Figure 5-8: Optical connectors have a fiber-optic cable and a special plastic connector called a Toslink connector.

ADAT Optical

The *ADAT* (Alesis Digital Audio Tape) Optical (also known as *lightpipe*) format can send eight tracks of digital audio at once. Developed by Alesis, ADAT Optical has become a standard among digital audio products. It consists of a fiber-optic cable using a special Toslink connector (see the "S/PDIF" section earlier). Audio interfaces allow you to use the ADAT optical for either eight channels of ADAT information or for Optical S/PDIF connections — but you can generally only use one or the other at one time. You choose your preference from your audio recording software hardware menu.

USB

USB stands for *Universal Serial Bus* and is a com
computers currently made. Chances are good t
than one USB jack and you've plugged a USB c
you'd like to remember.

In case it's been a while since you've had to mess with you.
take a look at Figure 5-9. As you can see, USB has two different plugs ιυ ι.
different jacks: rectangular and square. The rectangular connection is called
the "A" connection and is for any receiving device such as your PC or a USB
hub. The square connection is called the "B" connection and is used for a
sending device, such as your USB audio interface or printer.

Aside from two different types of jacks and plugs, USB also has two different
standards: USB 1.1 and USB 2. USB 1.1 can handle a data rate of up to 12 Mbps
(megabits per second), and USB 2 can handle 40-times that rate — 480 Mbps.
Currently, USB interfaces primarily use USB 1.1 and, because of the relatively
slow transfer speed, have limited input and output options. USB 2 has considerable faster transfer rates, so expect audio interfaces to use this approach
more in the future. (Chapter 4 has more on audio interfaces.)

Figure 5-9:
USB uses
two types of
connections:
the "A"
connection
(left) and
the "B"
connection
(right).

FireWire

Developed by Apple Computer, FireWire (also known as IEEE 1394 or iLink) is a high-speed connection that many audio interfaces, hard drives, digital cameras, and other devices use. Even though FireWire was developed by Apple, you can find FireWire ports on devices from many manufacturers. FireWire connectors (see Figure 5-10), unlike USB connectors (see the preceding section), are the same on both ends.

Figure 5-10:
FireWire is a high-speed data transfer protocol.

Like USB, FireWire supports two types: FireWire 400 (the regular one) and FireWire 800. FireWire 400 supports data transfer speeds up to 400 Mbps, and FireWire 800 can handle transfer rates of, yep, you guessed it, 800 Mbps. A lot of audio interfaces currently use FireWire 400 as a way to connect with your computer. These interfaces can handle quite a few inputs and outputs without any problems. I expect that you'll soon see interfaces supported by FireWire 800 in the not-too-distant future. (I'll admit that this isn't exactly a risky assumption.)

Getting Hooked Up

Hooking up all your gear can be a truly rewarding experience. That is, if you get everything working without a hassle. Getting hooked up properly isn't rocket science, you need to take some issues into consideration when doing it to make sure that you don't break anything and that you don't degrade the sound of your system. This section walks you through the process.

Connecting your computer

A computer has lots of different connectors; which ones you actually have to mess with depends on the type of other gear (such as an audio interface) that you have. Here are some things to remember when plugging into and unplugging from your computer:

✔ **USB and FireWire can be *hot-swapped*.** In other words, you can plug and unplug stuff from these ports without having to turn off your computer. You computer senses the change in components when you switch and adjust accordingly.

✔ ***Always* turn off and unplug your computer before opening the computer's case.** Your computer has a lot of electrical components inside it, and touching them when your computer is plugged in can cause electrocution.

For many audio interfaces, you don't need to worry about opening your computer. However, in the case of adding RAM or connecting a PCI interface (see Chapter 4) you need to open the case.

✔ **De-static yourself before touching any internal components.** Before you touch any of the computer components inside the computer case, touch the metal of the computer's case to ground yourself and release any built-up static electricity. Touching a component without releasing the static first can case a static charge to damage the component.

If you put your computer's CPU unit in another room (Chapter 2 has more on this), make sure that you get the proper cable and signal boosters so that your signal doesn't degrade. For example, USB cables can be run for about 15 feet before you need a powered hub to boost the signal. Likewise, the Mac LCD displays are powered by the computer and can only handle a 10-foot extension to the cable before the signal drops to the point of being unreliable.

Interface

The audio interface is the core of your audio recording computer. It contains all the components that you need to turn your analog music into something your computer can work with. And it also turns the digital bits back into your music again. As important as this piece of equipment is, it's extremely easy to hook up.

As I describe in Chapter 4, several different types of audio interfaces exist, and each one connects to your computer differently. The following sections describe each type and show you how to connect the interface to your computer.

PCI-based systems

PCI-based interfaces require that you install the PCI card into an available PCI slot inside your computer. For some people, opening up a computer to connect the PCI card can be nerve-wracking. These instructions cut the problem down to size:

1. **Shut down your computer and unplug it from the wall outlet.**

   You're going to be messing around inside the computer case and you *really* don't want any power connected to it.

2. **Open the case.**

   This step usually requires removing a couple screws from the rear of the case to allow removal of the side panel on the left.

3. **Touch the metal frame of your computer.**

   This step discharges any static electricity you might have built up.

   It takes only a small spark of static electrical discharge to ruin sensitive electronics on the card or in your computer. So, whenever you handle electronic components, be certain to discharge any built-up static charges, and never touch anything inside your computer case — or on the PCI card — that you don't absolutely have to.

4. **Remove the interface's PCI card from its static-free bag.**

   Grip it from the edges (like holding a CD of your favorite music) and be careful not to drop it.

5. **Locate an open PCI slot (consult your computer's manual if you don't know where this is) and gently push the PCI card into the slot — it goes in only one way.**

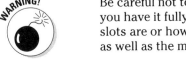

   Be careful not to bend the card or use excessive force, but make certain you have it fully seated into the PCI slot. If you're unsure where the PCI slots are or how the PCI card fits, consult both your computer's manual as well as the manual that came with the audio interface you're using.

Take your time and don't rush this step. I've seen more than one audio interface that had intermittent problems because of an improperly installed card.

6. **Screw in the screws for the PCI card to fully seat the card.**

7. **Close your computer case.**

If your interface doesn't have a break-out box, you're ready to boot up and install your software. Chapter 8 has the details for this procedure.

On the other hand, if your PCI interface consists of a PCI card and a break-out box (Chapter 4 has more on these items), you need to connect the PCI card to the break-out box. This particular type of audio interface unit comes with a special cable to do this and involves these simple steps:

1. **Attach one end of the cable to the long connector on the back of the PCI card (which you can now find at the back of your computer).**

2. **Connect the other end to the connector (generally labeled *Computer*) on the back of the break-out box.**

3. **Double-check your connections to make sure the cable is securely connected.**

4. **Plug in your computer's power cord and boot up your computer if you don't have any other installations to make.**

You're ready to install the software. Consult Chapter 8 (or your interface and software manuals) for the specifics.

FireWire

Compared to connecting a PCI interface, hooking up a FireWire interface to your computer is child's play:

1. **Shut down your computer.**

   Although FireWire can be hot-swapped, your system needs to be turned off before you make the connection the first time. The disconnection allows your computer to find the new device when you turn it on. After the first time, you can plug and unplug the interface even with the computer turned on.

2. **Attach the FireWire cable to the FireWire connector on the back of the interface.**

3. **Plug in the other end of the cable to the FireWire connector on your computer.**

4. **Connect the power cable to your FireWire interface and plug it into the wall power socket.**

5. **Turn your computer back on and install your software.**

Most manufacturers recommend that you avoid using any FireWire hubs and instead connect the interface directly to a FireWire port on your computer.

USB

Even though USB ports are hot-swappable, it's a good idea to turn off your computer before you install your USB interface for the first time. Here are the steps:

1. **Shut down your computer.**

2. **Attach the included USB cable to your interface's USB jack.**

3. **Plug in the other end of the cable to the USB connector on your computer.**

   Don't use a USB hub; plug the cable directly into your computer. This keeps your signal from being interrupted by having too much data trying to get through one USB line.

4. **Turn your computer back on and install your software.**

Input devices

Your keyboard, guitars, and mics need to be plugged in somewhere. For most home recordists just starting out — people unlikely to have external mixers, preamps, and direct boxes — the plug-in place of choice will be the audio interface. Here's a quick rundown on how to connect these input devices:

✔ **Keyboards and other electronic instruments:** Plug an instrument cable from the output of your instrument to one of the instrument inputs of your interface. This type of input usually lacks a preamp and sometimes doesn't even have an input gain (volume) control, but depending on your interface it might be an input with a preamp and/or gain control in it.

If your interface's input doesn't have a gain control, you use the main volume control on your instrument to control the volume level going to your computer. If your interface's input has a gain control — either with a preamp or not — you need to balance the level of your instrument output to the level of your input gain control so that you get a good sound. Chapter 9 details this process.

✔ **Guitars and other string instruments with electric pick-ups:** Plug a guitar cable from the output of your guitar (or other instrument) to an input in your interface that can handle guitar signals. Which type of input this ends up being depends on your interface. Most interfaces can handle a guitar in one of the preamp inputs, but many can also handle it in one of the instrument inputs. (You can often tell whether this is the case by the instrument inputs having a gain (volume) control on them — no gain no way, yes gain yes way.) Check your interface's manual to see which inputs can handle the signal from a guitar.

When you record, you adjust both the guitar output and the interface's input gain to get the level you want. Chapter 10 offers more detail on this process.

✔ **Microphones:** Plug an XLR microphone cable from the output of your mic to one of the preamp-equipped inputs of your interface. You use the gain control on your interface and the placement of your mic to set the level of your mic signal. Again, check out Chapter 10 for tips on getting a good signal level all the way to your computer.

If you use an external preamp to record your mic signals, you plug your mic cable's output into the preamp's input and run the appropriate cable (usually an unbalanced TS or a balanced TRS, depending on your equipment) from the output of your preamp to one of the instrument inputs of your interface. The level is adjusted at the external preamp and not your audio interface.

Monitors

Hooking up your monitors is the last step in the process of being able to get your sound into and back out of your computer. How you connect your monitors to your audio interface depends on whether you have powered or unpowered monitors and the type of connectors that are included in your monitors.

Powered

Powered (active) monitors can be connected directly to your audio interface's main outputs. For most home recording equipment, this means using either a TS instrument cable or balanced TRS cable. Some interfaces and monitors can handle both — check the manual for each of these components to see what you need to buy.

If your interface and monitors only use TS connectors, keep the length of your cords as short as possible because long runs of unbalanced cords can develop noise. If you have the option of balanced cords, go that route. Also, and this is getting kinda tweaky, use the same length cords for both monitors even if one monitor sits closer to the interface than the other. This ensures that the sound gets to both monitors at the same microsecond. (I told you this is kinda tweaky.)

Some monitors also have balanced XLR connectors, but you won't find them on many of the interfaces currently available. They're used primarily on professional gear such as separate high-end converters.

To make the connection, simply run the cord from the main outputs of your interface to the inputs of your speakers. Pretty simple, huh?

Unpowered

Unpowered (passive) monitors require an amplifier between your audio interface and the speakers. In this case, you run unbalanced TS or balanced TRS, depending on your interface and amp specifications (check your owner's manuals for details), from the main outputs of your interface to the inputs of your amp. Then run speaker cables from your amp to your monitors. The jack/plug configuration — and in turn the cords — will depend on your equipment. Some amps use banana plugs (two-pronged connectors used for professional speakers) for the outputs while others use TS plugs. Monitors might use either of these as well.

If you use your home stereo speakers as your studio monitors, you need to get some special cords because your interface will have either TS or TRS jacks, and your stereo receiver will have RCA jacks. In this case, get cords that have TS on one end and RCA on the other. Plug the TS end into the main outputs of your interface and the RCA end into one of the Aux inputs of your stereo receiver. Then just hook up your speakers (if they aren't already hooked up), and you're set to go.

If you use your home stereo to power your speakers, you need to turn the volume on your receiver up a bit to get sound from your interface. Because your interface also has an output level adjuster, you need to do some experimenting with the volume of both the interface output and the receiver volume to get a decent sound. If your stereo receiver's volume is too low, you need to crank your audio interface output to get your music loud enough. This can result in a thin sound or in distortion. Likewise, if you have your stereo receiver's volume too high, that can make the volume control on your audio interface too touchy, and you can easily end up with distortion. Finding the right balance between the two volume levels will take some time. You know when you've got it right when you can get a good solid sound without distortion at a volume that is comfortable to listen to.

Part III

Choosing and Installing Recording Software

The 5th Wave   By Rich Tennant

"I know we're on a budget, but don't you think it's time to break down and replace the old sound card?"

In this part . . .

Part III explores the software needed for audio and MIDI recording. Chapter 6 introduces you to the many functions that audio and MIDI recording programs perform to help you decide what features you should look for in your system. In Chapter 7, you examine some of the most popular and powerful options available, and I help you choose the best option for your needs. Chapter 8 explains the process of installing your software — whether you use Windows XP or Mac OS X — and helps you get set up properly and as quickly as possible.

Chapter 6

Understanding Computer Recording Software

*O*ne of the first things you'll notice when you start digging through all the software options available for audio recording programs is that much of this stuff pretty much performs the same basic functions. All the major programs let you record and edit audio, record and edit MIDI data, add effects, and process audio a number of ways, and they also let you mix and master your audio to make your music sound the way it does in your head. The difference is the degree to which you can perform the various functions in your chosen program and the ease at which you can perform these functions.

With so many different programs out there, it's hard to keep them all straight. In this chapter, I offer what assistance I can by introducing you to many of the basic functions available in computer-based recording software and showing you what to look for so that you can choose the best program for your needs.

Even though you might find that certain programs share similar basic features, not all audio recording software is equal. In fact, as you look around and dig into the specifications of each program, you'll discover some big differences among the various contenders. This chapter explores the many different functions that are available in audio recording programs so that you can determine which features are important to you when you buy a program. Chapter 7 details some of the most popular programs and explains what each can and can't do. Between these two chapters, you can get a good idea of which programs you want to try out.

Audio Recording and Editing Basics

Audio recording is one of the primary recording functions in a computer. With that fact out of the way, you should also know that you need to consider three main areas when looking at the audio capabilities of a program: track counts, recording formats, and editing functions. This section details these functions.

Track counts

Even though the overall number of tracks you can record and play in your computer system is dictated by the power of your processor and your hard drive speed, some programs constrain you even further by limiting the number of audio tracks that you can have active in a song. This limitation is generally seen on the lower-end programs offered by software manufacturers and is simply a way for manufacturers to give you an incentive to upgrade to one of their higher-priced versions. For example, Pro Tools LE has an active track limit of 32 tracks, whereas Pro Tools TDM extends this limit to 192 audio tracks.

If you plan to work on music that requires a lot of instruments and/or effects, you need to think long and hard about track limitations before purchasing. Although many people consider it excessive, pop tunes often have as many as 100 or more tracks (dozens of which are for just the vocals), so filling up 32 isn't as difficult as you might imagine.

Recording

All audio recording programs record audio (if you find one that doesn't, don't buy it), but how they do it differs. These differences involve the following options:

✔ **Sample rate:** The sample rate refers to the number of times per second that the audio is sampled. This relates to the frequency range that can be captured by your computer. Sample rates typically include 44.1 kHz, 48 kHz, 88.2 kHz, and 96 kHz. Some programs, such as Logic, can go as high as 192 kHz or higher. For audio work that ends up on CD, 44.1 kHz is fine, but if you want to record audio for DVD, you need to have the capability to record at 96 kHz. Some other reasons to record at a higher sample rate exist — the most relevant being that as your sample rate goes up, your *latency* (the delay between the sound entering your system and coming back out to your ears) goes down.

That said, most musicians still record at 44.1 kHz. This sample rate captures a sufficient frequency range — well beyond the human hearing limit — and keeps you from having to do a sample rate conversion (SRC)

process to get your music to CD level. In addition, this lower sample rate puts less stress on your computer because half as much data is moving through your system at a given time compared to 88.2 kHz. As an added bonus, recording at 44.1 kHz means half as much hard drive space is needed for your audio files.

✔ **Bit depth:** As I describe in Chapter 4, *bit depth* is the amount of information contained in each of the samples (see the sample rate bullet) taken of your audio. You find two different bit depths in current audio recording software: 16 bit and 24 bit. There is no comparison between these two — go with 24 bit. Even though 16 bit is the bit depth of CDs and your music most likely will end up there, having the extra 8 bits available to mess around with is important if you do any processing of your signal.

Audio recording programs also have what's called *internal* bit depth. This is the bit depth that the programs use when performing digital signal processing tasks such as volume changes and EQ. This internal rate is set much higher than the bit depth you record at so that your system can process your audio when you do things like equalizing or changing the volume of your track. Typical rates you see in recording programs include 48-point fixed rate or 32-point float. Don't buy into the hype about one approach being better than another. They all work similarly, and all the professional-level programs sound very much alike. Make your choice based on the computer platform you use and the features you want in a program.

✔ **File format:** Most recording programs let you choose from a variety of file formats in which to record. Although no universal file format exists to ensure compatibility between different programs, most programs can record and play back Broadcast Wave (`.bwav` or `.wav` extension). This is an important function because as you grow in your music-recording skills — and as recording programs develop — you might find that you want to use a different program to continue recording or to mix your songs. By using a program that has the ability to work with Broadcast Wave files, you future-proof yourself (a bit anyway).

Editing

All audio recording programs can edit audio, but the way they do it and the degree to which you can make difficult edits (such as replacing a single note within a complex musical phrase) vary a lot.

Pro Tools, the heavy-weight champion of the audio editing world (in my experience, anyway), has some very thoughtful features that make editing audio very fast and easy. These include:

✔ **Shuffle:** This is an editing mode that lets you move sections of audio around while keeping the beginnings and endings of adjoining sections lined up tightly. (See Figure 6-1.) This particular feature is showing up in more programs — Logic Pro 7 just added some features similar to the shuffle feature, for instance — and is useful for working on your song's arrangements, especially the drum parts where there's no break between sections.

Figure 6-1:
Being able to shuffle audio regions makes creating arrangements easy.

✔ **Tab to Transient:** This is by far my favorite feature. It's a real time-saver when you have to cut up sections of a recorded audio. Tab to Transient lets you move from one transient peak (the start of a vocal phrase or the initial crack of a drum hit, for example) to another, as shown in Figure 6-2. In programs without this feature, you have to zoom way in to the waveform display of your audio and manually locate the very start of a section. This can take a lot of time. The Tab to Transient feature makes it as easy as pressing Tab on your computer keyboard.

✔ **Spot:** This is an essential feature if you want to link an event to a specific point of another event in your song. For example, if you have a piece of video that needs a sound effect added, you can place the start of the sound effect to the exact spot in the video using this feature. Then if you move the video over one way or the other, the spotted audio moves with it automatically. This feature is common in programs like Nuendo and Logic — ones that work well with video, in other words.

✔ **Scrub:** In the olden days of tape decks, if you wanted to find a specific place in your song, you rocked the tape against the playback head of your tape deck to hear your audio. This action, called *scrubbing,* allowed you to find the start of a drum hit, for instance. Most self-respecting audio programs have a scrub feature. (See Figure 6-3.) Some scrub features are a bit cumbersome to use, but others mimic the process of scrubbing on a tape deck very well. If you plan on doing any audio editing, make sure that the program you're considering has a scrub function and that it works well for you.

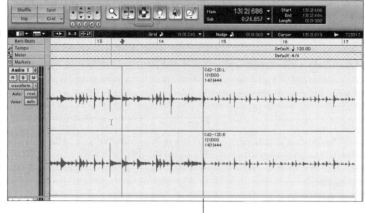

Figure 6-2:
Some
programs
let you
use the
Tab key
to find the
beginning
of a note
or phrase.

Tabbing to a transient

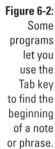

You can find many other audio editing functions in the gazillion different audio recording (and editing) programs out there. If the multitrack recording program you like to use doesn't have all the editing capabilities that you find you need, you don't need to trash your current program. Instead, you complement it by getting a stereo audio editor program such as WaveLab or Cool Edit Pro.

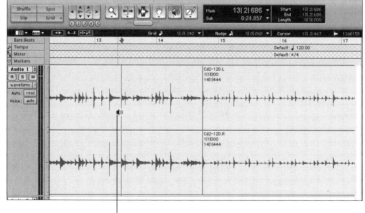

Figure 6-3:
The Scrub
feature lets
you hear
specific
sections
of audio,
much like
rocking the
tape on a
tape deck.

The Scrub feature lets you hear a certain section.

Making Sense of MIDI Capabilities

Most recording programs have some sort of MIDI capability. Some are pretty rudimentary (Pro Tools, anyone?), but others (such as Logic or Sonar) are quite extensive. Regardless of what recording program you're looking at, if it has MIDI capabilities it's going to let you record MIDI data, play the data back, and edit it. So if you intend to use only an occasional soft-synth or keyboard in your music, just about any recording program that has MIDI capabilities will meet your needs. If you see yourself using a lot of MIDI or if you want to be able to do extensive edits or perform MIDI operations on your data, you need to look closely at your options to find the program that meets your needs (and desires).

Here are some things to look for in MIDI-capable recording programs:

✔ **Quantization:** Quantization is the ability to adjust the timing (rhythm) of your performance to match a grid. Basic programs let you use a fairly simple grid — such as 16th notes — whereas more sophisticated programs allow you to quantize to a grid and keep the feel of your music by not adhering strictly to the grid lines. Instead, these programs can fix your timing mistakes while injecting a bit of human-type feel to your performance. If your sense of rhythm isn't that great, being able to quantize with feel can mean the difference between a track that kinda works and one that rocks.

✔ **Multiple windows:** The most rudimentary MIDI programs offer a simple piano roll window (the graphic looks like the roll of paper with holes punched in it that old-time player pianos used). This window shows the MIDI notes as small rectangles representing the pitch, time location in the song, and duration. You can edit within this window, but if you do much editing this is a cumbersome way of going about it. MIDI-intensive programs give you the ability to edit your MIDI data by using a window that looks like a piece of sheet music and/or has a list of MIDI events in column form. Having several windows to choose from allows you to use the one that best fits the type of editing you want to do, thus speeding up the process. Figure 6-4 shows a couple alternative windows in Logic — one of the most capable MIDI programs available.

✔ **Transposition:** Being able to change (or *transpose*) the key of a performance is high on the list of must-have functions for many people. Most MIDI-capable programs offer this option. The difference you find between the various programs is in the ease with which you can do this and the specific steps you need to take to get it done.

✔ **Scoring:** Scoring is the ability to take your MIDI data and print it out as a piece of sheet music. If you're a composer that creates your music to be played by other musicians, being able to score your music from MIDI data might be an important feature.

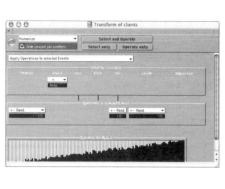

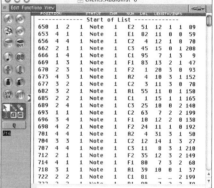

Figure 6-4:
Powerful
MIDI
programs
tend to
have
several
windows
that you
can work in.

Looking at Looping

Looping, simply put, is the ability to take a short snippet of music (called, logically enough, a *loop*) and arrange it with other loops in a song until you have a composition that you like. Loops can be snippets that you make from your recorded performances, or they can be pre-recorded files that you can buy from a large variety of loop makers.

I've got mixed feelings about looping. On the one hand, you can take a pre-recorded snippet of audio and put it in your song and create a composition without having to actually play an instrument. This can be a real time-saver when composing. On the other hand, you don't need to learn how to play an instrument to do this. This can result not only in not taking the time to learn how to play an instrument, but also in not taking the time to really under-stand music composition and theory. Don't get me wrong. I've never been a rule follower (musically, anyway), but I've found that breaking the rules works only if you know the rules in the first place. My experience is that, with looping, the temptation is to skip the rule-learning process, which makes breaking the rules less of a creative decision and more of a decision made because the recordist doesn't know any better. But I digress.

Anyway, I'll leave the ethical struggle to you over whether using loops in music constitutes a real musical composition or a fast-food version of music-making. (I have no bias, really. No really, I mean it. Really. . . .)

Loops, whether you like them or not, are here to stay. In fact, looping has become pretty much standard in songs that you hear on radio stations favored by the teen set, and it's even gaining popularity among serious composers.

Most audio recording programs have some ability to use loops. At the very minimum, almost all programs let you insert loops into your song and arrange them to meet your needs, as shown in Figure 6-5. Here the loop automatically adjusts its tempo to fit your song and can be transposed up or down to fit the key of your composition.

Beyond these basics, many programs — ACID is one example — offer you ways to manipulate the loops to make them unique. A short sampling of what you can do includes the following functions:

Figure 6-5:
Using loops
is as
simple as
clicking and
dragging
one into
your song.

✔ **Edit:** The contents of the loop often show up in your program either as MIDI data or as audio waveforms. If it's MIDI data, you can edit the notes just like you would any other MIDI data, including changing duration, placement in time, and pitch. Audio waveform data can be cut and pasted and otherwise edited by using the same techniques you'd use to edit standard audio data.

Sophisticated looping programs give you more editing power to create your own unique loops and effects from the included loops.

✔ **Quantize:** You can adjust the timing of your loops in many loop programs (*quantize* is the term of choice here). Basic programs allow you to quantize only MIDI-based loops, but full-featured programs offer the ability to quantize audio loops as well. This can be handy because adding a bunch of loops together — where each has a slightly different feel — can result in a sloppy-sounding groove. Quantizing all the loops in one fell swoop can fix the problem.

You can also find groove-quantizing features that make it easy for you to morph existing loops into a different feel. This tool makes your loop library go further and allows you to create even more unique music.

✔ **Lots of loops:** More powerful loop programs come with more extensive loop libraries. Of course, if you buy a less expensive looping program, you can always add more loops.

✔ **Beat mapping:** This feature is handy for remixing. With this tool, you can map the tempo of an existing song so that you can add looped passages to it easily. You're not likely to find this feature in lower-end programs; it's been relegated to more powerful loop programs.

✔ **Effects:** Some programs offer the ability to create effects such as real-time reverse of your loop, DJ stuttering effects, and many others. More likely than not, the more powerful the program, the more powerful the effects you can perform on your loops.

Connecting two (or more) programs

Chances are that, as you build your computer-based studio, you'll find more than one program that you want to use. And chances are good that you use one program for one thing and the other for something else. For example, maybe you want to use Pro Tools for recording and mixing audio and ACID for composing with loops. (Chapter 7 has more about these and other programs.)

To top it off, you're probably going to want to use both these programs at the same time and you're going to want them to synchronize with one another. If this is the case, you're in luck because there's a program that is made to handle this scenario. It's called ReWire (www.propellerheads.se/ technologies).

If you have a vague inkling that you might one day want to hook one program to another, make sure that it's ReWire capable, because as the audio recording world stands now, the ReWire way is becoming the standard way to connect programs.

Making Use of Mixing

Mixing is one of the essential elements of all audio recording programs. Mixing is the ability to blend your individual tracks together into a single pair of stereo tracks. Simple mixers let you control the volume and panning information (left to right positioning in the stereo field), whereas full-featured mixers give you nearly complete flexibility over numerous elements of your tracks. These include

- ✔ **Automation:** Being able to automate your mix — changing volumes, panning, effects send levels, and others — is important because when you mix with your mouse you can adjust only one thing at a time. To have a complex mix where each of your tracks has changes throughout the song requires decent automation capabilities. Powerful programs let you adjust everything: volume, panning, muting, soloing, send levels, effects parameters, and so on.

- ✔ **Send effects:** Sends are signal routing functions that let you send part of your audio signal to a different place in the mixer. Basic programs limit the number of Sends available to you for each track to as few as 5, whereas more sophisticated programs raise this limit to 64 or more. This feature is important if you do complex mixes that use numerous effects. (For this, you also need a very powerful computer or a host-based effects processor. Chapter 15 has much more on Sends, including host-based plug-ins).

- ✔ **Inserts:** Inserts are signal routing functions that let to place an effect inline with the audio signal as it works its way through the mixer. Like Send limitations (see preceding bullet) many basic programs have low limits on the number of insert effects you can plug in to each track. Full-featured programs raise this limit to where you have much more flexibility in what you can do.

- ✔ **Surround mixing:** Being able to mix beyond a two-channel stereo format can be helpful if you mix for video or DVD audio. Basic programs don't offer this option, so if this important to you, you need to look for a full-featured (read: more expensive) solution.

- ✔ **Offline bouncing:** Offline bouncing lets you mix your song as quickly as your computer's processor can process the data rather than in real time. This is a handy feature if you have a lot of songs to mix or if your songs are long. The alternative is real-time bouncing, where your song plays at regular speed (and you hear it all through speakers). With long songs, the wait can be agonizing (for me anyway). This feature is one I consider a necessity, though it might not be one for you.

Digging Into Digital Signal Processing

Being able to digitally process your audio after you've recorded it is one of the pluses that computer-based recording has going for it. This processing is either done with plug-ins that you can add to your chosen audio recording program (see Chapter 15) or is one of the functions available in the program you buy.

Plug-ins can easily be added to any program, so the digital signal processing (DSP) abilities contained in a program are going to be only a minor concern for you when you're program shopping. Regardless, here are some processing functions that you might find in your audio recording programs:

✔ **Duplication:** Being able to quickly and easily duplicate a selection allows you to mess with your audio data without the risk of losing your original data. Even though most audio editing operations are done non-destructively (meaning they don't change the original audio data), many DSP functions do alter your data, so you need to make sure you work on a duplicate in case you do something that you dislike and want to go back to the original.

✔ **Consolidation:** As you edit your audio tracks, you often end up with a bunch of short snippets arranged end to end to make your song. Although you can leave these individual sections separate, it's often better to consolidate them into one continuous audio file when you mix. This takes some of the load off your hard drive and makes it easier later on if you want to export or import the track to another program to work on it there (such as taking it to a professional mixer). In this case, being able to consolidate is important. Not all programs have this function, so look closely if you want to be able to do this.

✔ **Quantization:** Being able to quantize MIDI is a common feature, but quantizing audio files requires a more elaborate program. This feature is easily abused, but when you need it (you've recorded a track that you know you can't replicate, but it needs some timing adjustment, for example), it can save you tons of hassle.

✔ **Transposition/pitch shifting:** Like quantization, being able to transpose a MIDI phrase is a no-brainer, but being able to do this to an audio file takes a more sophisticated program. Having this option can save you from having to re-record all your tracks when you finally realize (or admit) that you can't sing your song in the key you recorded it in.

Finishing Up with Mastering

The final step in recording your music is to master it. Mastering is the process of optimizing the dynamics and tonal balance of your music, arranging the sequence of your songs, and getting it to the format needed to make copies for distribution.

For an audio recording program to be able to do mastering, you need the following capabilities:

- ✔ **Parametric equalizer:** A parametric equalizer is an EQ where you can adjust precise frequencies. This type of EQ is necessary in mixing as well as mastering. Because of this, most audio recording programs have one. If not, or if the one supplied with the programs doesn't sound very good (all too common, unfortunately), you can get a third-party plug-in to do the job in your existing program. Chapter 15 has more about finding third-party plug-ins.

- ✔ **Multiband compressor:** A multiband compressor is a compressor that lets you apply different levels of compression to specific frequency ranges. You won't find a multiband compressor in many of the audio recording programs, so you might need to get a third-party plug-in for this.

- ✔ **Limiter:** A limiter is essential if you want to squeeze out a bit more volume in your music. Most audio recording programs come with a limiter; the question is going to be whether the limiter included with the program is good enough to do the job necessary in mastering. A mastering limiter should be absolutely transparent — it should have no sound of its own when plugged in.

- ✔ **Dithering:** If you follow my recommendations, you'll get a program that can record in 24 bits. This means that when you're done recording, mixing, and mastering your music, you need to get your music from 24 bits to 16 bits so you can put it on a CD. You want to do this without messing with the sound of your music, so you want to have the option of being able to apply *dither* — a process that adds random noise to your music to make it sound better as it fades out. Most full-featured programs come with a decent selection of dithering algorithms that you can apply when you create a bounce of your mix.

Most audio recording software can handle most of the basic tasks you put before it, but audio recording programs aren't often set up to handle the last step — putting your music on CD. In this case, you need to get a CD-burning program that can create Red Book audio CDs from your CD-Rs. I cover the elements of mastering and provide a list of programs you can use for this last step in Chapter 14.

Chapter 7

Finding the Right Software for You

*T*he most important decision you can make when getting a computer-based recording system up and going involves choosing which software you want to use. The software plays an important role in how you do your day-to-day audio recording work, but it also impacts lots of other facets of your recording experience — what hardware you can use, the types of recording and editing you can do, and the number of tracks you can work with, to name just a few. Understanding how you work and the strengths and weaknesses of the various software programs that are on the market can keep you from spending your money on a program that doesn't fit your needs.

In this chapter, I help you clarify your needs and goals and offer you an overview of many of the most common software programs available. I cover audio and MIDI capabilities, maximum track counts, editing abilities, and the compatibility of software and hardware, among others. In all, this chapter helps you easily find the right software and hardware for your needs.

Audio recording software can have many different types of features. Not all software programs have all the features you want, so you might end up needing to get more than one program to do what you want. This is just one of the inevitable facts of life. Don't stick with just one software program that does a lot of things well and a few things badly; go out and plunk down some cash to get a program that fills in the holes for you. Almost all programs let you save your audio files as BWAV (Broadcast Wave) files, so you can freely share files among programs.

In this chapter, I discuss the different tasks for which you use recording software, such as recording, editing, looping, processing, and so on. If any of these tasks are unfamiliar to you, check out Chapter 6, where I explain these different areas in detail.

Determining Your Needs

Before you go out and buy a recording program, take a few minutes to clarify what you need and want in a program. Doing so can save you a ton of hassle because not all programs are made alike — each program offers different features and has its own particular strengths and weaknesses. Knowing your needs and how they relate to a program's available features can keep you from getting the wrong program and having to learn a whole new program that does meet your needs.

Here are some things to consider before buying any software:

- **Setting your budget:** Recording software runs from free to over a thousand dollars. That's quite a range, so narrowing down your budget to, say, around $100 can weed out a lot of options. When setting your budget, think about all the aspects of recording that you want to cover with your system. For example, if you set a budget of $300 for a software program and also plan on forking over $800 for soft-synths or a hardware synthesizer, getting a program such as Logic Pro — which gives you both the soft-synths and the recording program in one fell swoop — might actually put you back less than buying everything separately.

- **Examining your musical style:** The style of music you make and the way you work can narrow down your software options. For example, if you intend to record mostly soft-synths and you do a lot of MIDI work, Pro Tools wouldn't be your best choice because it's more aligned with people who want to record live instruments and edit and mix audio tracks rather than MIDI tracks. Plugging in soft-synths and running MIDI-intensive music isn't what Pro Tools does best. If this is your desire, you're better off with Logic Pro (on a Mac) or SONAR (on a Windows PC).

- **Exploring computer platform compatibility:** Certain software runs on only one computer platform. Logic Audio or Digital Performer, for example, can only run on a Mac, whereas SONAR requires a Windows machine. Other software, such as Pro Tools or Cubase, can run equally well on both platforms. So if you already have a computer or know which type you intend to get, your choices do narrow down a bit. In the sections that follow I explain the platform limitations (if any) of each program.

- **Exploring hardware compatibility:** Some software programs do require specific hardware in order to run. For example — and this is the most extreme example — Pro Tools simply won't run without Digidesign hardware. If you have hardware other than Digidesign, Pro Tools won't boot up. In less extreme cases, you might find that certain programs don't work very well with certain types of hardware. This is becoming less of an issue as manufacturers work to keep their products compatible with other products, but hardware compatibility is something to keep in mind as you decide on the particulars of your system. Pay special attention to your hardware's drivers (the software that comes with your audio interface hardware) — make sure that the software you intend to use supports those drivers.

Because there are so many variables in hardware and software, not all manufacturers of software can test all the hardware variations. The best thing you can do to ensure that certain hardware works with certain software is to see whether other users have had success with the combination. Internet forums are good places to find this information. (Check out Chapter 20.) The Web site of the hardware and/or software manufacturer is another great place to look for compatibility issues. Be sure to do your footwork before you buy. This action will minimize the chances of you not being able to get your system working.

✔ **Exploring software compatibility:** Many people want to run more than one audio recording program at a time or they want to use third-party plug-ins with their main program. If this describes you, make sure you understand what other software is compatible with your main recording program. For example, there are several plug-in formats (see Chapter 15), and each recording program uses one (or sometimes two) of them. So if you want to use a compressor that is in, say, VST format, you need to make sure that you get a recording program that supports VST plug-ins.

✔ **Planning for the future:** If your budget is limited or you aren't sure how deeply you want to get into computer-based recording, you'll probably be tempted to get a basic, entry-level recording program to give you a taste of the process. This is well and good, but I encourage you to think about the future and choose an entry-level program that has an upgrade path built in to it. I say this because software makers fashion their programs with a certain workflow and graphic look, and having to abandon that workflow and look just because you've outgrown a particular software version would be a pain.

Need more convincing? If you get used to a program that doesn't have an upgrade option, you'll be forced to learn a new program's ways of working, which could take you weeks to figure out. On the other hand, if you think ahead, you can get into a basic program for very little money and upgrade to a fuller-feature version of that same program, saving you the hassle (and headache) of learning a program from scratch. In the following sections, I foster this idea of "planning for the future" by describing several recording program options for each manufacturer so you can find an entry-level program that has a simple upgrade path.

Tons of audio recording programs are available. Because I believe in being able to upgrade to a better program as your needs grow, I include only the most popular programs that have a decent upgrade path. I believe this saves you money and hassle in the long run. Because developing software is expensive and risky for the manufacturers, buying a product from a company that has several versions of its program for different users increases the chances that the software you get good at using is available down the road.

Examining Popular Programs

As you'll see when you scope out the many (and I mean *many;* hundreds of different programs are available) audio recording programs that are out there, they all offer different features, and each has strengths and weaknesses to contend with. This section explores the most common programs and gives you a good sense of what they offer.

Because I can't possibly cover all the different programs available, I encourage you to go online and look for other programs. You might find the perfect program for you — one that I don't even list here. (Okay, okay, that's highly unlikely given my masterful command of all things audio, but stranger things have happened.) Also, because space is limited in this chapter, I can't go into great depth about the programs I do describe. Before you buy, take some time to check out the Web sites of the programs that look good to you. There you can find a much more comprehensive description, some screen shots of the programs, and more often than not, a free trial download.

If at all possible, try the software you're interested in before you buy. If you can't get your hands on a demo, try to find someone in your area that uses the program and ask to see it in action. (Many local music stores have demos ready to go and will walk you through the program.) This is an important step in the decision-making process because each software program operates differently and what's intuitive for one person might be counter-intuitive for another. A perfect example here is Logic Audio. For whatever reason, some people have trouble wrapping their puny brains around the way it works, but others find the way it works completely logical and truly the only intelligent way of ever doing anything (Sorry, I couldn't help myself.) Fifteen minutes spent fiddling around with the various windows is usually enough for many people to get a grasp of the program and to see whether it makes sense to them.

Pro Tools

Chances are good that you've heard of Pro Tools. Pro Tools is the most-used audio recording program in professional studios. Does this mean it's the best audio program available? Of course not. Pro Tools became the most-used program because, when it first came out, Digidesign (the maker of Pro Tools) was one of the first companies to develop hardware that guaranteed a certain level of stability and performance. The company did this at a price point that was attractive to commercial studio owners at the time. And the company had a very good (make that excellent) marketing department.

Pro Tools comes in two versions:

✔ **TDM:** Pro Tools TDM uses DSP (digital signal processing) chips that you install into your computer. These chips run Pro Tools, so your computer's own CPU never actually does any processing of your audio. Using DSP chips guarantees certain track and plug-in counts, so TDM is the version that many commercial studios use. The advantage of this system was dramatic when computers were slower, but now, for most people, it's not needed. The only advantage to TDM now (unless you record and mix over 100 tracks at a time) is in the quality of some of the plug-ins you can find, such as equalizers, reverbs, and compressors. This is because the DSP chips in the TDM system allow for some power-hungry, great-sounding plug-ins and also because having these plug-ins run on the DSP chips keeps them from being *cracked* (counterfeited). Complete TDM systems start at around $10,000.

✔ **LE:** Pro Tools LE is a host-based version of Digidesign's popular product. *Host-based* means that the software runs off your computer's processor, so the number of tracks and plug-ins you can have is dictated by the power of your computer. With the speed of today's computers Pro Tools LE is plenty powerful enough for the needs of most recordists. Unfortunately, Digidesign has chosen to limit the capabilities of Pro Tools LE by imposing a pretty arbitrary track count limit of 32 audio tracks on the program. Still, 32 audio tracks is plenty for most people. You can get an entire LE system for under $500, including both the software and the audio interface to run it. (Chapter 4 has more on audio interfaces.)

Seeing the strengths of Pro Tools

Pro Tools excels at several things, including

✔ **Audio recording:** Pro Tools began its life as a no-frills audio recorder and editor and was therefore set up with audio recording in mind. The layout of the interface is similar to that of a tape deck and analog mixing board, as shown in Figure 7-1 — which means that if you're an analog dinosaur and you want to get into digital recording, this interface might be the easiest for you to get used to. Also, if you plan to record mostly audio with only the occasional MIDI track to spice things up, this program might be the easiest way to get started.

✔ **Audio editing:** Editing audio is Pro Tool's strongest suit. With this program, you can make even the most exacting edits quickly and accurately.

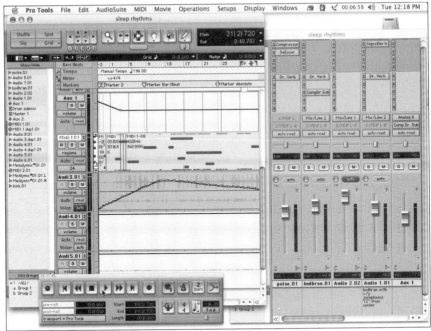

Figure 7-1:
Pro Tools in
all its glory

Frankly, editing audio is the only reason I use Pro Tools in my studio. I record into another program, import the tracks into Pro Tools if they need editing, edit them there, and import the edited version back into my other program to mix. As crazy as it might seem, this process saves me tons of time and makes editing a joy instead of a chore. (It's "crazy" if you call using the best tool for the task at hand "crazy," which, come to think of it, doesn't sound that crazy after all.) If you anticipate doing a lot of audio editing (for example, say you want to create your own personal loop library), Pro Tools is the best program available.

✔ **Integrated hardware:** Pro Tools requires that you use one of Digidesign's audio interfaces for it to run. This can be advantageous because you're pretty much guaranteed that you won't run into any hardware problems. This can offer some peace of mind for people new to digital recording. Of course, you still need to think about the compatibility of your computer hardware, but at least by using Pro Tools you can be assured that your interface will work as advertised. (Chapter 3 has details about computer hardware compatibility.)

✔ **Compatibility with commercial studios:** Most commercial recording studios use Pro Tools TDM. Because Pro Tools LE is essentially the same software, you can take your Pro Tools sessions (song files with all the editing, plug-in, and mixing data added) to a commercial studio to record without hassle. This means that if you don't have a good room in which to record drums, you can go to a studio that has a top-notch drum room and record your rhythm tracks. You can then go back home and record the tracks that you can do well at home. You can also send all your recorded and edited tracks to a professional mix engineer to mix without having to convert them. (Check with your mix engineer about this because he might want you to send him raw data files instead of a Pro Tools session even if he uses Pro Tools to mix. It's often easier this way for him.)

Compatibility between different software programs is quickly becoming a non-issue. Most programs can record in the Broadcast Wave format (BWAV or WAV extensions). Almost any audio recording program can read Broadcast Wave format, which means that you can record into one program and import the audio file into another program to do other work. (See my example in the "Audio editing" bullet earlier in this section.)

Waking up to Pro Tools weaknesses

Like all audio recording programs, Pro Tools has some areas where it isn't perfect. Here are the major issues working against Pro Tools:

- ✔ **Limited MIDI capabilities:** Pro Tools didn't start with MIDI capabilities and (unfortunately) the MIDI implementation that got added in to Pro Tools at a later date is less than optimal for people who use MIDI a lot. The basic functions are okay if all you want to do is record some MIDI performances and maybe do some simple editing of it, but if you're a MIDI power-user, this isn't the best program for you. (In this case, look to Logic or SONAR.)

- ✔ **Limitations of track counts:** Digidesign has put an arbitrary track limitation in Pro Tools LE of 32 *voices* (mono tracks playing). This means you can have up to 32 mono tracks or 16 stereo tracks (or any combination adding up to 32 total voices) playing at one time. For many people, this track limit doesn't seem like a, well, limitation because 32 tracks are still quite a bit for a home recordist.

- ✔ **No plug-in delay compensation:** Most of the other professional-level programs, such as Digital Performer, Logic, and SONAR, automatically compensate for the delay that's introduced in a track by a plug-in (Chapter 15 has more about this feature), but so far Pro Tools (currently up to version 6.7) doesn't. This can be a big deal for some users depending on their choice and use of plug-ins, so be aware that this is an area that Digidesign doesn't see as a priority.

- ✔ **No hardware choice:** If you use Pro Tools, you're stuck with Digidesign's hardware. This has its advantages (as I describe in the preceding section) but the downside is that you're left without a choice in the matter. It's generally accepted that Digidesign's interfaces for Pro Tools LE aren't the best quality you can find, so if you want the best possible sound from your system and you want to use Pro Tools software, you need to shell out for some external preamps and converters (which is what I did). This will cost you quite a bit more than if you just bought the high-quality components, so factor the external preamps and converters into the cost of your system.

In reality, the sound quality of Digidesign hardware is plenty good enough for most home recordists starting out and isn't that much different than the quality of any of the all-in-one audio interfaces. (See Chapter 4 for more on interfaces.) More important than the sound quality of any Digidesign hardware are your skills as a recordist. So if you want to go the Pro Tools route, you don't have to get external devices to record music that sounds pretty darn good.

Finding out more

To find out more about Pro Tools, check out www.digidesign.com. This site has all the available product information as well as the DUC (Digidesign Users Conference) forum for Pro Tools users.

ACID

Produced by Sony Media Software (and originally created by Sonic Foundry), ACID is the most popular loop-based recording program. (See Chapter 12 for more on looping.) ACID and similar loop-based programs use pre-recorded musical snippets that you can manipulate a number of ways to create your musical compositions. ACID is available for Windows PC only and comes in three iterations:

- ✔ **ACID Xpress:** This is a free version of ACID and as such is a very limited edition compared to the other versions. ACID Xpress has a limit of 10 tracks and supports only 16-bit recording. Both these limitations make it a less-than-ideal choice for any professional work. Still, it's a great way to get an idea of how ACID works for free.

- ✔ **ACID Music Studio:** The next step up, ACID Music Studio, is a much more featured program than ACID Xpress. Even though it adds a lot of functionality, it's still handicapped by being limited to working at a bit depth of 16 bits. This makes it unsuitable for professional work.

- ✔ **ACID Pro:** ACID Pro is the flagship looping program. ACID Pro has tons of great features and is used by many professionals who create their music in a loop-based format and extends the bit rate to the current industry standard of 24 bits. ACID doesn't limit the number of tracks you can record and mix, so the sky (and your computer) is the limit here. This style of working is commonly used for musical genres such as hip-hop and techno.

Examining the advantages

ACID has some real advantages for some composers. These include:

✔ **Loop-based recording:** For many composers, working with loops makes creating music easy. Because the loops contain audio that sounds good right from the start, you don't need to learn basic recording skills to start making music. You don't even need to learn how to play an instrument very well. For artists whose goal is to quickly create "listenable" music, this can be a real asset.

✔ **Huge number of loop libraries:** Because ACID was the first powerful and successful loop-based program, it has had the time and money to develop an extensive loop library. These loops can be used in most loop-based programs, so you're not restricted to using ACID in order to benefit from this library. Still, because they were developed for ACID, it puts ACID at an advantage overall.

✔ **Powerful loop-manipulation functions:** ACID lets you do some pretty cool things with loops. Like all loop-based programs, you can speed up or slow down the loops, but beyond that you can customize the loop's sound in your songs in ways that many other programs don't allow. For example, ACID offers a sophisticated groove mapping function that lets you apply different groove templates (timing maps) to your loops quickly and easily. It also lets you extract the timing from a loop and apply it to a different loop and lets you manipulate your groove templates in many different ways.

Detailing the disadvantages

For all the advantages that ACID has, you should be aware of some disadvantages if you're considering using this program. These include:

✔ **Windows PC only:** If you're a Mac user, you can't use this program (unless, of course, you buy a Windows PC).

✔ **Loop-based:** I include this feature in both the Advantages as well as the Disadvantages list because if you aren't interested in working with loops, many of the features in this program are useless to you. If you're more interested in recording and editing audio and MIDI, you have many more appropriate choices.

✔ **Limited audio and MIDI functionality:** Don't get me wrong — you can record and edit audio and MIDI by using ACID, but because most of the focus for this program is on loops, audio and MIDI functions take a back seat. Such functions are clearly best done in other programs — programs whose strong suit is audio or MIDI (or both like Logic and SONAR).

Finding out more

Sony's Web site (http://mediasoftware.sonypictures.com) has tons of information and downloads (both free versions and demos) on its products including ACID. The site also has a user forum.

Cubase

Cubase is made by Steinberg and is one of the most popular audio and MIDI recording programs available. Cubase has been around for a while and is used by many hobbyists and professionals. This program runs on Windows PCs as well as Macs, although it's been historically more stable on Windows PCs.

Cubase comes in several versions. These include

- **Cubase LE:** This is the entry-level offering. As with all entry-level products, it has its limitations. These include maximum tracks counts (48 audio and 64 MIDI), a limited number of physical inputs and outputs (4), a limited number of inserts (2), and others. The one area that Steinberg doesn't limit their entry-level version is in bit depth. With this low-cost version, you can record in 24 bits.

- **Cubase SE:** As you might expect, Cubase SE is a step up from the LE edition. Cubase SE still has limitations, but they are markedly fewer than what you find in LE. In this version, you can have 48 audio tracks and an unlimited number of MIDI tracks. You also get more inputs and outputs (eight) and more inserts (five), among other extras. This is a decent starter program if your needs are modest.

- **Cubase SL:** Stepping up to Cubase SL adds a lot of functions that you don't get in the slimmer versions. In this version, you have an unlimited number of both audio and MIDI tracks at your disposal and you can have up to 128 physical inputs and outputs, more than enough for most users. You also get improvements such as an unlimited Undo feature, an additional Mix window, and many others.

- **Cubase SX:** This is Steinberg's top Cubase option. You are going to find all the basics here in spades, but you also find functions that professional users need, such as improved automation functions, surround mixing, beefed-up mixing and editing capabilities, and video functions. This is a top-notch professional product.

Cubase: What works well

Cubase is a great program that clearly has some areas where it excels. These include:

- **Cross-platform capabilities:** Cubase can work on both Windows PCs and Macs. It seems that the Windows version is still more stable, but I don't hear a lot of complaints about the Mac version, either. This is one of the few programs that is truly cross platform.

- **MIDI integration:** The MIDI functionality of Cubase is very good. It ranks between Sonar and Logic (on the excellent end) and Pro Tools (on the no-frills but functional end). Working with soft-synths and MIDI instruments is easy, and you have a lot of flexibility in how you can work. This is a good program for anyone who's looking for a decent blend between audio and MIDI capabilities.

✔ **Easy to get started on:** I found that Cubase was easy to get going on when I first tried it out. Its layout is logical, and the functions are relatively easy to grasp. (Actually, the look of the layout drives me nuts. See the following section.) Cubase is a good program for people who aren't well-versed in computer-based recording and want to get going relatively painlessly. In addition, the introductory versions record in 24 bit so they tend to stand out in my mind as decent beginner applications because you can get decent raw tracks to import into full-function programs later on.

Cubase: What doesn't work well

Like all audio recording programs, Cubase ain't perfect. Here are some areas where it isn't the top contender:

✔ **Cluttered interface:** Call this a personal problem, but I find the visual look of Cubase to be cluttered and distracting. It might be because of the relatively little time I spend using it compared to some other programs, so take a gander at it for yourself to see whether you like the way it looks. Even though the look of a piece of software doesn't affect its functionality, you spend a lot of time looking at a program's windows, palettes and menus when you work. If you find a program distracting to look at, it makes getting work down more difficult.

✔ **Audio editing:** Audio editing in Cubase leaves a bit to be desired. It seems to me that Steinberg might have intentionally chosen to leave this an area where Cubase lacks functionality, given that the audio editing capabilities in one of its other programs, Nuendo, is far superior. So, they know how to do it well, they just chose not to do it well in Cubase. This might not be a big deal for the users out there who just want to do some basic editing, but if audio editing is a priority for you, consider trying some other programs in addition to (or instead of) Cubase before you settle for Cubase.

✔ **Automation:** The automation in Cubase isn't up to the same standard as some of the other audio recording programs. (Logic would be a good example here.) Because most people record within the computer, automation is an important part of the mixing process, and the limited automation features in Cubase can slow you down a bit. However, I do expect Steinberg to improve on its automation features soon — soothe Steinberg folks have received too many complaints to ignore. Keep an eye on future versions of Cubase for these improvements. (Version 5 is current as of the writing of this book.)

Finding out more

Check out Steinberg's Web site for more information about Cubase, including updates to the program. (Steinberg was getting ready to introduce an update as I wrote this section.) The Web address is: `www.steinberg.net/list products_sb.asp?Langue_ID=7`.

Cakewalk

Cakewalk makes several different recording programs. These are divided into the home recoding and professional lines. The home studio line includes these popular products:

- **Guitar Tracks Pro:** As its name suggests, Guitar Tracks Pro is geared toward guitar players and focuses on audio rather than MIDI or a combination of the two. This program has a track limit of 32. On the plus side, it records at 24 bits and lets you record in file formats that you can always import into a more feature-rich program later if you want. It also supports using loops. (Figure 7-2 gives you a look at Guitar Tracks Pro.)

- **Home Studio 2:** This is a MIDI, loop, and audio recording program that records at 24 bits. This is a decent basic system for people just getting into home recording because it gives you an unlimited number of audio and MIDI tracks. There is an XL version that adds some soft-synths and effects.

- **Music Creator Pro:** This program is a step up in features from the Home Studio 2 version. The 24-bit recording and unlimited tracks in conjunction with loop-based composition tools make this a fairly full-featured program.

Cakewalk plusses

The Cakewalk home studio programs excel in certain areas including

- **Easy to use:** The Cakewalk programs are designed with the beginner in mind, and so they're easy to understand, and getting some recording done quickly is a snap.

- **Inexpensive:** The programs are relatively inexpensive for the features they offer, and they're a good value for the home recordists who are just getting started.

Cakewalk minuses

Programs made by Cakewalk are designed for people starting out and can't really be compared with powerhouse programs such as Pro Tools, Logic, Digital Performer, and SONAR. But even when you compare Cakewalk programs with its basic home recording program peers, it could still stand to improve in some areas, including

Figure 7-2:
Cakewalk
has
something
for you
guitar
players out
there.

✔ **Limited editing functions:** Although you can edit both audio and MIDI in these programs (except Guitar Tracks Pro, which doesn't have MIDI capabilities), you're limited at what you can do and how quickly you can do it. In all honesty, though, for the price you really can't expect the power of some of the other programs.

✔ **Scaled-down user interface:** These programs don't offer much in the line of windows in which to work. Don't get me wrong, you can do all you need to with the windows, but certain windows, such as the MIDI piano roll window, make working with Cakewalk programs less than ideal.

Finding out more

To find out more about Cakewalk home recording programs, go to: www.cake walk.com/homemusicians.asp.

SONAR

Although SONAR is a Cakewalk program and could easily be put in the Cakewalk section in this chapter, I separated SONAR from the other Cakewalk offerings because it's in a different league. Unlike Guitar Tracks Pro, Home Studio 2, and Music Creator Pro, SONAR is a full-featured professional program set that competes with the other heavy-hitters such as Pro Tools, Logic, and Cubase.

SONAR comes in two configurations:

- **SONAR Studio Edition:** SONAR is an audio and MIDI program that also supports loops. This program is on par with the other professional-level programs such as Logic, Digital Performer, Cubase, Pro Tools, and Nuendo. SONAR Studio Edition offers unlimited audio and MIDI tracks.

- **SONAR Producer Edition:** This edition of Sonar is essentially the same as the SONAR Studio Edition except that it adds some functions such as improved surround sound support, more plug-ins, and an enhanced mixing environment, a shown in Figure 7-3.

Examining SONAR's strengths

SONAR is a top-notch program that has some definite strengths. These include

Figure 7-3:
SONAR comes in a Producer Edition.

✔ **Plug-in delay compensation:** This is an important feature for people who use a lot of plug-ins on their tracks because the program automatically compensates for any delay that is introduced by processing the plug-in.

✔ **Looping:** Even though all the better (and beyond) programs have looping functions, SONAR's loop manipulation abilities are on par with ACID, the "Loop Master" program.

✔ **Freeze function:** Logic started the freeze function trend (and I'm glad Logic did so — it's a great feature), and SONAR has included it as well. The freeze function lets you apply the plug-ins you've assigned to a track (you create a new file with the plug-in applied to the track) and play it back without having to process the plug-in while the song plays. This function is handy if you have lots of tracks with plug-ins and you want to take the stress off your system. SONAR makes this process easy.

SONAR weaknesses: The gory details

Some parts of SONAR could be improved upon, including:

✔ **Windows PC only:** Sorry Mac users, SONAR is available only for Windows PCs. I wouldn't expect this to change, so if you're a Mac user. I recommend trying Logic.

✔ **Not very customizable:** This is a key feature if you spend a lot of time recording (or plan to). SONAR still isn't where some of the other programs are in this regard. (Logic and Nuendo, for example, are markedly better in this regard.)

✔ **Audio editing:** Because I've complained about the audio editing capabilities (or workflow styles, anyway) of many of the programs that I list in this chapter, I have to be consistent and say that SONAR is no better. In fact, in some ways SONAR is behind most of the other programs when it comes to audio editing. If extensive audio editing is a top priority for you, you may want to look at Pro Tools or Nuendo.

✔ **File management:** Managing your files in SONAR is definitely harder than in programs such as Pro Tools and Logic. This can be a time-suck for people who do a lot of recording or who share audio clips between songs.

Finding out more

To find out more about SONAR, check out the Cakewalk Web site at: `www.cake walk.com/professionals.asp`. This site also has an excellent user forum.

Logic

Logic is one of the most-used and most powerful audio/MIDI recording programs available. Logic has been around for quite a while; it started out as Emagic's baby, but has since been bought by Apple. Logic is available in two forms:

✔ **Logic Express:** Logic Express is the introductory version of Logic. It has many of the functions of Logic Pro except for a couple of very important distinctions — at least they're important for professional users. First, Logic Express doesn't support Broadcast Wave or AIFF file types, which means you can't import or export files from and to other programs. (Importing into Logic Pro is no problem.) Second, it has a limit of 12 hardware inputs. On the other hand, Logic Express does record 24-bit files, so you can record high-quality tracks in this program and easily upgrade to Logic Pro later on if you want.

✔ **Logic Pro:** Logic Pro is one of the most feature-rich programs available. With Logic Pro, you have unlimited tracks and hardware inputs, awesome automation, MIDI, and software synthesizer features (including many included soft-synths). This is one of the top professional recording programs and is used by many commercial studios and professional composers.

Logic: The strengths

Logic is a powerful program that offers some great features. Some of the most important are

✔ **Extensive MIDI capabilities:** Logic started out as a MIDI sequencing/ editing program. As a result, it has functions that many of the other programs don't have. Because of this, working with MIDI is a joy in Logic, as is working with software synthesizers. (See the "Soft-synth support" bullet in this list.) If MIDI is high on your list of functions, you have to give Logic a try. (If you use a Mac, see the following section.)

✔ **User flexibility:** Logic is a powerhouse of a program. One of the big advantages for some users is the ability to customize your working environment to your needs. (Such flexibility is also a hindrance for some users — see the following section.) Being able to make these customizations can save power-users a boatload of time. (Need I say that this is one of the things I love about this program?)

✔ **Soft-synth support:** Logic is one of the best programs out there for using software synthesizers. Plugging in soft-synths and actually using them is easy with this program. In addition, Logic Pro ships with a ton of really good software synthesizers and samplers, which can save you a lot of money. If you intend to use soft-synths in your music, definitely check out this program.

✔ **Freeze function:** The freeze function allows you to freeze a track with its plug-ins. This is a quick way to create a new file of your track with its plug-ins recorded to it so that your system isn't processing the plug-in in real time. This takes a lot of strain off your system, especially if you use several plug-ins and have numerous tracks in your mixes. This function was introduced by Logic and quickly copied by a bunch of other programs because it started to level the playing field between host-based recording systems (such as Pro Tools TDM) that have their own processors and native recording systems (ones that use the computer's processor to function).

✔ **Linking computers:** As of version 7, Logic added the ability to link more than one computer together to share the processing burden among them. This allows you to have more plug-in and soft-synths happening before your system starts to bog down. Other program designers had tried to add this feature before, but they never made it stable or easy to use. Apple seems to have done this, and the ability (currently) puts Logic above all the other native systems for people who need lots of power.

✔ **Tight integration with Mac OS:** As of version 6, Logic is owned by Apple. This means that, as the program develops further, you can be assured that it will be as tightly integrated into the Mac OS as any program can be. This translates into more available power, unique features tied to the OS, and improved stability. (Not that Logic is unstable now; in fact, it's very stable, but so are most programs.)

Logic: The weaknesses

On the flip side, Logic has some limitations for some users. These include

✔ **Mac only:** Windows PC users can't use the latest versions of Logic (versions 6 and up). Earlier versions (5 and down) were supported for Windows PCs, so if you don't need the latest features, you could go with an older version of Logic. This isn't something I'd recommend because the features introduced since version 5 are the ones that set Logic apart from many of the other programs.

✔ **Cumbersome audio editing:** By cumbersome, I mean that it just can't compete with Pro Tools when it comes to audio editing flexibility. This doesn't mean that it won't do the job or that it doesn't do it well; it's just that, when compared to the superb audio editing capabilities of Pro Tools, Logic is harder to work with. If intricate editing of your audio is a priority for you, I recommend that you try Logic for yourself to see whether you can work it the way you want to — and while you're at it, try Pro Tools if possible so that you can compare it with Logic.

✔ **The Environment:** Logic uses a concept called the Environment to work in. Basically, the Environment is a display feature that allows you to customize your working environment in an almost unlimited number of ways. As you might imagine, it's a unique way of working that takes some people some time to get a handle on. Many people don't take the time to learn how to use the Environment effectively and walk away in disgust with this program. I included the user flexibility of the Environment in the Advantages list, too, because when you get it figured out you're able to harness the awesome power of this program. If at first glance the Environment is confusing to you, I recommend finding someone in your area who's well-versed in Logic to get you going with it or try one of the excellent resources offered for this program. (Check out the Apple Web site for one such resource.)

Finding out more

You can find out more about Logic at the Apple Web site. The address is
www.apple.com/logic. You can also find an excellent user forum for Logic
users at http://community.sonikmatter.com/forums.

Digital Performer

Digital Performer (shown in Figure 7-4) is made by MOTU (Mark of the
Unicorn), the people who make the MOTU audio and MIDI interfaces. Digital
Performer is a full-featured program for Macs that does both audio and MIDI
well. Digital Performer is available in only one edition, but MOTU includes
a distant cousin (and extremely stripped-down) version called Audio Desk
with its interfaces. You can upgrade to Digital Performer (DP) for just a few
hundred dollars.

Surveying DP's strengths

Digital Performer is a solid program that offers the following strengths:

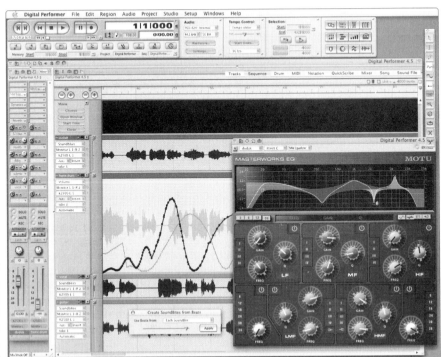

Figure 7-4:
Digital
Performer
piles on the
features.

✔ **Tight hardware integration:** MOTU makes audio interfaces as well as the Digital Performer software program. As a result, its hardware and software products work well together. Even though most programs have solid hardware support, having one manufacturer make both hardware and software reduces the possibility of compatibility issues.

✔ **MIDI capabilities:** MIDI is one of the areas where DP excels. If you do a lot of MIDI recording and, more importantly, editing, you'll find that Digital Performer offers plenty of functions that make working with MIDI easy and fast.

✔ **Soft-synth support:** DP, like Logic, is a soft-synth users dream. Incorporating software synthesizers into your song is simple. (In addition, MOTU makes some decent software synthesizers such as the sampler MachFive.)

✔ **Customization:** DP can be customized for your working style. As far as I'm concerned, for people who do a lot of recording this is undoubtedly one of the most important functions of an audio recording program. By being able to customize your working environment, you can save yourself quite a bit of time performing the tasks that you do often.

Exploring DP's weaknesses

Digital Performer has some areas where it could be improved on. (But don't we all?). These include:

✔ **Mac only:** Digital Performer is limited to Mac users only. This program has never been available for Windows PC users, and there's no plan to expand beyond Macintosh computers.

✔ **Audio editing:** Compared to Pro Tools and Nuendo, Digital Performer is weak when it comes to audio editing. As was the case with Logic, DP's audio editing capabilities do exist, but performing tight edits takes time. If it turns out that you do only an occasional intense edit (for example, cutting a single drum hit in a track with a complex part), you'll do fine with DP, but if you intend to do a lot of this type of edit, you might be better off using Pro Tools or Nuendo.

✔ **Cluttered interface:** Digital Performer has a lot of eye candy. This might look nice to some people, but it creates a couple of potential problems: It can slow down your system and it can cause you to divert your attention from what your music sounds like to what it looks like.

Finding out more

For more information about Digital Performer, go to MOTU's Web site at: `www.motu.com/products/software/dp`. You can find a forum for Digital Performer users at `http://osxaudio.com/forums/viewforum.php?f=23`.

Nuendo

Nuendo is made by Steinberg, the maker of Cubase. Nuendo is designed and marketed as a media production program and is used most often by people in post-production sound design. Nuendo is available only in one edition. This line has no entry-level products; only the top-of-the-line version is available (which I guess would make it the only-one-in-the-line version).

Surveying Nuendo's strengths

Nuendo is becoming the professional's choice for post-production work. It handles audio beautifully. Here are some of its strengths:

- **Audio editing:** Nuendo rivals Pro Tools in the audio editing department. Although it works differently, Nuendo does many of the same basic functions, so you can swiftly make intricate audio edits. If you intend to do a lot of audio editing, this program is definitely worth looking at.

- **Customization:** Nuendo, like Logic, offers users considerable flexibility in how the program looks and functions. Being able to customize your working environment is important to working quickly. If you like being able to tweak your settings, you might like working in Nuendo.

- **Network linking:** Nuendo, like Logic, offers the ability to link more than one computer together. This lets you share the processing duties between two computers. Even though it came up with this function before Logic, getting it working in Nuendo isn't as easy or intuitive (to me anyway). Still, this ability can make complex songs easier to work with (assuming you have more than one computer).

- **Surround mixing:** For surround mixing, Nuendo is great. Surround mixing lets you place the tracks in your mix in a variety of locations beyond just the left and right possible with stereo mixing. Surround mixing isn't common yet for music, but it's necessary if you work on video. Nuendo version 3 adds quite a few enhancements over previous versions, so Steinberg has clearly made surround mixing a priority for this program. You can expect this strength to be amplified in future versions. If you want to mix for film, this program is one of the best (also check out Logic if you use a Mac).

- **Cross platform:** Nuendo works on both Macs and Windows PCs. Most power-users are using Windows PCs when they work in Nuendo. I've heard of complaints about stability on Macs in version 2. Given the number of complaints and the cost of the program, I expect that Steinberg fixed this for version 3 (which hasn't yet been released as I write this section).

Exploring Nuendo's weaknesses

Nuendo has some weaknesses. These include

- ✔ **Limited MIDI capabilities:** Like Pro Tools, Nuendo doesn't have the best MIDI implementation. Because it's designed as a post-production program, Steinberg assumes that MIDI isn't a priority for its users, so it hasn't endowed this program with the kind of MIDI capability that you find in programs such as Logic or SONAR. So if you want to do any MIDI work, you're better of with a different program.

- ✔ **Expensive:** Nuendo retails for $2,000. This is more than double the price of many of the other professional-level audio recording programs. The reason this is the case is a mystery, but that's the reality. If you want to focus your work on film-based post-production, the cost shouldn't be a deterrent, but for basic audio recording (which is where this program excels) you can find other options for less that work just as well.

Finding out more

You can find more information about Nuendo at Steinberg's Web site located at `www.steinberg.net/ProductPage_sb.asp?Product_ID =2444&Langue_ID=7`.

Chapter 8

Installing Your Software

· ·

· ·

*I*nstalling recording software is pretty much the same as installing any other type of program on your system. The only difference is in how you get your system ready for the software installation. Without optimizing your system settings — getting it so that it can deal with the high demands that come with audio recording — you can run into problems down the line with audio dropouts (silences), clicks and pops, and limited track and plug-in counts.

In this chapter, I guide you through the process of getting your system ready and optimizing your operating system's settings to ensure (as much as possible, anyway) that your system will be stable and will perform at its best. Just so you know that I'm not necessarily choosing sides in the platform wars, I go out of my way in this chapter to take you step by step through both a Macintosh OS X and a Windows XP system.

Getting Ready to Install

Before you install your audio programs, you really need to do a few things to make the process quick and easy. These are:

 ✔ **Update your system software to the most recent version.** This doesn't necessarily mean buying the most current version available (though this is often a very good idea); instead, it means that you download and install the most recent iteration of the version you have. For example, if you have Mac OS 10.2.1 on your computer, an update is definitely in order.

 ✔ **Check the documentation on the packaging of the recording software you intend to install.** There might be restrictions on what operating system versions you can use. For example, Pro Tools 6.3 won't work with Mac OS 10.2 — it needs at least version 10.3. In this case, you might need to upgrade your OS version. Be sure to check the documentation on the side of the box before you buy your recording software and budget in the OS upgrade if necessary. Trust me on this one: It's a bummer to have a program you can't install until you get other software installed first.

✔ **Make sure your hardware is up to snuff.** Check with the manufacturer of your software to make sure that your computer and audio interface components are compatible with the program. Depending on the age and composition of your computer, you might need to make some upgrades. Chapter 3 discusses the whole hardware upgrade issue in greater detail.

✔ **Get the drivers for your audio interface ready.** You're going to install your audio interface drivers before you install the audio program itself, so have the discs with the drivers ready. (I cover the actual process of installing these drivers later in the PC and Mac sections.)

✔ **Reboot your computer.** You want to install the programs from a fresh boot, so if you've been doing other tasks on your computer, turn it off first. When it's booted up, you can move on to the steps that I list in the next section.

After you take care of the stuff that I list here, you're ready to move on to configuring your operating system and installing your programs. If you use a Windows PC, go to the next section. If you use a Mac, skip to the Mac section later in this chapter.

Putting Software on a Windows XP PC

Getting your PC ready to face any and all audio recording tasks will take you a few minutes, but it's well worth your time because it makes your system both more stable and more efficient. In this section, I cover some basic things to keep in mind when you're configuring (or purchasing) a PC system for use with audio recording software programs.

Configuring the Windows XP operating system

Before you can actually install your audio recording software, you need to get your system configured for it. This section describes the procedures and helps you make sure that your system will run trouble-free (at least as much as can be expected).

After you make all the adjustments in this section, you need to reboot your computer for them to take affect.

Windows settings

Although for the most part you can run almost any audio program just fine on a standard Windows XP configuration, a few system adjustments will free up system resources, allowing more of your computer system's power to be available for use by your music programs. This is important because almost all the audio programs that you could possibly install on your computer are designed to transform your system into a native DAW (Digital Audio Workstation) — one that relies solely on the host computer's processing power with no additional DSP (digital signal processor) cards for support. (The exceptions that prove the rule are the Pro Tools TDM systems, which have their own computer chips to take the load off your computer; you can see Chapter 7 for more on this particular animal.) Some of the adjustments I recommend here — such as enabling direct memory access (DMA) for all your IDE hard drives — are crucial for running audio programs successfully. The sections that follow lay out the basic system settings that I recommend.

Windows XP Classic mode

You can accomplish the same basic housekeeping and setup tasks in Windows XP in many ways. Because I don't know how your system is set up right now, I lead you through the process from square one. The first thing you want to do is set your system display — the way stuff looks on-screen — to Windows Classic mode. Here's how:

1. **Choose Start➪Settings➪Control Panel.**

   The contents of the Control Panel folder appear on-screen.

2. **Double-click the Display icon.**

   The Display Properties dialog box appears.

3. **Select the Themes tab and then select Windows Classic from the Theme drop-down list, as shown in Figure 8-1.**

   This resets your system to its classic theme and disables your active desktop setup.

4. **Click the Apply button.**

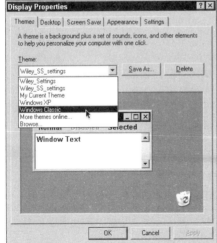

Figure 8-1:
Select
Windows
Classic
under
Themes.

5. **Select the Desktop tab and then select None from the Background list box, as shown in Figure 8-2.**

6. **Click OK.**

This procedure disables the active desktop in Windows, which might free up some valuable system resources depending on how your system was set up to begin with.

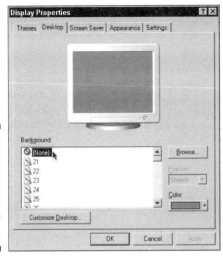

Figurer 8-2:
Under the
Desktop tab,
select None
from the
Background
options.

Choosing Control Panel settings

Windows XP is remarkably stable, but for those rare times when it (or a program running under Windows) crashes, it generates an error report and asks whether you want to send the report to Microsoft. This feature, called Error Reporting, takes system resources to run — and because you'd rather have those resources working hard to keep your recording software running smoothly, you need to disable Error Reporting. Here's the drill:

1. **Choose Start⇨Settings⇨Control Panel.**

   The contents of the Control Panel folder appear on-screen.

2. **Double-click the System icon.**

   The System Properties dialog box appears.

3. **Select the Advanced tab.**

4. **Click the Error Reporting button.**

   The Error Reporting dialog box appears, as shown in Figure 8-3.

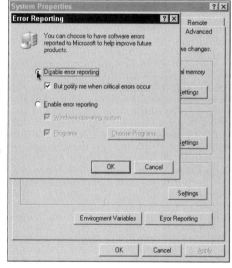

Figure 8-3:
Select the
Disable
Error
Reporting
option.

5. **Select the Disable Error Reporting radio button.**

6. **Click OK to close the Error Reporting dialog box.**

7. **Click OK in the System Properties dialog box to close it. Leave the Control Panels window open.**

Standby power should be set to Always On for whatever audio recording system you use. This ensures that your computer doesn't go to sleep while you're recording. To do this, follow these steps:

1. **Open the Control Panel if you closed it already. (Choose Start➪ Settings➪Control Panel.)**

2. **Double-click the Power Options icon.**

   The Power Options Properties dialog box opens.

3. **Select the Always On option from the Power Schemes drop-down list.**

4. **In the Settings for Always On Power Scheme section of the dialog box, select Never from the Turn Off Monitor drop-down list, as shown in Figure 8-4.**

Figure 8-4:
Select the Always On and Never options to keep your monitor from shutting down during a long song.

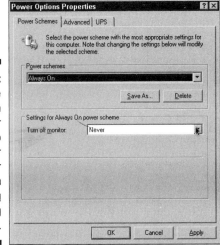

5. **Click Apply to accept these settings.**

6. **Click OK to close the Power Options Properties dialog box.**

7. **Leave the Control Panel open. You have more settings to adjust.**

You also want to make sure that no screen saver appears on your screen as you record because if it does you won't be able to see what's happening on-screen and the screen saver might crash your system to boot. The following steps show you how you can make sure that no screen saver makes an unplanned appearance:

1. **Open the Control Panel if you closed it already. (Choose Start⇨ Settings⇨Control Panel.)**

2. **Double click the Display icon.**

   The Display Properties dialog box makes an appearance.

3. **Select the Screen Saver tab and then select None from the Screen Saver drop-down list, as shown in Figure 8-5.**

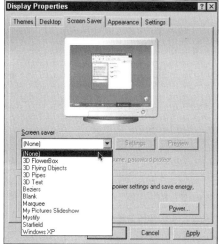

Figure 8-5:
To keep a screen saver from disrupting your recording session, select None from the Screen Saver list.

4. **Click the Apply button.**

5. **Click the Appearance tab and then click the Effects button in the lower-right corner of the tab.**

   The Effects dialog box opens, as shown in Figure 8-6.

6. **Make sure that none of the seven options listed in the window are selected with a check mark. If any of them are selected, simply click those pesky check marks so they disappear.**

7. **Click OK to close the Effects dialog box.**

8. **Click OK to close the Display Properties dialog box.**

9. **Leave the Control Panel open; there's still one more thing you have to do.**

Figure 8-6:
Turn off
all display
effects by
making sure
none of
the check
boxes in
this dialog
box are
selected.

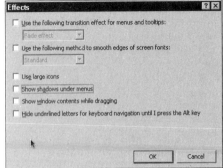

Your system sounds need to be disabled to prevent potential problems with audio programs — problems such as clicks, pops, or dropouts in your audio or having your system crash when you record or playback audio. To disable your system sounds, follow these steps:

1. **Open the Control Panel if you closed it already. (Choose Start➪ Settings➪Control Panel.)**

2. **Double-click the Sounds and Audio Devices icon in the Control Panel.**

   The Sounds and Audio Devices Properties dialog box opens.

3. **Click the Sounds tab.**

4. **Select No Sounds from the Sound Scheme drop-down list, as shown in Figure 8-7.**

Figure 8-7:
Selecting
No Sounds
from the
Sound
Scheme
drop-down
list silences
those pesky
internal
sounds.

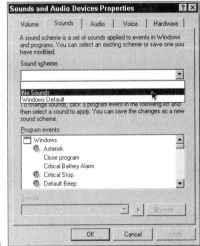

5. **Click Apply to accept this change.**

6. **Click OK to close the Sounds and Audio Devices Properties dialog box.**

7. **Close the Control Panel by clicking the X at the upper-right corner of the window.**

Congratulations! You've just configured your system settings.

Enabling DMA

All IDE hard drives on your system *must* have DMA (direct memory access) enabled before your recording program can effectively write and read data to and from your hard drives. This takes the central processing unit (CPU) out of the process and improves the transfer of data from your RAM to your hard drive. To enable DMA, do the following:

1. **Right-click the My Computer icon on the Windows desktop.**

2. **From the contextual menu that appears, choose Properties to access the Properties dialog box, and then click the Hardware tab.**

3. **On the Hardware tab of the Properties dialog box, click the Device Manager button.**

4. **In the Device Manager dialog box, double click the IDE ATA/ATAPI Controllers branch of the navigation tree.**

   The navigation tree expands to show the controllers associated with your system.

5. **From the listing, double click the Primary IDE Controller branch and select the Advanced Settings tab.**

   If it doesn't already say DMA If Available under the Transfer Mode option, change it so that it does. If you have several disk drives on your system, you have to do the same for each drive.

6. **Click OK and repeat the same steps for the Secondary IDE controller.**

   It's in the Device Manager navigation tree, directly below the Primary controller.

Disabling AutoPlay

AutoPlay is a feature of Windows XP that automatically runs certain programs or plays music on a CD when you insert it into your computer's CD drive. This is a handy feature in everyday life, but can cause problems with audio recording software because resources are used in your computer to run this feature, which can slow your system down. In addition, AutoPlay has been known to cause glitches in audio recording or playback on some systems. For the sake of your music, disable AutoPlay for all CD drives on your system. Here's the drill:

 1. **Double click the My Computer icon on the Windows desktop.**

    The My Computer window duly appears.

 2. **In the My Computer window, right-click the icon for your CD drive.**

 3. **From the contextual menu that appears, select Properties to access the Properties dialog box and then select the AutoPlay tab.**

 4. **On the AutoPlay tab, select Music Files from the Select Content Type drop-down list.**

 5. **At the bottom of the Properties dialog box, select the Prompt Me Each Time to Choose an Action option.**

 6. **Repeat Steps 4 and 5 with the Pictures, Video Files, Mixed Content, Music CD, and Blank CD options for the Select Content Type drop-down list.**

 7. **Click OK.**

 8. **Repeat Steps 2 through 7 for each CD or DVD drive on your computer.**

Disabling virus protection

Virus protection is an important thing to have on any computer that connects to the Internet, but virus protection can also adversely affect audio recording performance. Ideally, your computer would be dedicated to recording, editing, and mixing your music. However, you will likely be using an all-purpose computer that you will use for many tasks, such as surfing the Web for business, pleasure, and/or helping with your children's homework. In that case, be sure to turn off your virus protection whenever you're running any audio recording program. Check with the documentation that came with your virus-protection software for the best way to do this. (And don't forget to re-enable virus protection before you log on to the Internet again.)

I hate to repeat myself, but I will: If you're really serious about having a bulletproof system, try to keep any extra software (such as games, finance, publishing, graphics, and so on) off your audio computer. At the very least, keep all other applications closed while you work on your music.

Connecting your hardware

When you have your system fine-tuned (which I cover in the previous section), you can connect your hardware. Shut down your computer and do what needs to be done to connect your audio interface. (Not sure what needs to be done? Each piece of hardware has its own installation procedure, as spelled out in it's accompanying manual, but I do give you some general guidelines in Chapter 5.) When you have the hardware connected, turn on your computer.

Then, after the Windows desktop appears, turn on the power to your audio interface. (If you're using a product that doesn't have a power switch, you can obviously ignore this particular step.)

On Windows PCs, it's important to wait to install any software until after you've attached your hardware, and, if needed, powered it on. The complete details for attaching hardware are located in Chapter 5.

Installing your software

After you complete the Windows system-setup adjustments that I list in earlier sections, you can install your audio program. You need to check the documentation that came with your software for the specific procedure, but most software installations work pretty much the same way. With that in mind, here's a rundown on the steps involved when installing Pro Tools, one of the more popular audio programs out there. As you can see, it's pretty simple. Just follow these steps:

1. **Connect your interface to your computer.**

   As I explain in Chapters 5 and 7, Pro Tools runs only with Digidesign hardware, so your interface of choice had better be a Digidesign model. If you have a 002 or 002 Rack, this means connecting the FireWire cable, whereas the Mbox requires a USB connection, and the 001 requires plugging in the PCI card into an open PCI slot and making the connection between the PCI card and the break-out box — the rest of the 001 system.

2. **Boot up your PC.**

   The Windows desktop appears.

3. **If your Digidesign interface has a separate power switch, this is the time to turn on the interface.**

   If it doesn't have a separate power switch, jump right to Step 4.

4. **Insert the Pro Tools software CD in your computer's CD drive.**

5. **Double-click the My Computer icon on the Windows desktop.**

   The My Computer window appears.

6. **In the My Computer window, double-click the icon for your CD drive.**

   The contents of the CD are displayed in a new window.

7. **Double click the Pro Tools LE Installer folder.**

   The contents of the Pro Tools LE Installer folder are displayed for all to see.

8. **Double-click the Setup icon.**

9. **After the Installer dialog box appears, click Next to continue.**

10. **Accept the default paths for installation — they're fine, and it's less hassle — and then click the Install button.**

11. **Wait for the installation to complete.**

12. **Restart your computer.**

Installing Software on a Mac

Getting up and going on a Mac is easy. When you have a computer that has the right specs (I spell out specs in Chapter 3), it will take you less than 15 minutes to be ready to plug in your hardware (Chapter 5 covers this) and start recording (as Chapter 10 details). This section takes you through, step by step, the process of turning your Mac into a lean, mean, audio recording machine.

Recording, editing, and mixing audio on a computer takes a toll on your system's resources. The best (and time-tested) way to ensure that you have as few problems as possible is to keep your computer lean by dedicating it to audio only. Use a different computer for all your other chores such as home finance, word processing, or games. If you have only one computer, I strongly suggest that you keep all other applications turned off while you record.

That said, I'm going to contradict myself and tell you that I've done a lot of testing by using audio programs on different Mac computers with OS X and my experience is that it's a very robust operating system that seems to handle having more than just audio on the computer. In fact, I've successfully run an Internet browser while downloading music, a graphics program, a photo-editing program, a word processor, and an e-mail program while mixing 8 tracks of audio and didn't have any problems. I don't recommend that you have these other programs on while you work, but my experience is that OS X seems to be up to the task of at least having other programs on your system.

If you decide to use your everyday computer for recording audio, use a dedicated hard drive for the audio data and defragment it frequently. Also, don't put any other data on this drive — ever. If your system gets sluggish and you start to experience audio clicks, pops, or dropouts, it's time to defragment your drive.

Setting system settings

Before you install any audio recording software, check to make sure that you have the latest version of OS X. (Also check your software manufacturer's Web site to make sure the latest version of OS X is supported.) Then follow these steps to prepare your system for the software installation:

1. **Log on to your computer by using an administration account.**

   Your OS X documentation spells out this procedure for you.

2. **Choose Apple↪System Preferences, as shown in Figure 8-8.**

   The System Preferences dialog box appears.

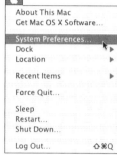

Figure 8-8:
Systems
preferences
are located
under the
Apple menu.

3. **Under the Hardware Options, click the Energy Saver icon.**

   A new dialog box opens.

4. **Under the Sleep tab, slide the slider for Put the Computer To Sleep When It Is Inactive For option over to Never, as in Figure 8-9.**

   This keeps your computer from shutting down if you record a long song because you don't touch any keys while recording.

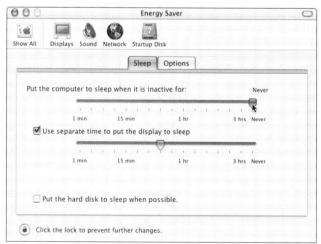

Figure 8-9:
Turn off
the sleep
function
for the
computer
in the
Energy
Saver
dialog box.

5. **Leave the Put the Hard Disk to Sleep When Possible option deselected.**

   This keeps your computer from going to sleep during long sessions.

6. **Go back to the main Systems Preferences dialog box by pressing the Show All button in the upper-left corner of the dialog box.**

7. **Select Software Update from the System options at the bottom of the dialog box.**

8. **When the new Software Update dialog box opens, deselect the Automatically Check for Updates When You Have a Network Connection option, as shown in Figure 8-10.**

   This keeps your system from dedicating resources to look for and download software updates.

9. **Close the dialog box by clicking the red button in the upper-left corner of the dialog box.**

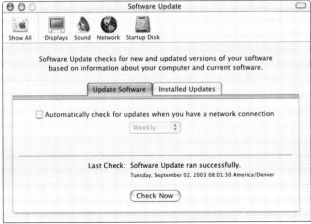

Figure 8-10: Deselect the automatic software update option in the Software Update dialog box.

Installing your software

After you complete the system-setup requirements in the preceding section, you can install your audio program. You need to check the documentation that came with your software for the specific procedure, but most software installations work pretty much the same way. I highlight the Pro Tools software program as an example of a Windows-base software program earlier in this chapter, so for the sake of consistency I'm sticking with Pro Tools for the Mac section as well. Here's a rundown:

1. **Insert the Pro Tools software CD in your computer's CD drive.**

2. **In the new window that appears, double-click the Install Pro Tools icon.**

    The OS X Administration window appears, asking you to enter your password.

3. **Enter your OS X administration password and click OK.**

    The Pro Tools installer opens.

4. **Select the Startup hard drive as the destination drive.**

    The installation path is set.

5. **Click the Install button.**

    Pro Tools is installed on your computer. (This might take a few minutes, so sit back and contemplate the fun you're going to have once it's finished installing itself.)

6. **Restart your computer.**

Wait to open the program until after you attach your hardware. The complete details for attaching hardware are located in Chapter 5.

Configuring Your Hardware

If you think that after installing your software you can start documenting your musical genius right away, think again. Before you can do any recording, you need to configure your hardware in your audio recording program. This involves several steps, including installing hardware drivers and choosing hardware settings, choosing I/O buffer settings, and selecting input and output routing. These steps are detailed in this section.

Setting up your interface

Hardware settings are the configurations that relate to your audio interface and include such things as the clock source, bit depth, sample rate, and digital input/output routing selections. The options that you have to choose from as well as the steps you perform to select these settings vary depending on the hardware you use. To give you an idea of this process, I detail the set up procedures for two interfaces — a Digidesign model and a MOTU model — in this section. And because I use a Mac for most of my recording, the steps in this section use a Macintosh running OS X. The procedures for Windows XP are similar.

Installing interface software

Every audio interface comes with software that allows you to run it with your audio application. Unless the maker of your audio recording software is the same as the manufacturer of your audio interface, you need to install this software separately from your audio recording software. To do this, follow the steps that I list in "Installing your software" section of the Mac OS X and Windows XP sections of this chapter — depending, of course, on which operating system you have installed on your computer.

After you have the interface software installed and have restarted your computer, you're ready to perform the setup procedure.

Opening the Hardware Setup dialog box

Depending on your hardware/software choice, you need to open your audio recording application or your audio interface software program. For example, if you use Pro Tools software (which requires one of the Digidesign audio interfaces), follow this procedure to open the Hardware Setup dialog box:

1. **Turn on your interface by depressing the power button located on the front panel.**

2. **Double-click the Pro Tools icon in the Applications folder of your computer — or wherever Pro Tools is installed on your system — to launch Pro Tools.**

   Pro Tools boots up without any open windows.

3. **Choose Setups⇨Hardware Setup from the menu at the top of your screen.**

   The Hardware Setup dialog box opens. (See Figure 8-11.) You're now ready to adjust the settings.

Figure 8-11: The Hardware Setup dialog box is where you configure your hardware device.

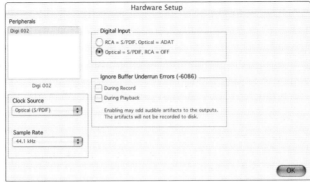

If you use an audio interface that isn't joined at the hip with your audio program, you need to open the interface's software to make the hardware setting adjustments, rather than adjusting your audio program. As an example, here's how you adjust hardware settings when using a MOTU application:

1. **Turn on your interface by flipping the switch on the front panel.**

2. **Double-click the MOTU icon in your application folder to open the software.**

   The setup dialog box for your particular device opens.

3. **Click on the tab for the interface you have to access your setup options, as shown in Figure 8-12.**

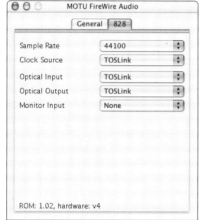

Figure 8-12:
Your audio interface hardware settings dialog box lets you choose the settings you want to use.

Making your selection

Getting to the Hardware Setup dialog box is only half the battle. You still have to actually change some of the settings. This section gives you some guidelines on what to do.

With the hardware setup dialog box open, you can see a bunch of settings you can tweak. Each device's setup dialog box has different options. The most common settings include the specific hardware device, clock source, sample rate, and digital/optical inputs and outputs. Some devices, such as the MOTU interfaces (see Figure 8-12), give you monitoring options for some version of low-latency monitoring. (*Latency* refers to the delay caused by your audio being converted from analog to digital and back again so you can hear what you play, and *low latency* refers to a setting that reduces this latency by routing your signal to skip either part of the software or part of the hardware in your system. Chapter 10 has more on low-latency monitoring). Here's a rundown of the most common (dare I say, important) selection areas:

✔ **Device:** The device is the piece of hardware you have. If the manufacturer of your interface makes more than one device, you might have the option of choosing from their various models. As you can see in Figures 8-11 and 8-12, the dialog box lists the device (or devices) that you have connected to your system. If you have more than one device, you need to select the one whose settings you want to adjust. This is as easy as clicking the name of the device. For the Pro Tools example, you can find the device name in the Peripherals list box (refer to Figure 8-11); in the MOTU example, the device selection option is located as a tab at the top of the Hardware Setup dialog box. (Refer to Figure 8-12.)

✔ **Clock Source:** The clock source is the device that controls the digital clock (the exact time that each sample takes place). This drop-down list allows you to choose your source for the digital master clock, thus making sure that if you have more than one device (a separate A/D converter connected to your interface, for example), all devices are synchronized. If you use just your connected interface, simply choose Internal in this menu, but if you have other digital devices, such as a digital mixer or external converter, select your clock source based on the device that has the best clock. Your choices here depend on your interface and how it defines the different possibilities. For example, the Digi 002 (see Figure 8-13, left) includes these options:

   • **Internal:** Uses the digital clock inside the Digidesign interface.

   • **ADAT:** Synchronizes from a signal sent into the ADAT input of your interface. ADAT stands for Alesis Digital Audio Tape. (For more on ADAT inputs, see Chapter 5.)

   • **S/PDIF:** Synchronizes to a signal sent via the coaxial S/PDIF input. S/PDIF stands for Sony/Phillips Digital Interface Format. (For more on S/PDIF inputs, see Chapter 5.)

   • **Optical (S/PDIF):** Synchronizes to a S/PDIF signal coming in the ADAT optical input. You can choose this last one only if you have the lower option selected in the Digital Input check box. (See the "Digital/Optical Input and Output" bullet.)

The MOTU 828 (Figure 8-13, right), on the other hand, contains these options:

   • **Internal:** Uses the digital clock inside the MOTU interface

   • **ADAT 9-pin:** Synchronizes from a signal sent into the 9-pin ADAT connector of your interface.

   • **Toslink:** Synchronizes to a signal coming in the optical ADAT or S/PDIF input. (For more on Toslink connections, see Chapter 5.)

Figure 8-13:
You can
choose from
several
clock
sources
for most
interfaces
(Digidesign
Digi 002, left
and MOTU
828, right).

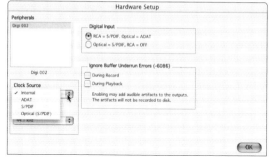

With some interfaces, such as the Digidesign units, you have to connect your desired device to your Digidesign hardware before opening the Hardware Setup dialog box if you want to use one of the digital connections as a clock source. If the device isn't connected beforehand, it won't show up in the dialog box.

If you have more than one digital device connected (such as a digital mixer connected to your Digidesign interface), do some experimenting by recording with different clock sources; compare the chosen sources to see which one gives you the best sound. (Digital clocks vary in quality.) Also, if you have more than three digital devices connected to your system, consider using a specialized master clock and distribute this clock source to all your devices. This will likely give you a better sound because it ensures that all your devices are following the same clock timing.

✔ **Digital/Optical Input and Output:** The digital/optical input and output parameters let you choose how the digital/optical inputs on your interface function. Most devices that have an optical input and output let you select how they function. The optical jacks are able to handle either ADAT (eight channels of digital audio) or S/PDIF (two channels of digital audio) signals, but not both. Aside from being able to select between the two data types, some interfaces also allow you to select None for this parameter. Figure 8-14 shows you the options that the Digidesign and MOTU hardware setup dialog boxes have to offer.

✔ **Sample Rate:** The Sample Rate drop-down list allows you to choose the *sample rate* — how many times every second digital data is collected — in which to work. Depending on your interface, you might be able to choose from 44.1 kHz, 48 kHz, 88.2 kHz, or 96 kHz. Figure 8-15 shows you your options in both the Digidesign and MOTU hardware setup dialog boxes.

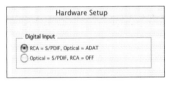

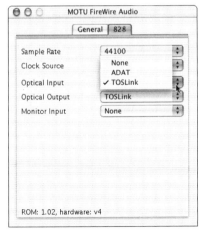

Figure 8-14: You choose the way the digital/ optical input and output jack transfer information (Digidesign Digi 002, left and MOTU 828, right).

For some devices, such as the Digidesign interface, the Sample Rate drop-down list is editable only when you don't have a song file open. If you have a song file open, this drop-down list box shows the sample rate chosen when this song file was created but won't allow you to make any changes. To choose a different sample rate for any future song files, close the song file you have open and then choose Setups⇨Hardware Setup from the main menu, make your choice, and then click OK. Then open a new song file. This new song file is in the sample rate that you just chose.

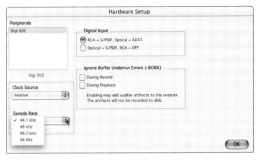

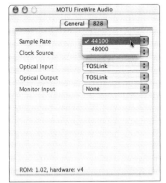

Figure 8-15: You can select your interface's sample rate from a drop-down list (Digidesign Digi 002, left and MOTU 828, right).

After you make your selections, you can close the Hardware Setup dialog box. This can be accomplished by either clicking the OK button, as with the Digidesign device, or by clicking on the Close button at the top of the window (the red button on the left side for Mac OS X and the X button on the right side for Windows XP).

Configuring your audio application hardware settings

You need to adjust a few settings in your audio application to get your system up and running and to give you the best performance possible. For example, you need to assign drivers and adjust buffer settings. This section outlines these areas.

Setting up your hardware

If you use an interface and audio recording program from different manufacturers, you need to set up your interface within the recording program in addition to setting it up in its own software. Just to give one example, if you use Logic Pro, follow these steps:

1. **Double-click the Logic Icon in your application folder (or wherever Logic is located in your computer) to launch the application**.

   Logic opens with a new song file. (Chapter 10 has more about opening a song file.)

2. **Choose Audio⇨Audio Hardware & Drivers, as shown in Figure 8-16.**

   The Audio Hardware and Drivers panel of the Preferences dialog box opens.

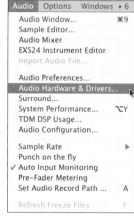

Figure 8-16:
Open the hardware settings dialog box in your recording program to select your interface.

3. **Select the check box for the type of driver that your interface uses.**

   The driver type expands to show the hardware options.

   Note: The MOTU 828 and the Digidesign Digi 002, the two interfaces I've been using as examples in this chapter, both use Core Audio drivers in Mac OS X as well as in Windows XP.

4. **Select your audio interface from the Driver drop-down list, as shown in Figure 8-17.**

5. **Click OK to accept your selection and close the Audio Hardware and Drivers dialog box.**

Adjusting buffer settings

Audio recording programs allow you to control to some degree the amount of stress you put your computer through. These settings are in the form of buffers, which store data and parcel it out as appropriate to help your system run most efficiently. Buffers come in several varieties, depending on the particular software you use, but I cover the most important ones in the following sections.

Inputs and outputs

In Logic, this particular buffer is called the *I/O buffer;* in Pro Tools, it's referred to as the *H/W buffer size.* Regardless of what you call it, this setting lets you determine how many samples are placed in memory before being written to disk. The specifics of each recording program vary, but the bottom line here is that tweaking this setting determines how much latency (delay) you have from the audio coming in to your system and the audio going out again to your headphones or speakers.

This is an important setting because this latency can be noticeable when you record and can easily make it harder for you to get into a groove. (Chapter 10 has more on latency and recording.)

Every audio recording program offers you several settings to choose from. These can be as low as about 64 to as high as 1024 or more. (These numbers refer to the number of audio samples that are placed in the buffer at a time.) Here, lower numbers mean a lower degree of latency — with an accompanying greater strain on your processor — whereas higher numbers mean more latency.

To adjust the hardware buffer size, follow these steps:

In Pro Tools:

1. **Choose Setups⇨Playback Engine.**

   The Playback Engine dialog box opens.

2. **Select the setting that you want from the H/W Buffer Size drop-down list.**

3. **Click OK to accept the setting and close the dialog box.**

In Logic Pro:

1. **Choose Audio⇨Audio Hardware and Drivers.**

   The Audio Hardware and Drivers dialog box opens.

2. **Select the setting that you want from the I/O Buffer drop-down list.**

3. **Click OK to accept the setting and close the window.**

I suggest that you keep this setting as low as possible while recording (especially when you do overdubs). How low you can go depends on how many tracks you record at once — and whether you want to use plug-ins such as reverb while recording. Using lots of tracks and lots of plug-ins requires lots of memory, which might force you (rats!) to bump up the hardware-buffer size. Higher buffer sizes mean higher latencies, which can make overdubbing tracks more difficult, so I reserve high buffer sizes until after I'm done recording all my tracks.

When you're ready to mix, go ahead and raise the buffer size — it doesn't matter if there's a delay within your system because you're not trying to record a new track to it. This puts less stress on your system and allows you to have more plug-ins going at a time before you run into performance problems.

Playback or disk/process buffer

The playback or disk/processor buffer deals with the amount of memory the audio engine uses to manage the hard drive's buffers. As with the hardware buffer, you want as low a setting as you can get without sacrificing system performance. If the setting is too high, you experience a delay between when you hit the Play command and when your program starts playing the recording.

Too low a setting, on the other hand, can create problems such as audio dropout when you record or play back tracks — the sound can just cut off. Start with the default setting and make adjustments as needed. To set this buffer, follow these steps:

In Pro Tools:

1. **Choose Setups⇨Playback Engine.**

   The Playback Engine dialog box opens.

2. **Select the setting that you want from the DAE Playback buffer size drop-down list.**

3. **Click OK to accept the setting and close the window.**

In Logic Pro:

1. **Choose Audio⇨Audio Hardware and Drivers.**

   The Audio Hardware and Drivers dialog box opens.

2. **Select the buffer setting that you want from the Process Buffer Range drop-down list.**

3. **Click OK to accept the setting and close the window.**

Congratulations! Your system is ready to start recording.

Part IV
Revving Up the Recording Process

The 5th Wave   By Rich Tennant

INTENSE BUT UNINFORMED AUDIOPHILE BILLY WIGGINS ENJOYS HIS CUSTOM BURNED CD COLLECTION OF DIAL UP MODEM WARBLES

In this part . . .

Part IV explores the computer-based recording process. Chapter 9 gets basic with an exploration of ways to get the best source sound, whether it's from a guitar, a keyboard, or a microphone. In Chapter 10, you start the recording process by discovering ways to record and edit audio data. Chapter 11 focuses on the process of recording and editing MIDI (Musical Instrument Digital Interface) performance data. Chapter 12 introduces you to the world of loops and helps you get set up to use them in your music. Chapter 13 ups the ante by helping you understand and use software instruments (called soft-synths) in your music. Chapter 14 completes this section by walking you through the process of mixing and mastering your music in your computer.

Chapter 9

Getting a Great Source Sound

The quality of your recording relies heavily on two things: the sound of your instruments and how well you do getting that sound into your computer without messing it up. The problem is that anyone can easily mess up the sound or at least fall short of getting the best possible sound.

This chapter gives you the knowledge to keep bad sound — or sound that's not as good as it could be — from happening. In this chapter, I describe signal flow and the role that it plays in shaping the sound of your instrument. I also give you tips on how to get great guitar sounds and killer keyboard sounds without hassle. To top it off, I spend a few pages getting you up to speed on miking effectively.

Making Sense of the Signal Chain

The *signal chain* is the path that your sound travels from its creation (your guitar, keyboard, or voice) to your recorder (the computer). This path often includes several steps — and pieces of gear — that need to have their levels optimized so that you don't end with too much or too little sound going to your system. Figure 9-1 shows a typical signal chain for a mic.

Figure 9-1:
The signal
chain is the
sound data
highway.

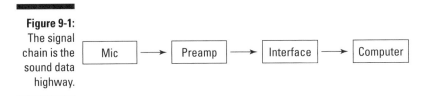

In this example, the sound originating from your voice, enters the microphone, travels to the preamp where it's amplified, is sent to the interface where it's turned into digital information, and finally it gets sent into your computer's recording software program and the hard drive where it's stored.

The key to a good instrument or mic sound is getting the levels of each step in the chain set to its optimal level. This chapter focuses on three distinct steps in the chain:

✔ **The source:** In the example you see in Figure 9-1, the microphone's placement has a huge effect on the signal level that goes into your computer. Moving the mic just a couple inches can have a significant impact on your signal level at the preamp. A good, solid level keeps you from having to crank up your preamp too far, which causes noise. If the level is too hot though — *hot* in the sense of a solid signal between –12dB and –6dB, not in the sense of "burn your fingers" hot — you risk getting distortion at the mic. This same concept holds true for keyboards or other electronic instruments, as well as guitars plugged directly into your interface.

✔ **The preamp/interface:** You adjust this level so that the level at your software is where you want it (see next bullet). The trick here is that you don't want the level set so high that it creates noise in your track, but you don't want it so low that you're forced to set your source volume so high that it creates distortion.

✔ **Your software:** If you record at a 24-bit rate (Chapter 4 has more about bit rates), you want your levels peaking at about –10 to –12dB. This approximate level gives you the necessary headroom (room for transient peaks) so that your signal doesn't overdrive your converters and software and produce distortion. If you record at a 16-bit rate, you need to raise this level a bit (peaks no higher than –6dB) and keep a very close watch to make sure that you don't clip (distort) the signal.

Setting the best level for each stage of your signal chain is more of an art than a science. You need to use your ears and carefully listen as you make adjustments to each stage. Having one level set too high increases the likelihood of distortion, which ruins your sound, and it forces the next stage to be too low, which often results in a thin sound. Take your time setting the levels and use your ears.

Getting a Great Guitar Sound

Do you wanna know how to get the absolute best, most rich, engaging guitar sound? Well, I wish I could tell you, but alas I can't. This is something you're going to need to figure out by listening as you tweak your gear. That said, you can get your sound into your computer in four ways, and each way has its plusses and minuses:

✔ **Directly from your guitar into your interface:** This assumes that your interface can handle a direct connection from a guitar. (Most can, but check to make sure that the one you have or want has this capability. If it doesn't, you need to get a direct box to put between your guitar and your interface. I talk about direct boxes in Chapter 1.) By using this method, the sound you get from your guitar is pretty much the same sound you're going to get recorded.

You might not like the sound. In fact, I'll bet that you won't. The solution to this unfortunate state of affairs is to use a plug-in (or more than one) in your recording program to get the sound you want. This is a common way to get a guitar sound, and tons of good plug-ins can help, including plug-ins for providing distortion, delay chorus, and even special amp simulators that are designed to sound like popular guitar amplifiers. One advantage to this approach is that you can tweak the sound of your guitar as much as you want after it's recorded. The disadvantage is that you can easily become afflicted with indecision disorder and be unable to pick the sound you want. Also, many guitar-tone connoisseurs feel that the sound this way isn't as good as miking up an amp with the sound you want.

✔ **From your guitar to an amp simulator, from the amp simulator into your interface:** Amp simulators are like the plug-ins that you can get for your software, only they're standalone units that have the various sounds in them already. A bunch of standalone amp simulators are available on the market, and most offer decent simulations of the most popular guitar amps. This can be a good solution for many people, but the disadvantage of doing this instead of adding your effects in the computer is that after you record your sound through an amp simulator, that's the sound you're stuck with. Of course, if you often get hit with indecision disorder, this might be a good solution for you.

✔ **From your guitar into your amp and from your amp's line output to your interface:** Recording a guitar this way is great for people who have an amp that they like the sound of but who don't want to mic a speaker. When you follow this approach, you have three volume controls to adjust to get your level into your recorder — your guitar, your amp, and your interface. You might have to take some time tweaking these settings to get the best possible sound.

✔ **From your guitar into your amp with a mic picking up the speaker's sound:** This is the old standby approach because you get to record the actual sound you're used to hearing coming out of your amp. With this method, having the right mic and mic placement makes all the difference in the world. I offer some specific guitar-amping mic techniques later in this chapter.

There is no one way to get a great guitar sound. Don't be afraid to experiment. You might just come up with a sound that really moves you.

Creating a Killer Keyboard Sound

They key to a killer keyboard sound is making sure that you get the sound into your system without messing it up (no pressure here). Depending on your gear, keyboard sounds can be brought into your system one of two ways:

✔ **Using an external keyboard:** For an external keyboard containing the sounds you want to record, plug an instrument cord from the main outputs of your keyboard to the corresponding number of inputs in your audio interface. Turn your keyboard volume up between ½ and ¾ or until you get a decent signal to register in your software. If your interface input has a volume (gain) control, adjust it and the volume of your keyboard until you get a solid sound without distortion.

✔ **Using a soft-synth:** If you want to record a software synthesizer, you first need to connect a MIDI controller to your system. This can be in the form of a MIDI connection (through a MIDI port), or it can be a USB connection if you have a USB-equipped keyboard. Chapter 5 explains how to make the connections for this. After you have your keyboard hooked up, you need to set up a soft-synth in your song. The steps vary depending on the particular software that you use. I detail some specific soft-synths in Chapter 13.

Follow the guidelines that I list in the "Making Sense of the Signal Chain" section, earlier in this chapter, to get your signal levels to be optimal.

Making the Most of Microphones

Finding a great sound from a mic is key to getting a great-sounding recording. To do this, you need to use the best mic for the application and place it where it can sound its best. This requires not only knowledge of the different types of mics that are available, but also how these mics are used for a variety of instrument. In this section, I give you a quick tutorial on microphones and mic-placement techniques to get you started.

There are as many different ways to mic an instrument as there are people doing the miking, so the following sections just provide some general guidelines. (If you want more detail — including some cool drawings — check out my *Home Recording For Musicians For Dummies,* 2nd Edition, also published by Wiley.) Most importantly, don't be afraid of the experiment; let your ears be the judge of what works for your instrument in your song.

Tracing typical microphone techniques

Regardless of the style of microphone you use — or the type of instrument you record — you can use one or more of the following mic-placement techniques to capture the sound you want:

- ✔ **Spot (or close) miking:** Spot miking (also called close miking) involves placing your microphone within a couple feet of the sound source. People with a home-recording setup use this technique most often because it adds little of the sound of the room (the reverb and delay) to the recorded sound.

- ✔ **Distant miking:** When you use distant miking, you place mics about 3 or 4 feet away from the sound source. Distant miking enables you to capture some of the sound of the room along with the instrument. An example of a distant-miking technique is the overhead drum mic. With it, you can pick up the whole drum set to some extent. Coupled with a few select spot mics, you can record a natural sound.

- ✔ **Ambient miking:** Ambient miking is simply placing the mic far enough away from the sound source so you capture more of the room sound (the reverb and delay) than the sound of the actual instrument. You might place the mic a couple feet away from the source but pointed in the opposite direction, or you might place the mic across the room. You can even put the mic in an adjacent room, although this is an unorthodox technique, I'll admit. The distance that you choose varies from instrument to instrument.

Ambient mic placement works well in those places where the room adds to the sound of the instrument. (Home recordists sometimes use stairwells, bathrooms, or rooms with wood paneling to liven up the sound.) The sound that you record is ambient — steeped in the sonic qualities of the surroundings (hence the name *ambient miking*). If you mix this in with a spot mic, you can end up with a natural reverb. If your room doesn't add to the sound of the instrument, you're better off not using any ambient mics. You can always add a room sound by using effects in the mixing process. (See Chapter 17.)

✔ **Stereo miking:** Stereo miking involves using two mics to capture the stereo field of the instrument. A variety of stereo miking techniques exist, and things can get pretty complicated when using two mics to record. (For all the details, check out my *Home Recording For Musicians For Dummies,* 2nd Edition, also published by Wiley.) You can also find stereo mics that — on their own — do a good job of capturing the stereo field of an instrument.

Stereo miking has the advantage of capturing a natural stereo image. When you listen to performances that were recorded with well-placed stereo miking, you can hear exactly where on the stage each instrument performed.

✔ **Combined miking strategies:** Many times you'll want to use more than one mic. The possible combinations are almost limitless: You can use several spot mics on one instrument, you can use a spot mic and an ambient mic, you can have a distant mic and a spot mic, or . . . Well, you get the point.

Taming transients

The single most difficult part of getting a good sound by using a microphone is dealing with sudden, extreme increases in the sound signal. These blips are called *transients,* and they regularly happen when a drum is first struck; when a vocalist sings certain syllables (for example, those that begin with *p*); and when a guitar player picks certain notes. In fact, because you can't always control the amount of force that you apply to an instrument, transients can happen at any time, with any instrument, and without warning. (Highly trained musicians produce fewer transients because they have a greater mastery over their muscular movements.)

In digital recording, all it takes is one slight, unexpected note to cause clipping and distortion, ruining what might be a perfect musical performance. Believe me, nothing is so heart-wrenching as listening to the perfect *take* (recorded performance) and hearing the unmistakable sound of digital distortion. Although you can't eliminate transients completely (they're part of an instrument's character), you can tame the extreme transients that often cause digital *overs* (a thick signal at too high a level, resulting in distortion). You can lash 'em down in three ways:

✔ **Level 'em.** Set your levels properly so the transients don't overload the converters. Transient are fast. So fast, in fact, that the meters in your preamp (assuming it has meters), interface (if it has any meters), or your computer often don't show transients, so be sure to set your levels low enough to accommodate these extra signals since they're also higher in level than the body of the sound. This is especially important for transient-rich instruments such as the acoustic piano. I recommend giving yourself an extra 6dB of room for these transients.

✔ **Mic 'em.** Make sure you have proper mic placement. A microphone that's too close to a loud sound source (or pointed too directly at the point of attack) can easily pick up extreme transients. In most cases, all you have to do is to pull the mic away from the instrument a little or turn it ever so slightly so that it avoids picking up too high a signal. (I cover mic setup thoroughly in the following section.)

The main thing to keep in mind when placing your mics is to experiment. Don't be afraid to spend time making small adjustments. After all, the track you save could be your own.

✔ **Run 'em through.** Run the signal through a compressor when recording. A compressor is a piece of hardware (not included in your audio interface) that controls the dynamics of your signal to keep your levels from getting too high. However, to do this with a computer-based system and an all-inclusive audio interface (one with preamps in it), your interface has to have *line inserts* — doohickies that let you *insert* a compressor between the preamp and the converter within the interface. (Check the specs of your interface to see whether you have this option.) If your interface doesn't have inserts (most of them don't), you need to use an external preamp and plug the compressor between the preamp and the interface.

If you follow my advice in the "Making Sense of the Signal Chain" section earlier in this chapter and you keep your recording levels peaking no higher than about –10 to –12dB, you don't need a compressor to take care of the transients because they likely won't exceed the maximum level that your system can handle.

Setting Up Your Mics: Some Suggestions

When you start to record, you discover an almost infinite number of ways to set up your mics. I can't go into all of them here (as if I really knew all of them anyway), but what I can do is share the miking approaches that I use and have found to work for me. Okay, they're not just *my* approaches; they're pretty common ways for miking a variety of instruments.

Vocals

Regardless of the type of studio you have or the style of music that you record, you'll probably record vocals at some point. And unfortunately, vocals are one of the most challenging instruments to do well. First, you have to find the right mic for the person who's singing, and then you need to try different approaches to get the best sound out of him or her. Fortunately, you're in luck. In this section, I lead you through the (sometimes complicated) process of getting good lead and backup vocal sounds.

You have a lot of options for miking vocals. The type of mic that you use dictates where you place it. The following bullet list gives you the gist. (Need a refresher on the different types of mics out there? Check out Chapter 4.)

- **Dynamic mic:** Dynamic mics sound best when you place them close to the singer's mouth. The effect that you get is gritty. (Huh? Okay, by gritty, I mean *dirty.* That's no help either? Let me see. . . .)

  Dynamic mics produce a midrange-dominated sound because the high frequencies aren't reproduced well. When a singer sings with the mic right in front of his or her mouth, the sound has even fewer high frequencies due to the proximity effect — the close range enhances the low-frequency response. What you get is a deep, bass-heavy sound that's often described as gritty or dirty. This type of sound can be great for matching the mood of some styles of rock and blues music.

- **Large-diaphragm condenser mic:** Large-diaphragm condenser mics are those most commonly used for vocals. These mics can clearly reproduce the entire audible frequency spectrum, emphasizing the low mids slightly at the same time. What you get is a nice, warm, full-bodied sound (that sounds like I'm describing a wine). The *proximity* effect (how close the singer is to the mic) determines how nice and warm-bodied the sound is. The closer the singer is, the deeper and richer the tone can be.

  When you set up a large-diaphragm condenser mic for vocals, place the mic in such a way that the spiteful *sibilants* (the sound from singing *s* and *t* sounds) and pesky *plosives* (the pops from singing *p* syllables) don't mess up your recordings. To deal with plosives and sibilants, you can use a *pop filter* (a screen that reduces the impact of sibilants and plosives going to your mic) or have the singer sing past the mic instead of right into it. If you want the singer to sing past the mic, you can

  - Place the mic above the singer and set it at an angle pointing away from him or her (Figure 9-2, left).

  - Put the mic off to the side and face it toward the singer (Figure 9-2, center), but not squarely in the path of the vocal.

  - Set up the mic below the singer and angle it away from him or her (Figure 9-2, right).

Figure 9-2:
Place the mic at different angles to control sibilance and plosives.

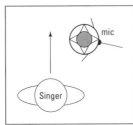

✔ **Small-diaphragm condenser mic:** Small-diaphragm condenser mics create a much brighter, airier sound than their large-diaphragm cousins. You don't get the low-mid warmth of the large-diaphragm beast, so the small-diaphragm mic probably won't be your first choice as a vocal mic — unless (for example) you're recording a female vocalist with a soprano voice and you want to catch the more ethereal quality of her higher frequencies.

✔ **Ribbon mic:** The ribbon mic is a good choice if you're looking for an intimate, crooner-type sound. (Think Frank Sinatra.) The ribbon mic is thought to add a silky sound to the singer's voice — produced by a slight drop-off in the high frequencies (which aren't as severe as you'd get from a dynamic mic). To my drum-abused ears, ribbon mics have a kind of softness that large-diaphragm condenser mics don't have. The sound is more even, without the pronounced low-mid effect.

Electric guitar

Miking your electric guitar is a personal thing. Every guitar player, it seems to me (although I don't play guitar, so what do I know?), spends an awful lot of time getting his or her "sound." If you're a *real* guitar player, you undoubtedly take great pride in getting your sound *exactly right* on tape, er, disc. You likely spend countless hours tweaking your amp and adjusting the mic to get it just right. On the other hand, if you're not a (harrumph) *real* guitar player, you might just want to record the part and get it over with. Either way, you can start looking for that perfect guitar sound by placing your mics in one (or more) of the ways that I outline later in this chapter.

The actual type of mic you choose depends largely on the type of sound you're looking for. For example, if you're looking for a distorted rock guitar sound with effects, you can get by just fine with a dynamic mic. If you favor a clean sound, a small-diaphragm condenser mic might work better for you. If you're going for a warm, full-bodied sound, try using a large-diaphragm condenser mic.

No matter which type of mic you use, you get the best sound from your amp speakers by putting the mic about 2 to 12 inches away from the cabinet, pointing the mic directly at the cone of one of the amp speakers (specifically, the center of the speaker, which *is* that cone-shaped thing in the box). You can see this positioning in Figure 9-3.

If you can't quite get the sound that you want from your amp with the one mic pointed at the speaker cone, try adding a second mic about 3 or 4 feet away — also pointed directly at the speaker cone — to get a more ambient sound. This arrangement might also give your sound more life, especially if you have a room with natural reverberation.

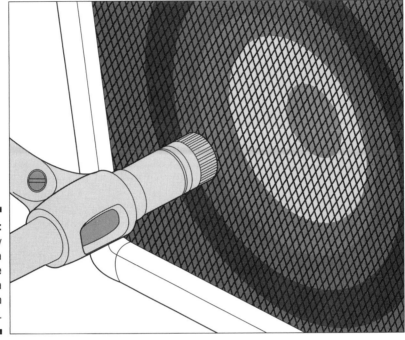

Figure 9-3:
Start by placing a mic near the cone of a speaker in your amp.

Electric bass

When you mic an electric bass, getting a good sound can be a real bear. Your two adversaries are muddiness (lack of definition) and thinness (a pronounced midrange tone). These seem almost polar-opposite characteristics, but they can both exist at the same time. Don't be afraid to be creative. Try recording your bass in different rooms or with different mic combinations. Look for a room with a warm sound to it.

Because the bass guitar produces low frequencies, a dynamic mic or a large-diaphragm condenser mic works well. I personally avoid small-diaphragm condensers and ribbon mics for the electric bass, but try them if you want. Who knows — you might end up with an awesome bass track.

Mic placement for the electric bass is similar to the guitar; you place a single mic 2 to 12 inches away from one of the speakers. Sometimes, with bass, you can angle the mic and let the speaker's sound kind of drift past the diaphragm. Potentially it's a great sound. For a bass, skip the distant mic (which generally just adds muddiness to the sound).

Acoustic guitars and such

At the risk of offending banjo, dobro, or ukulele players, I'm lumping all guitar-like (strummed or picked) acoustic string instruments together. I know, they all sound and play differently, but the microphone-placement techniques are similar for all these instruments. Allow me to explain.

Because all these instruments have a resonating chamber and are played with the instrument facing forward, you can pretty much use the same mic placement for any of them. You use different *types* of mics for different instruments, and I get to that in a minute.

I prefer to use condenser mics when recording acoustic instruments. The type of condenser mic you use depends on the overall tonal quality that you want to capture or emphasize. For example, if a guitar has a nice woody sound that you want to bring out in the recording, a large-diaphragm condenser mic is a good choice. On the other hand, if you're trying to capture the brightness of a banjo, a small-diaphragm mic is a better choice.

You can position your microphone in a variety of ways, and each accents certain aspects of the instrument's sound. Even a slight adjustment to the mic can have a significant impact on the sound. You might have to experiment quite a bit to figure out exactly where to put a mic.

To help with your experimentation, listen to the guitar carefully and move the mic around (closer in and farther out, to the left and right) until you find a spot that sounds particularly good. You need to get your ears close to the guitar to do this. After some experimenting — and a great deal of patience — you should be able to get the sound you want.

Drum set

If you're like most musicians, getting great-sounding drums seems like one of the world's great mysteries. (You know, along the lines of how the pyramids were built or how to cure noise hangover.) You can hear big, fat drums on great albums, but when you try to record your drums, they always end up sounding more like cardboard boxes than drums. Fret not (hey, at least I don't say that in the guitar section), for I have solutions for you.

First things first: Tuning your drums

The single most important part of getting killer drum sounds is to make sure your drums are tuned properly and that they have good heads on them (okay, that's two things). Seriously, if you spend some time getting the drums to sound good in your room, you're already halfway to the drum sound of your dreams. There isn't space to go into detail here (especially if you play a large kit), but if you want specific drum-tuning guidance, you can do a search on the Internet or (ahem) check out a copy of my book, *Drums For Dummies* (Wiley Publishing, Inc.).

When the tuning of your drums is perfect, you're ready to start placing some microphones. You can choose from an unlimited number of miking configurations, only a few of which I can cover here. (It would take a whole book to cover them all.)

The room and the drums

The room influences the sound of the drums more than it influences that of other instruments. If you're looking for a big drum sound, you need a fairly *live* room (one with lots of reflection).

I know you're thinking, "But all I have to work with is a bedroom for a studio, and it's carpeted." No worries — you can work with that. Remember, if you have a home studio, potentially you have your whole *home* to work with. Here are a couple ideas to spark your imagination:

- ✔ Buy three or four 4-x-10-foot sheets of plywood and lean them up against the walls of your room. Also place one on the floor just in front of the kick drum. This adds some reflective surfaces to the room.

- ✔ Put the drums in your garage (or living room, or any other room with a reverberating sound) and run long mic cords to your mixer. If you have a laptop-based system, you can just throw it under your arm and move everything into your garage or, better yet, take all this stuff to a room with great acoustics and record.

- ✔ Set up your drums in a great recording room and place an additional mic just outside the door to catch some additional ambient sound. You can then mix this in with the other drum tracks to add a different quality of reverberation to the drums.

Kick (bass) drum

The mic of choice for most recording engineers when recording a kick drum is a dynamic mic. In fact, you can find some large-diaphragm dynamic mics specifically designed to record kick drums.

No matter where you place the mic, you can reduce the amount of boominess that you get from the drum by placing a pillow or blanket inside the drum. Some people choose to let the pillow or blanket touch the inside head. I prefer to keep it a couple inches away from the inside head, but sometimes it's okay to let it touch the outside head.

That said, you can place your mic in several ways:

  ✔ **Near the inside head:** This produces a sharper sound with more of the instrument's initial attack.

  ✔ **Halfway inside the drum.** This works if you have just one head on your drum and you want less attack and more of the body of the drum's sound.

  ✔ **Near the outside head:** This is preferable if you have both heads on your drum and you want a full-bodied sound.

Try all three ways and see what fits best with the kind of musical mood you want to call up.

Snare drum considerations

The snare drum is probably the most important drum in popular music. The bass guitar can cover the kick drum's rhythm, and the rest of the drums aren't part of the main groove. A good, punchy snare drum can make a track, whereas a weak, thin one can eliminate the drive that most popular music needs.

Because the snare drum is located so close to the other drums (especially the hi-hats), a cardioid pattern mic is a must. The most common mic for a snare drum is the trusty Shure SM57. The mic is generally placed between the hi-hats and the small tom-tom about 1 or 2 inches from the snare drum head. Point the diaphragm directly at the head. You might need to make some minor adjustments to eliminate any bleed (sound) from the hi-hats. This position gives you a nice punchy sound.

If you want a crisper tone, you can add a second mic under the drum. Place this mic about 1 or 2 inches from the head with the diaphragm pointing at the snares. Make minor adjustments to minimize any leakage from the hi-hats.

Tom-toms

The tom-toms sound best when you use a dynamic mic. For the mounted toms (the ones above the kick drum), you can use one or two mics. If you use one mic, place it between the two drums about 4 to 6 inches away from the heads. If you use two mics, place one above each drum about 1 to 3 inches above the head.

If you want a boomy sound with less attack, you can place a mic inside the shell with the bottom head off the drum.

Floor toms are miked the same way as the mounted tom-toms:

  ✔ Place a single mic a couple inches away from the head near the rim.

  ✔ If you have more than one floor tom, you can place one mic between them or mic them individually.

Hi-hats

The hi-hats are generally part of the main groove — as such, they're important enough that you want to spend some time getting a good sound. You'll probably have problems with a few other mics on the drum set picking up the hi-hats, particularly the snare drum mic and overhead mics. (Some people don't even bother miking the hi-hats for this reason.)

You can use either a dynamic mic or, better yet, a small-diaphragm condenser mic for the hi-hats. The dynamic mic gives you a trashier sound, and the small-diaphragm condenser mic produces a bright sound. Place the mic about 3 to 4 inches above the hi-hats and point it down. The exact placement of the mic is less important than the placement of the other instrument mics because of the hi-hats' tone. Just make sure your mic isn't so close that you hit it instead of the cymbal.

Cymbals

Small-diaphragm condenser mics capture the cymbals' high frequencies well. You can mic the cymbals by placing mics about 6 inches above each cymbal or by using overhead mics set 1 to 3 feet above the cymbals. (See the next section for more on mic placement.)

The whole kit

Most of the time, you want to have at least one (but preferably two) ambient mics on the drums — if for no other reason than to pick up the cymbals. These (assuming you use two mics) are called *overhead mics,* and (as the name implies) you place them above the drum set (usually by means of a boom stand). The most common types of mics to use for overheads are large- and small-diaphragm condenser mics because they pick up the high frequencies in the cymbals and give the drum set's sound a nice sheen (brightness).

To mic the drum set with overhead mics, do one of the following:

- ✔ **Use X-Y mics.** Place two mics right next to each other so that the diaphragms are at almost right angles about 2 feet above the drummer's head.

- ✔ **Use a spaced pair.** Place the two mics so that they're 3 feet apart (if 1 foot above the cymbals) or 6 feet apart (if 2 feet above the cymbals). Point the spaced mics down toward the drums, and you're ready to record.

Figure 9-4 shows both of these setups.

Figure 9-4:
Overhead
mics
capture the
cymbals
and the
drums.

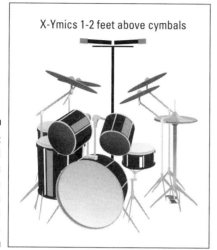

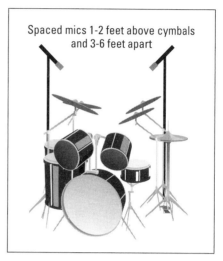

Chapter 10

Recording and Editing Audio

I'm sure you remember how to record to a regular tape deck: Turn it on, plug everything in, and click the Record button. One of the problems with computer-based recording is that nothing is as simple as recording to a tape deck. (Of course, the advantages far outweigh the disadvantages here.) For many musicians (and I don't necessarily mean you) the added complexity of recording to a computer can end up pushing the limits of what they feel comfortable doing when trying to get their ideas down on tape (oops, I mean disc).

What could be a problem for others isn't going to be problem for you for one simple reason — you have this book (and this chapter, in particular) to help you out. In this chapter, I walk you through the process of getting a song up and going in your audio program and I help you perform the necessary steps to turn your ideas into finely shaped bits of digital information.

Each recording program has its own way of working, and each has its own set of quirks and features. Because I can't possibly detail how to carry out every task possible in each program on the market, I concentrate on Logic and Pro Tools, two popular programs that put their own distinctive spin on the recording and editing processes. The examples I use should give you a general idea of the range of approaches out there when it comes to using recording software. You still might find that the program you use requires a look-see into the manual for specifics.

Setting Up a Song to Record

The first step in the recording process is to create a new song file in which to record. This is a pretty simple process in both Logic and Pro Tools — all you really have to do is open a new song file and adjust your hardware settings for your interface.

Creating a new song file

To open a new song file in Pro Tools, do the following:

1. **Double-click the Pro Tools icon to boot up the software.**

   The main menu appears.

2. **Choose File➪New Session.**

   This opens the New Session dialog box, as shown in Figure 10-1.

From this dialog box you have a bunch of settings to make for your song file. Here's a rundown of the different parameters and what they mean:

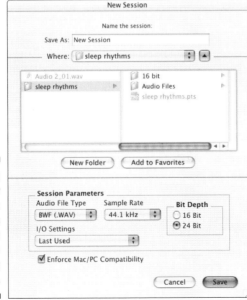

Figure 10-1: The New Session menu is where you set up a new song file.

- ✔ **Save As:** This is where you type the name of this new song.

- ✔ **Where:** You can use this drop-down list to choose where you want to save the file on your hard drive. I recommend that you use the handy New Folder button to create a new folder for storing the session file and that you name the folder the same as your session file. This makes your session file easy to find on your hard drive — especially if you haven't worked on the session for a while.

- ✔ **Audio File Type:** This drop-down list lets you choose among BWF (Broadcast WAV File), AIFF, or SD2 file types. Choose the one that works best for you. (I always use BWF files because they're compatible with other software I use. Your needs might be different.) If you aren't transferring your files from one program to another, I suggest using the default BWF option.

- ✔ **Sample Rate:** Here you choose the sample rate of your session. In Pro Tools, your options depend on the Digidesign hardware you have. For example, if you have the Digi 001 or Mbox, your choice is between 44.1 kHz and 48 kHz, whereas if you have a Digi 002 or 002R, you can choose among 44.1 kHz, 48 kHz, 88.2 kHz, and 96 kHz.

  The higher the sample rate, the more work your computer's processor has to do. Often you have to balance your desire for the highest-resolution music possible against the capabilities of your system.

  I recommend getting to know your system before you record a lot of music with it. Experiment with different sample rates and track counts to see what your computer can handle. With this information, you can get a good sense of how hard you can push your system before you reach the limits of its performance.

- ✔ **Bit Depth:** In this area, you can choose between 16- and 24-bit rates. Choose 24 bit.

- ✔ **I/O Settings:** In this drop-down list, you can choose between the most recently used setting or a stereo-mix setting of the physical inputs and outputs of your interface.

- ✔ **Enforce Mac/PC Compatibility:** Selecting this check box ensures that if you transfer your session from a Mac computer to a PC, you can still open the session and work in it. Leave this check box selected.

After you make all your choices and click the Save button, a new song file (session) opens in Pro Tools. This session doesn't have any tracks yet for recording your music, so before you actually start to record you need to create some tracks. I describe this procedure — along with all the intricacies associated with the various kinds of tracks — in the "Taking a look at tracks" section, later in this chapter.

In contrast to Pro Tools, opening a new song file in Logic Pro (choose File⇨ New) automatically opens the Autoload song. The Autoload song is a song template you can create that already has the number of the various track types embedded in it that you want in your song. (If you haven't created an Autoload song, don't worry; Logic Pro opens a basic song file with a bunch of tracks in it to get you started.) You can still make changes to these tracks, but it saves you time from having to put them in your new song manually. You also don't have to choose the settings that Pro Tools offers in its New Session dialog box. These settings are scattered throughout a variety of menus. For example, you set the sample rate by choosing Audio⇨Sample Rate.

Logic Pro also doesn't force you to immediately name and choose a location for your new song. If your program takes this live-and-let-live approach, I highly recommend that you immediately save your new song right away so that if something happens and your program shuts down on you nothing gets lost. It also gets the whole song-naming thing out of the way because the first time you click Save, you'll be asked to type in a name and file location. If you're in a groove recording, the last thing you want to do is stop and think about what to call your song and where to put it.

Each audio recording program has its own peculiarities when you open and work with a song, so check your manual to find out the exact procedures for your software.

Taking a look at tracks

Within your song file, all your work is done with tracks. Tracks are like the channels in your mixer or physical tracks on a tape deck. These tracks represent your audio data in your song. The one big advantage with computer-based recording is that you can choose how many and what kind of tracks you want in your song.

Understanding track types

To repeat the mantra throughout the book, every program is different (is there an echo in here?), but many programs use certain basic types of tracks. The basic track types include the following:

✔ **Audio Instrument Tracks:** These are like MIDI tracks — they record MIDI data — but they don't send the MIDI signal back out of your system again. Instead you route the signal to a software synthesizer. These tracks can be mono or stereo.

✔ **Audio Tracks:** An audio track contains audio files and can be mono or stereo.

✔ **Bus, Aux, or Auxiliary Input Tracks:** Tracks with these names are used as effects sends, for submixes, or for other routing purposes. These can be mono or stereo.

✔ **Master or Master Fader Tracks:** This track type contains the summed output for all the tracks routed to it or that are in your song, depending on your audio recording application. Master Fader tracks can be mono or stereo, although stereo is most common.

✔ **MIDI Tracks:** MIDI and audio instrument tracks contain MIDI data — instructions to MIDI devices on how to create specific digital sounds. (For more on MIDI, check out Chapters 4 and 11.) These tracks are available only in mono.

✔ **Output Tracks:** These tracks control the signals that are routed to the physical outputs of your interface. In Pro Tools, this can also be the Master Fader track. Output tracks can be either mono or stereo.

Creating tracks

If you use Pro Tools to record your music, you first need to create some tracks in a new song because no tracks were included by default when it was created. (Non-Pro Tools users shouldn't skip over this section. Even if your song opens with some tracks already in it, as with Logic Pro, you might want to create some new tracks in your song. This section explains how to do this.)

To create a new track in Pro Tools:

1. **Choose File➪New Track or press ⌘+Shift+N on a Mac (or Ctrl+Shift+N on a PC).**

   The New Track dialog box opens, as shown in Figure 10-2.

2. **Select the number, format, and type for your track.**

   These options include:

   - **Number of new tracks:** The default here is 1, but you can pretty much create as many new tracks as you like. Just keep in mind that you can have only 32 voices playing at one time in your session.

   - **Track format:** Here you choose stereo or mono.

   - **Track type:** Clicking the arrows opens a menu that lets you choose between an Audio, Auxiliary Input, Master Fader, or MIDI track.

3. **Click the Create button to create your new track.**

   This track then appears in your screen.

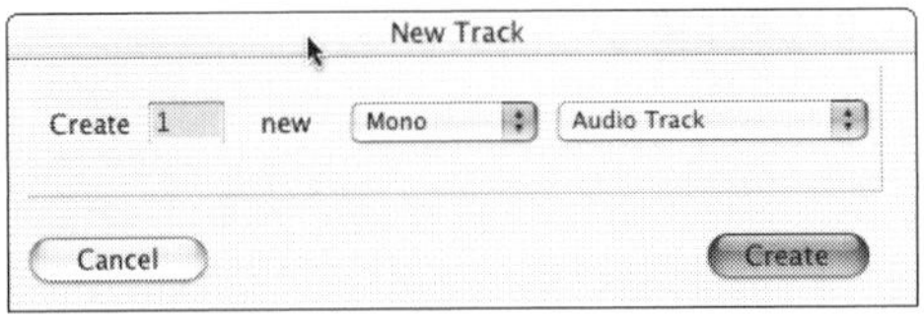

Figure 10-2:
The New
Track dialog
box awaits
your
command.

Creating a new track in Logic Pro is almost as easy:

1. **Choose Functions⇨Track⇨Create from the menu at the top of the Arrange window, as shown in Figure 10-3.**

   A new track appears in your song in the same format (and with the same name) as the track directly before it.

   Note: If the Arrange window isn't showing, choose Windows⇨Open Arrange to make it appear.

Figure 10-3:
Creating a
track in
Logic Pro
starts with
this menu in
the Arrange
window.

2. **To assign an audio object to the new track, click and hold on the track name in the Arrange window.**

   A pop-up menu appears, as shown in Figure 10-4.

3. **Drag your mouse to the Audio menu option and then to the type of audio object you want.**

   Your choices here are Audio Instrument or Audio Track. Choose Audio Track if you want to record a miked instrument that's plugged in to your audio interface, and choose Audio Instrument if you want to use a soft-synth. Select one of the options from your audio object list to assign an audio object.

Figure 10-4:
Assign an
audio object
to your new
track from
the pop-up
menu
located
under the
track icon.

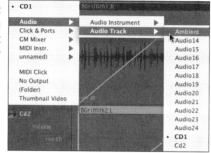

4. Release the mouse.

Your new track is assigned to the selected audio object.

You can change the type of any new track you create by clicking and holding over the track name in the Arrange window until the Track Type Selector pop-up menu appears. Then just drag your mouse to the track type that you want and release.

Naming tracks

As you start recording your ideas — and as you build up a pretty impressive list of tracks — you have to find a way to keep (ahem) track of what you recorded on each of them. The best way to do this is to give each of your tracks a unique name — something that gives you some idea of what exactly you recorded (lead guitar, kick drum or whatever). Naming tracks is essential for a multitracking musician. It's also very easy.

In Pro Tools, follow this simple procedure:

1. Double-click the track name within either of the main windows in your session.

The Name Track dialog box opens, as shown in Figure 10-5.

2. Type the name of your track in the Name the Track text box.

If you want, you can also use the Comments text box to type in any notes that might help you later on.

3. Click OK to close the dialog box and accept the name and notes.

Figure 10-5:
The Name
the Track
dialog box in
Pro Tools
lets you
create a
unique
name for
your tracks.

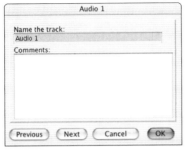

In Logic Pro, the track-naming procedure differs (as usual):

1. **In the Arrange window, click the track you want to rename.**

   The track becomes highlighted, and the track's fader and name appear on the left side of the window.

2. **Click the track name on the far-left side of the Arrange window.**

   The track name becomes highlighted, as shown in Figure 10-6.

3. **Type in your new name in the Name text box and press Return or Enter to accept it.**

   Your new name appears for your track.

Figure 10-6:
Logic also
lets you
name your
tracks with
unique
names.

Routing your input and output signals

With a new song file and a bunch of tracks to work with, you're ready to route the inputs from your audio or MIDI interface into the tracks that you want to record into. This process is pretty simple and is similar for most programs. Here's how you do it in Pro Tools:

1. **Choose Display➪Edit Window Shows➪I/O View to open the I/O section of the Edit window.**

   The I/O section of the Edit window shows the inputs and outputs for each of your tracks.

2. **Within the I/O section of your track in the Edit window, click and hold on the Input selector until the Input contextual menu pops up.**

3. **While still holding down your mouse button, move the mouse over the Input menu until it rests on the input listing you want, as shown in Figure 10-7.**

4. **Release the mouse button to select the input listing.**

   This menu closes, and the input you've selected appears in the Input selector.

Choosing your outputs requires pretty much the same procedure, although now you start things off by clicking and holding the Output selector instead.

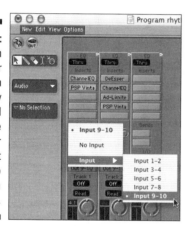

Figure 10-7: You assign an input (or output) in Pro Tools by clicking and holding the Input or Output selector to open a menu.

Logic Pro has slightly different procedures for assigning your inputs and outputs:

1. **In the Arrange window, click the track whose inputs and outputs you want to assign.**

   The track becomes highlighted, and the track's channel strip appears on the left side of the window.

2. **Within the I/O section of the track's channel strip (located directly above the track's fader on the left side of the Arrange window), click and hold on the Input selector until the Input contextual menu pops up.**

3. **While still holding down your mouse button, move the mouse over the Input menu until it rests on the input listing you want, as shown in Figure 10-8.**

4. **Release the mouse button to select the input listing.**

   The Input menu closes, and the input you've selected appears in the Input selector.

Assigning your track's output follows the same basic procedure, although now you click and hold the Output selector in Step 2 instead.

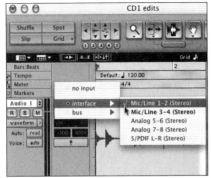

Figure 10-8: Assigning an input (or output) in Logic Pro is done by clicking and holding the Input or Output selector.

Preparing to Record

I'm sure you're just itchin' to click the Record button and start getting your ideas into your computer. Before you can do this, however, you need to cover some basics, such as enabling your tracks to record and setting proper levels. There's also a few more things you can do to make sure that you not only get your best possible performance, but also make the inevitable editing and mixing easier — things like creating a monitor mix and developing a song map. This section covers these details.

Enabling recording

For many computer audio applications, you need to enable recording in a track before you can hear the input source through your system.

Make sure that your instruments are plugged into your interface before you enable recording. I like to keep the volume off or set very low before enabling recording so that when I play my instrument it doesn't overload the system. You can turn up the volume when you have your track enabled.

Enabling a track for recording (the audio buzzword is *record-enabling*) is usually pretty easy: In Pro Tools and Logic Pro, for example, all you need to do is click the handy Record Enable button (labeled R) for that track. Figure 10-9 shows the Record Enable button in Pro Tools (left) and Logic Pro (right). After clicking, the button blinks a nice shade of red.

Figure 10-9: Click the track's Record Enable button (in Pro Tools or Logic) to enable the track for recording.

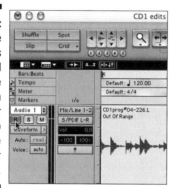 

Depending on your recording application, your track will either stay enabled for recording when you click another track's Record Enable button (in Logic Pro, for example) or it won't stay enabled (enable will turn off) when you click the Record Enable button on another track. (Pro Tools takes the "enable will turn off" route unless you hold down Shift as you enable additional tracks for recording.)

 Make sure that you understand how this whole enabling business works in your particular recording program. Check (and double-check) your application's manual to see how it treats this process. I can't tell you how depressing it is when you think you've recorded a track only to discover that, in fact, it wasn't enabled. I've lost some really good takes (performances) this way.

 When your track is enabled for recording, you should be able to hear (and see in your track's channel strip window) a signal when you play your instrument. If you can't see or hear anything, you need to check the following:

 ✔ Is your instrument plugged in?

 ✔ Is the track you've record-enabled set for the correct input and output?

 ✔ Are the volume controls on each of your pieces of gear (the guitar *and* the interface, for example) turned on at least a little?

✔ If you're recording with a condenser mic, is the phantom power — the low level of current necessary to get the microphone to produce a signal — turned on in your interface or external preamp?

✔ Are your monitors or headphones plugged in and the monitor or main output level on your interface turned up?

If you don't get a signal even after making sure that these conditions are met, go to the Hardware Setup window and make sure that your interface is displayed in the window and is selected. (In Logic Pro, choose Audio➪Audio Hardware and Drivers, and in Pro Tools choose Setups➪Hardware Setup.)

Setting recording levels

Setting the proper levels for recording is crucial if you want to record your music successfully. If you set your level too high, you get distortion; too low and you might end up with a weak signal that lacks fidelity. I discuss how to get your instrument levels into and through all your hardware at their proper levels in Chapter 9, so if you're not sure how to get your levels right, check back there. I'll wait here.

Hardware levels all set up? Now you need to adjust the most important level of all — the level going into your software. This level is displayed in the channel strip of your record-enabled track. (Figure 10-10 shows this channel strip in Pro Tools (left) and Logic Pro (right) when a level is coming into your system.)

For most computer-based recording systems, this is the only level that you can actually see as well as hear because most interfaces don't have input meters on them.

After you can both hear your instrument's signal and see it in the channel strip, you can make the final adjustments to your level until you get a good, *hot* (substantial) level without going over. This level is adjusted from *outside* the computer. That means tweaking your interface and messing with your other hardware — you know, twirling the knobs on the electric guitar, experimenting with mic placement, playing with your external preamp level, and so on. The fader in your software on your computer controls only the output volume of the track. Turning it up or down affects how loud the signal is to your ears, but it doesn't change the level going into your system.

Make your level adjustments on your hardware and leave the fader in your software set at unity gain (0 on some systems). (Refer to Figure 10-10 to see a fader set at this level in both Pro Tools (left) and Logic Pro (right) if you're not sure where unity gain is.)

Figure 10-10:
Your track's channel strip (in Pro Tools, left, or Logic, right) shows the level of your signal coming into your system.

The meter in your enabled track's channel strip should peak at –12dB to –10dB. Many programs — Logic Pro, for example — have a Peak Level display at the top of the meter that shows you the highest level achieved by the meter. Keep an eye on this as you set you levels. If your level gets too high and you reduce the gain into your system to compensate for that, you can then click the Peak Level display to zero it out again.

When you set your levels, set them a little on the low side because the tendency when recording is to get slightly nervous (okay, some people get *really* nervous), and this often results in playing that's a little louder. This is especially the case with vocalists. It's not uncommon for me to set the level as low as –18dB to –20dB for vocalists to start with.

Monitoring your inputs

The difference between a decent performance and a truly stellar one is based on inspiration. An inspired artist can perform at a level beyond his or her imagination. This is when magic happens. Well, when you have a set of headphones on and you're trying to record your ideas, you sometimes need a little extra push to get the inspiration faucet turned on. The best way to do this is to make sure that what you hear in your headphones as you play actually makes you want to play — and play better. You need to confront two issues when using a computer-based system:

- ✔ Getting the latency down to a manageable size.
- ✔ Creating an inspirational monitor mix.

The following two sections lay out how to accomplish both of these goals.

Getting a handle on latency

Latency, as I say a few times in this book, is the delay caused by the analog signal turning into digital bits and back into an analog signal so you can hear it. If your latency levels are high, what you hear in your headphones is going to sound out of sync with what you want to play — which can really mess up your mind (and more than likely your ability to play well). Latency is the Achilles heel of computer-based recording for many people.

Because this has been an area of concern, makers of both the hardware and software used for computer recording have spent a lot of time trying to fix this problem. Because of this, several approaches exist for reducing the latency in your system — each with its own advantages and disadvantages. These approaches are

- ✔ **Get a faster computer.** A fast computer allows you to use the lowest possible I/O or Hardware buffer settings. Lower buffer settings mean lower latency. (Chapter 8 has more on buffer settings).

- ✔ **Record at a higher sampling rate.** Because latency is determined by the total number of samples taken, increasing the sample rate of your recordings reduces that actual time of the latency. For example, when you use a 64-sample buffer setting and record at 96 kHz (the highest rate many interfaces can handle right now), your latency within your system drops in half.

- ✔ **Use the software's Low Latency or Software monitoring options.** Using one of these options can reduce latency a bit because you're monitoring off the software and not the hard drive. This can reduce latency to pretty low levels. One disadvantage with this option is that you might not be able to add any effects to your tracks and hear them while you record. This can make for a less-than-inspiring monitor mix.

- ✔ **Use the hardware's Direct Monitoring option.** Most audio interfaces have some sort of direct-monitoring option. That is, they split the incoming signal so that it is sent through the converters and on to the computer while sending the signal at the same time to the output monitor of the interface. While this is happening, the previously recorded tracks in your system are sent to your monitors with the unconverted signal, giving you a mix of the input signal and the previously recorded tracks in your headphones. This reduces the latency of your input signal down to effectively zero.

One problem with this approach is that you can't add any effects to the instrument that you're recording. (You *can* hear any effects placed on previously recorded tracks, though.) You can fix this by using an external effects box for monitoring purposes.

✔ **Use an external mixer or monitoring unit.** This approach is similar to using the direct monitoring option available on most interfaces. The only problem beyond those that come standard with direct monitoring is that you add another piece of hardware to your signal chain that, if it's not of high quality, will compromise the sound of your instrument. Also, if you use any of the preamps and such in your audio interface for your instruments, it's all but impossible to insert one of these units in the signal chain. To be honest, I recommend skipping the external mix/monitoring unit and going with one of the other options instead. It's just not worth the hassle.

Creating an inspirational monitoring mix

A *monitor mix* refers to an initial mix of tracks that you use as the foundation for adding more tracks. You *could* keep a monitor mix pretty bare bones — no effects, no prettifying whatsoever — but I recommend putting some effort into creating a monitor mix that actually sounds good.

To me, a good monitoring mix is one of the most important parts of the recording process. If you can make your voice, for instance, sound like you can actually sing (I know this is a stretch for many people), you'll be more likely to give the vocal a little extra and maybe end up surprising yourself when you listen to your performance. Here are some things you can do to make a monitor mix that encourages you to sound your best:

✔ **Add some effects.** Most vocalists love to hear some reverb on their vocals when they sing. Depending on the monitoring scheme you choose (see the preceding section), you might be able to do this within your software program. (Chapter 15 explains how to insert an effects plug-in into a track.)

✔ **Create a pleasing balance.** Take a few minutes to get a good mix of the tracks that you already have recorded so that it sounds as much like a complete song as possible. If you don't take the time to get a good monitor mix up front, you might end up wasting time when you have to re-record an uninspired part.

✔ **Mute distracting parts.** If any instruments distract you from the part you're trying to record (a counter melody to your guitar solo, for example), don't be afraid to turn them down or off in your mix. Use only the parts that make you play better.

✔ **Get quality headphones.** Because you'll often be wearing headphones when you record, I highly recommend that you get a decent pair — ones that you like the sound of because yucky-sounding headphones aren't very inspiring.

Following these tips will make the recording process much more enjoyable for you (and for your listeners when they finally hear your music).

Creating a click track

A *click track* is a metronome that you can listen to while you record — it ensures that you stay in time with the session. Recording to a click track can have many advantages, including being able to match the song's sections to particular bars or beats within the session. It also makes finding edit points and performing certain edits much easier. I always spend a few minutes setting up a click track for my songs, and I recommend that you give it a try, too.

All audio recording programs have some sort of metronome function. And all these programs have a way to create a click track within your system. Some are easy and some are, well, less intuitive. To help you out, I offer the basic steps for creating a click track and getting it to sound right in the two popular programs that I detail throughout this book — Pro Tools and Logic Pro.

The first thing you need to do before setting up your click track is open the dialog box that has the tempo/time signature data on it. Here's how you do it:

1. **Make sure the Transport window is showing in your song.**

   In Pro Tools, choose Windows⇨Show Transport; in Logic Pro, choose Windows⇨Open Transport if the Transport window isn't already showing.

2. **Open the MIDI/Time signature section of the Transport window.**

   In Pro Tools, choose Display⇨Transport Window Shows⇨MIDI Controls. In Logic, click the drop-down list arrow on the far-right side of the Transport window to open the Transport View Options menu. Select Tempo/Signature Display from the list. The tempo/time signature is displayed, as shown in Figure 10-11.

You're ready to start setting up your click track.

Figure 10-11:
The Tempo
and Time
Signature
fields are
located
in the
Transport
window of
Pro Tools
(top) and
Logic Pro
(bottom).

Setting the tempo

To set the tempo in these programs, follow these steps:

In Pro Tools:

1. **With the little Conductor icon engaged — it's blue — double-click the Time Signature icon (labeled ¼ as shown in Figure 10-11) or choose Windows⇨Show Tempo/Meter.**

   The Tempo/Meter Change dialog box appears.

2. **Select Tempo Change from the drop-down list.**

   The Tempo tab of the Tempo/Meter Change dialog box appears.

3. **On the Tempo tab, enter the data you want for your tempo.**

   This includes the location (enter **1/1/000** to set it at the beginning of the song), the tempo, the resolution (the note duration getting one beat, such as ¼ note), and whether the tempo starts at the beginning of the bar (called Snap to Bar).

4. **Click the Apply button to accept these settings and close the dialog box.**

   You now have a tempo for your song.

In Logic Pro:

1. **Use the Transport window or the Timeline to go to the location in your song where you want the tempo to begin.**

   Double-click the Stop button in the Transport window to get to the start of your song or click and drag along the Timeline (the numbers at the top of the Arrange window) to go to another location. You can also let the song play until it reaches the point where you want the tempo change to start and just stop the song there. Logic Pro puts the starting point for the tempo change wherever your song cursor is located, so make sure it's where you want it before you set the tempo.

2. **Double-click the Tempo field in the Transport window to highlight it.**

   In Figure 10-11, shown earlier, the Tempo field in Logic Pro's Transport window is showing 120.

3. **Type in the tempo value you want for your song and press Return or Enter to accept it.**

Choosing the time signature

Setting up a time signature (meter) for your click track is similar to setting the tempo. The basic steps are outlined in this section.

In Pro Tools:

1. **Double-click the time signature icon (labeled ¼, as shown earlier in Figure 10-11) or choose Windows⇨Show Tempo/Meter.**

   The Tempo/Meter Change dialog box appears.

2. **Select Meter Change from the drop-down list.**

   The Meter Change tab of the Tempo/Meter Change dialog box appears.

3. **On the Meter Change tab, enter the data you want for your time signature.**

   This includes the location (enter **1/1/000** to set it at the beginning of the song), the meter, the *click* (the note duration getting the click from the metronome, such as ¼ note), and whether the meter change starts at the beginning of the bar (called Snap to Bar).

4. **Click the Apply button to accept these settings and close the window.**

   You now have a time signature for your song.

In Logic Pro:

1. **Use the Transport window or the Timeline to go to the location in your song where you want the meter change to begin.**

   Click the Stop button in the Transport window twice to get to the start of your song or click-drag along the Timeline (the numbers at the top of the Arrange window) to go to another location. You can also let the song play until it reaches the point where you want the meter change to start and just stop the song there. Logic puts the starting point of the meter change wherever your song cursor is located so make sure it's where you want it before you set the meter change.

2. **Double-click the numerator (top number) of the time signature in the Transport window to highlight it.**

   In Figure 10-11, the time signature in Logic's Transport window is showing 4/4.

3. **Type in the beats per measure value you want for your song and press Return or Enter to accept it.**

4. **Double-click the denominator (bottom number) of the time signature in the Transport window to highlight it.**

5. **Type in the note division for the measure you want for your song and press Return or Enter to accept it.**

6. **Double-click the subdivision value (the note value that the measure is divided into) of the time signature (this is marked as 16 in Figure 10-11, shown earlier) in the Transport window to highlight it.**

7. **Type in the subdivision value you want for the measure.**

   This tells the click how many times each measure to play. For example, entering 16 tells the click track to play at 16th note intervals.

You now have your time signature set up for your click track.

Getting your click track to play

If you want to get your click track rolling and you're working with Logic Pro, just do the following:

1. **In the Transport window, click and hold the little Metronome icon and choose Metronome Settings from the pop-up menu that appears.**

   The Metronome Settings section of the Song Settings dialog box opens up, as shown in Figure 10-12, where you can choose various settings for your click track.

2. **Select the Klopfgeist check box (located in the upper-right corner on the Metronome Settings tab) to enable the internal metronome.**

   Note: You have to enable the internal metronome before you can actually use it.

3. **Close the dialog box by clicking OK.**

   Your metronome settings are saved.

4. **In the Transport window, click once again on the Metronome icon to highlight it (it glows blue).**

   Your metronome is turned on and will play when your song starts.

To turn off the metronome, click the Metronome icon to deselect it.

Contrast this relatively simple procedure with the way you get a click track going in Pro Tools.

Start by configuring your click track device. Follow these steps:

Figure 10-12:
The
Metronome
Settings
section lets
you choose
how your
click track
plays in
Logic Pro.

1. **Choose MIDI⇨Click Options or double-click the Click button or the Countoff button in the Transport window.**

   The Click/Countoff Options dialog box appears, as shown in Figure 10-13.

2. **Set when your click track plays by selecting one of the three options at the top of the dialog box.**

   The default is During Play and Record. This is usually where I leave it. However, if the click track is distracting when you play back your track, you might prefer the Only During Record option.

3. **In the Click/Countoff Options dialog box, click the Output drop-down list to select the device that will play your click track.**

   Choose None to use the click plug-in. The alternative is to select a MIDI device such as a drum machine. I'd go with the click plug-in because it's simple and it's included with Pro Tools so you don't have to buy any separate gear in order to use it.

4. **Adjust the pitch and/or the volume of your click by filling in the note (for pitch) and/or velocity (for volume) fields in the middle of the window.**

5. **Designate the duration of each click in the Duration field.**

   Increasing or decreasing the duration of the click can be helpful if you use a different sound (such as an external keyboard or a soft-synth) that's hard to hear with the default setting. If you use the click plug-in, the default setting works just fine.

6. **Enter the countoff amount in the Countoff field at the bottom of the dialog box and select or deselect the check box to the left.**

   If you want the countoff to play only when you record, select the check box. If you want the countoff to play during both record and playback, make sure that the check box is deselected.

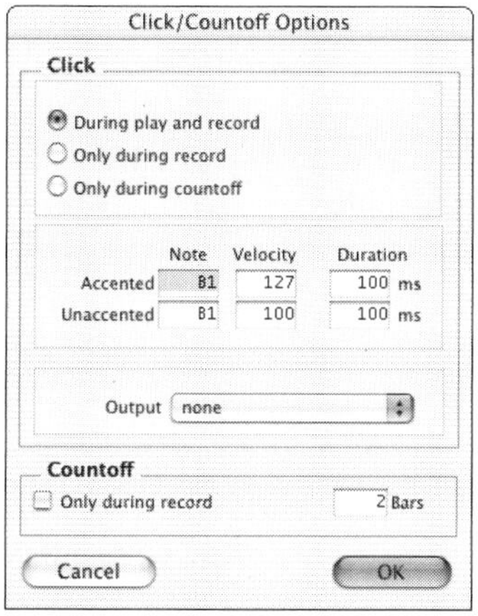

Figure 10-13:
The Click/Count off Options menu lets you configure your click track device.

Next you need to insert the click plug-in into an Auxiliary Input track. Follow these steps:

1. **Create a new auxiliary track by choosing File➪New Track or by pressing Shift+⌘+N (on a Mac) or Shift+Control+N (on a PC).**

   The New Track dialog box makes an appearance.

2. **Use the three drop-down lists to set up a single Mono Aux Input track.**

3. **Click the Create button.**

   Your track appears in the Edit and Mix windows.

4. **In either the Edit or Mix window, use the Input drop-down list for your new track to select any one of your hardware inputs.**

5. **Using the Output drop-down list for your new track, set your output to the main stereo outputs of your session.**

6. **Display your inserts options by choosing Displays⇨Mix Window Shows⇨Inserts.**

   The Inserts section for each channel strip appears in the Mix window.

7. **Choose Click Plug-in from the Inserts drop-down list for the track you just created.**

   The Click Plug-in dialog box opens. Here you can choose the volume for your accented and unaccented notes. Adjust them to taste, then close the window by clicking the Close button in the upper-left corner.

Wait, you're not done yet. You still have to enable the click track. This part is easy and can be done a couple ways:

✔ Choose MIDI⇨Click.

✔ Click the Click button in the MIDI section of the Transport window. When Click is engaged, this button is blue.

Okay, now you're ready to hear the click track when you play your song.

Hitting the Record Button

At last, the moment you've been waiting for: recording your music. This is the easy part. Well, at least the computer end of it is easy — you still have to create the performance of your life (no pressure).

Recording your first take

With your track record enabled, you can get to the business at hand. (If your track is not enabled yet, simply click the Record Enable button for your track — see the "Preparing to Record" section earlier in this chapter for details.) Because this is your first take, you probably want to start recording from the very start of the song. You have several ways of doing this, depending on your recording program. In Logic Pro, click the Stop button in the Transport window. (If the song is playing, you need to double-click the Stop button.) In Pro Tools, click the Zero Return button in the Transport window.

To start recording:

1a. In Logic Pro, click the Record button.

Your session kicks into gear.

or

1b. In Pro Tools, click the Record button, and then click the Play button.

Your recording session starts.

2. Click the Stop button to stop recording.

Your session stops.

How'd ya do? If you're not sure, you can play your track back to hear your performance. The following section details how to do this. If you know you messed up and want to fix a part or two, check out the "Punching in and out" section later in this chapter. If your performance was perfect, well, then congratulations; now you can go to the "Doing overdubs" section later in this chapter to add some more tracks.

Listening to your take

To hear what you've recorded (called your *take*), all you have to do is disengage the Record Enable button in the track you just recorded and click the Play button. You can adjust the volume level of your playback with the fader for the track in your software.

 Some programs — Pro Tools would be an example — allow you to hear your take while your track is still record-enabled. If you have Pro Tools and you'd like to monitor your tracks this way, you just need to make sure that you have the Auto Input monitoring option selected in the Operations menu at the top of your screen.

Punching in and out

Punching in and out is the process of re-recording a section of your track, thus replacing the original take with a new one. Punching in and out (often simply referred to as punching) is a mainstay of the multitrack recording process. In the bad old days of tape-based recording, punching in and out of a track to make corrections was a touchy process. Some tape decks could handle a tight punch (one where you have little room for error), but others were, to put it nicely, not as well calibrated. (Okay, they were sloppy and frustrating to use.)

This isn't the case with computer-based recording systems. In fact, the power of nearly all the audio recording programs available for punching makes it a joy to use. You also get lots of options when it comes to how you can punch. The following sections spell out the Big Three — Manual, Auto, and Loop.

Manual punching

Manual punching is where you play your song, manually press the Record button when you want to start the punch, and manually press the Stop button when you're done. (I wondered why it was called *manual.*) This is the old-fashioned way of punching that only really works if you have lightning-fast hands for mashing buttons.

I honestly don't know many home recordists who use this approach, for the simple reason that, when you're both engineer and the artist (as most home recordists are), it's darned difficult to do the punch and get ready to play without making a mistake.

Auto punching

Auto punching is the process of letting your computer do the punching in and out for you. This requires telling your recording program (Pro Tools or Logic Pro, for example) when to punch in and out.

Before you create your Start and End points for a punch, you need to decide where these points are going to be. To make this decision, you most likely need to play the track back to find the exact point where you want to punch — and then write down the coordinates, whether it be in bars and beats, minutes and seconds, or frames. If you're not sure how to do this, the "Listening to your take" section earlier in this chapter gives you the details on this process.

In Pro Tools, you can set up Auto punching one of several ways, but one of the easiest ways is to do it is by using the Transport window. Here's how:

1. **Select the Expanded view option of the Transport window by choosing Displays⇨Transport Window Shows⇨Expanded.**

2. **Click in the Start text box in the Basic Controls section of the Transport window and type in the beginning of the punch section you want.**

   The Start text box appears in the same format as the Main counter located at the top of the Edit window. In the case of Figure 10-14, it shows bars and beats. You might also have the options for minutes and seconds or for frames and subframes.

3. **Press Enter or Return.**

4. **Click in the End text box and type in the end of the range.**

   This text box, too, appears in the format selected for the main counter.

5. **Press Enter or Return.**

   You're now ready to perform a punch. Check out the "Performing the punch" section, later in this chapter, for steps on how to actually perform the punch.

Figure 10-14:
Type Start and End points in the appropriate text boxes.

In Logic Pro, do the following to set up Auto punching:

1. **Start by clicking and holding the arrow in the lower-left corner of the Transport window.**

   The Transport Views pop-up menu appears.

2. **Select the Locator Display check box on the Transport Views pop-up menu.**

   The locator fields appear.

3. **Click in the Start Point field in the Transport window and type in the Start point you want, as shown in Figure 10-15.**

   This text box is displayed in the same format as the main counter. In the case of Figure 10-15, the format is bars and beats.

4. **Press Enter or Return.**

5. **Click in the End Point text box and type in your desired value.**

   This, too, is displayed in the format selected for the main counter.

6. **Press Enter or Return.**

7. **Click the Autodrop button in the Transport window to engage the auto punch function. (In Figure 10-15, the button has the icon with two arrows — one facing down and one facing up — positioned over a bar.)**

Figure 10-15:
Type Start
and End
points in the
appropriate
text boxes.

To make the punch itself a bit easier, I recommend that you set a pre-roll. A *pre-roll* is a designated number of bars before the punch actually happens that your song starts playing from. This allows you to get into the groove of the song before you actually have to record. To create a pre-roll in your song, follow these steps:

In Pro Tools:

1. Choose Displays➪Transport Window Shows➪Expanded View.

The Pre-Roll and Post-Roll text boxes appear beneath the basic transport controls.

2. Click in the Pre-Roll Counter text box in the Transport window and type in the length you want, as shown in Figure 10-16.

This text box is displayed in the same format as the main counter. In the case of Figure 10-16, the format is bars and beats.

3. Press Enter or Return.

4. Click in the Post-Roll Counter text box and type in your desired value.

This value, too, is displayed in the format selected for the main counter.

5. Press Enter or Return.

6. Click the Pre-Roll and/or Post-Roll button in the Transport window to enable them. (The buttons are to the left of the counter text boxes that you used in Steps 2 and 4.)

All enabled buttons are highlighted.

Figure 10-16:
Enter a
value for the
pre-roll and
post-roll.

Logic Pro doesn't have pre- and post-roll text boxes. Instead, you can start playing your song anywhere before your punch-in point by simply clicking along the timeline (the location numbers at the top of the Arrange window). Instead of a post-roll, the song continues playing until you click the Stop button in the Transport window. (Note that recording itself stops at your designated End point.)

Performing the punch

Once you have set the Start and End points for your punch as well as your pre-roll and post-roll, you can record to that section using the standard editing features of your audio recording program. In Pro Tools, for example, you'd do the following:

1. **Choose either Non-Destructive or Destructive Record mode.**

   Non-destructive record mode is the default mode and is active if you have a Record button without any icon in it. The Destructive Record mode is selected from the Operations menu (Choose Operations⇨ Destructive Record from the main menu). When you have this mode selected a small "D" is visible in the center of the Record button in the Transport window.

   Only use the Destructive Record mode if you're *really* sure you don't want to keep the previous take in the selected section.

2. **Click the Record Enable button for the track you want to record onto.**

   The button will shine red.

3. **Click the Record button.**

   The Record light flashes red.

4. **Click the Play button when you're ready to record.**

   The session will start at the pre-roll time, the Record button will flash red, and you'll hear the previously recorded track until the pre-roll is over. The monitoring will switch to the input source and the Record light stops flashing — but remains red.

When you hit the end of the recording range, the session either stops playing or — if you have the post-roll enabled — stops recording. At that point, the Record button starts flashing again — and the monitoring switches back to the recorded region until the end of the post-roll period. When the session reaches that point, it stops playing.

Loop punching

Loop punching is basically an Auto punch that repeats until you press the Stop button. This allows you to do multiple takes of a section until you get it right. The process of setting up the Start and End points of the loop are the same as for Auto punching. The only difference here is you have to select the Loop Record mode before doing the punch. This is done by:

1. **Record-enabling the track you want to punch in and out of.**

   The "Enabling recording" section earlier in this chapter lays out how to do that.

2. **Engage the loop recording function (most audio recording programs have one).**

   In Pro Tools, choose Operations➪Loop Recording. In Logic Pro, click the Loop icon in the Transport window.

3. **Set the Start and End points.**

   Check out the preceding section for specifics.

4. **Click the Play button for your track.**

   This starts the session. After the track reaches the Start point, your song automatically starts recording until you reach the End point, where you are instantly brought back to the Start point (or the pre-roll — see the Tip icon in the "Auto punching" section for details) so you can go over the section again. This process keeps repeating until you get it right — or until you give up and settle for what you can get.

5. **Click the Stop button in the Transport window to stop the loop recording process.**

Depending on your choice of audio recording programs, these recorded loops show up in your session a number of ways. In Pro Tools, for example, each repetition through the loop shows up as a separate playlist in your track. In Logic Pro, the takes are each placed into a new track in your session.

Doing overdubs

Overdubbing is the process of recording additional tracks to the ones you've already put down. This process is at the core of what most home recordists — who act as engineer, producer, songwriter, guitar player, drummer, bassist, keyboardist, and so on — do day by day. Most people can play only one instrument at a time, so unless you've got a band at your beck and call you're going to have to record each instrument in its own pass. Luckily, this process is simple: Follow the steps to record your first take for the new track, and then create a monitor mix that makes it easy (or at least eas*ier*) to play and record your other instruments correctly and with feeling. For details on creating a monitor mix, check out the "Monitoring your inputs" section earlier in this chapter.

Editing Audio

Being able to make edits to a recorded performance has long been an important part of the multitrack recording process. Early tape-based recording systems required a deft hand and an acceptance of many limitations on what editing you could perform. The introduction of computer-based recording means that changing your recorded audio is now easy.

Some programs make editing audio easy — Pro Tools is an obvious example — whereas some programs require a little more finesse on the part of the user — Logic Pro, anyone? No matter which program you use, however, you're going to discover quite a few options for manipulating your tracks in ways that were unheard of when using tape.

Regardless of the specifics involved in making edits, some commonalities exist when it comes to using a computer to edit audio. These are

- **Selecting audio to edit:** Audio is represented visually in your recording program and can be selected for editing in a number of different ways. You can find a variety of different selection tools in most audio programs for making your selections.

- **Editing regions:** *Regions* are sections of your recorded audio. Editing regions involves taking sections of an audio file and moving them around in your song. In most audio programs, editing regions doesn't change the actual audio recorded in your computer — it simply changes the way your program plays it back within your song. Most programs allow you to save this region as its own unique audio file without altering the original file.

- **Editing audio data:** Editing audio data means changing the audio data that you've recorded. This alters the original audio file.

The upcoming sections examine these commonalities in a bit more detail.

Selecting audio to edit

The first step in editing audio is selecting what you want to edit. Making a selection in an audio recording program is very similar to making a selection in any computer program: Click and drag your mouse over the section you want, and then release the mouse. (See Figure 10-17.)

Figure 10-17:
Selecting audio to edit is as simple as dragging over the section you want to edit.

This type of procedure is pretty handy and is just the thing for a lot of simple procedures, such as selecting a section of a vocal that has some silence before and after it. But if you want to make more precise selections, such as fixing a single drum hit or editing a bad guitar note, you're going to need to fall back on more precise tools and features. Fortunately, most audio recording programs offer some very cool features and tools to help you select the exact audio you want to edit.

Because Pro Tools is the undisputed heavy-weight champion of editing audio, I list some ways that you can select material by using this program. If editing audio is important to you, make sure that whatever program you're considering for your studio can perform these tasks at least as easily.

Selecting an entire track

In Pro Tools, you can select all the regions in a track one of two ways:

- ✔ Triple-click one of the regions in the track.
- ✔ Click in the track with the Selector tool and choose Edit⇨Select All or press ⌘+A on a Mac or Ctrl+A on a PC.

 You call up the Selector tool by clicking the Selector button located at the top of the Edit window.

Selecting on the fly

You can make selections while your session is playing by using the arrow keys. Follow these steps:

1. **Engage the Link Edit and Timeline Selection button or choose Operations⇨Link Edit and Timeline Selection. Alternatively, you can engage the Edit and Timeline Link button in the upper-right of the Edit window.**

   The button becomes highlighted.

2. **Click the track somewhere before the place you want to start your selection.**

   This is where the session will start playing back. If you want to select a point near the beginning of the session, you can skip this step and just start playing from the beginning.

3. **Either click Play in the Transport window or press the spacebar to start playing the session.**

4. **Press the down-arrow key when your playback reaches the point where you want the selection to begin.**

5. **Press the up-arrow key when your playback reaches the point where you want the selection to end.**

6. **Click the Stop button in the Transport window or press the spacebar to stop the session.**

To scroll back to the selection Start point, press the left-arrow key; to scroll to the selection End point, press the right-arrow key.

Making a selection with the Tab to Transients function

Transients are the initial attack in an instrument. In Pro Tools, you can move from one transient in a region to another by engaging the Tab to Transients button and pressing the Tab key. This is one of the most useful functions in Pro Tools for editing, and it's the main reason that I use this program for audio editing. Tabbing to transients lets you quickly find the exact beginning of a phrase to edit. To use this function to choose Start and End points for a selection, do the following:

1. **Enable the Tab to Transients button.**

   The button here in the margin shows you what to look for.

2. **Make sure that you have the Edit and Timeline Selection option enabled by selecting the Link Edit and Timeline Selection check box on the Operations main menu at the top of your screen or engaging the Edit and Timeline Link button.**

3. **Using the Selector tool, click in the audio track somewhere before the Start point of the area you want to select.**

4. **Press Tab repeatedly to move from transient to transient until you get to the Start point.**

   If you go too far, you can back up by pressing Ctrl (on a PC) or Option (on a Mac) when you press Tab.

5. **Press Shift as you tab through the transients to the End point.**

   If you go too far, you can back up the End point by pressing Shift+Ctrl+Tab (on a PC) or Shift+Option+Tab (on a Mac).

Editing regions

Regions are visual representations of your audio within your song file. These are the waveform blocks you see in the Arrange window in Pro Tools (see Figure 10-18, top) and Logic Pro (see Figure 10-18, bottom). These regions can be sliced and diced, shuffled, deleted, copied, and pasted, to name but a few of the things you can do with them when you have them selected. (See the preceding section for all the selection stuff.)

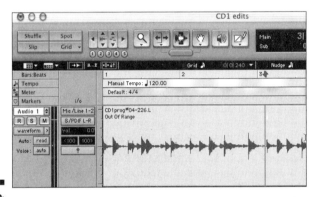

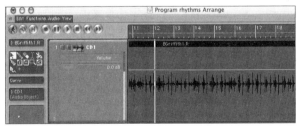

Figure 10-18: Regions are the visual representations of the audio you recorded for your song.

Being able to edit these regions without altering your original audio file lets you take sections of your performances and move them around at will. For example, say you have drum performance that you like for the first verse that you want to use again during the second verse. With a good audio recording program, you can get this job done in a few simple steps.

Pro Tools does it this way:

1. **Select the section you want to duplicate.**

   Check out the preceding section for directions on how to select material.

2. **Separate your selection from the existing region by choosing Edit⇨ Separate Region.**

   You now have three regions: the stuff leading up to the Start point you selected; the stuff between the Start and End points (the verse, in this example); and the stuff after the End point of your verse. Your selection — which is now its own region — is highlighted.

3. **Choose Edit⇨Copy to make a copy of the selection.**

4. **Click the Slip icon in the upper-left section of the Edit window to make sure you're in Slip edit mode.**

   In case you're curious, the other modes are Shuffle, Spot, and Grid. You don't want those modes — you want Slip.

5. **Click the start of the second verse where you want to put your drum section.**

6. **Choose Edit⇨Paste to place the first verse into the second.**

   Your first verse is placed in your track, and your original second verse is eliminated as a region, but the original audio data is still there if you want to use it later. The material before and after the place where you put your selection is turned into two more regions. At this point, your drum track now has five regions instead of the one it started with. These are: the stuff from the beginning of the song to the start of the first verse; the first verse; the stuff between the first and second verse, the second verse (which now has the same audio data as the first verse); and the material from the end of the second verse to the end of the song.

Editing regions involves these basic skills and can be done in almost all audio recording programs. The steps are obviously a little different, but the end result is the same.

Being able to edit regions like this without changing your original audio data makes it possible for you to try a variety of different arrangements in your songs. It also lets you restore your performance to the way they were without any loss in sound quality. This is called *nondestructive* editing. In the olden days of analog recording, by the time you've cut up a section of your perfor-mance you've essentially shredded the tape to the point that putting it all back together again is very difficult. (And even if you are physically able to do it, you'll discover that the sound of your track has been compromised to a great degree.)

Nondestructive editing is the single biggest advantage of computer-based recording and one that can be abused very easily if you're not careful. By being able to cut and paste your performances at will, you might be tempted to try to make your tracks "perfect" from a technical perspective. The danger in this is that you run the risk of making your performance soulless. When you start editing regions in your songs, be aware not only of the technical aspects of what you're doing, but also of the artistic side. Sometimes the less-than-perfect performance has the most feel and makes the best artistic statement. I'm a big fan of erring on the side of the artistic over the technical when it comes to editing regions.

Editing audio data

Aside from being able to edit the regions representing your audio data, you can edit the audio data itself, if you so choose. Depending on your audio recording program, you can perform a stunning variety of audio editing operations. These include such things as:

- **Copying data:** This makes a copy of your original file.

- **Redrawing the waveform:** This changes the shape of the sound-wave that is recorded.

- **Stripping silence:** This erases a section of your track to get rid of unwanted noise.

- **Normalizing:** This changes the volume of your tracks at the data level.

- **Quantizing:** This adjusts the timing of a section of your data to fit a grid.

- **Reversing:** This makes a section play in reverse.

Copying your track data

Performing editing operation alters your original audio data file permanently. Before you do this and end up regretting what you've done, make a copy of your file to work from. This gives you a backup of the original file in case you don't like what your edits have done to your music. Every audio program does backups a little differently. Here's how it's done in Pro Tools:

1. **Select the region you want to work on.**

2. **Choose AudioSuite⇨Duplicate.**

   The Duplicate dialog box appears, as shown in Figure 10-19.

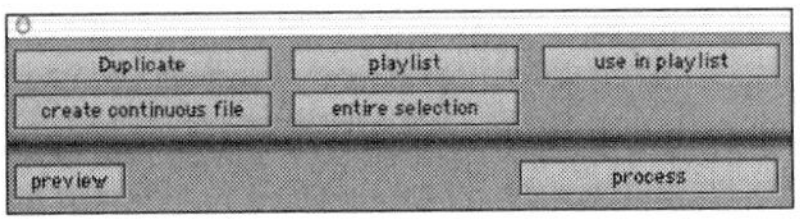

Figure 10-19:
The
Duplicate
dialog box.

Duplicate	playlist	use in playlist
create continuous file	entire selection	
preview		process

3. **Enable the Use in Playlist option on the right; make sure that the Playlist option (located in the top center) is enabled.**

4. **Click the Process button at the lower right.**

   You now a have a copy of the original region — a copy that's put in the track in place of the original.

When you have your copy, you can edit at will and not risk losing your original data.

Redrawing a waveform

Being able to redraw a waveform lets you get rid of a clipped note (distortion from overloading the converters in your computer). In Pro Tools, you take care of this little task with the help of the Zoomer and Pencil tools:

1. **Find the area in the region that you want to edit.**

2. **With the Zoomer tool enabled, click repeatedly on the spot you want to edit until you get into the sample level.**

   The waveform looks like a single wavy line. (See Figure 10-20.)

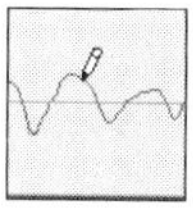

Figure 10-20: The Pencil tool in action.

3. **Select the Pencil tool.**

4. **Locate the exact spot to edit.**

   Your target, typically a moment of distorted sound, is usually easy to see because it looks like a sharp peak in the waveform. (See Figure 10-21, left.)

   If you have trouble seeing the problem, use the Scrub tool to listen to the audio.

5. **Draw over the waveform to round over the spot that was chopped off when the note got clipped (as shown in Figure 10-21, right).**

   Take it easy on making changes to the waveform. All you want to do is smooth out the peak, not change the sound too much.

Figure 10-21:
On the left is the cropped peak. On the right you see the fixed waveform.

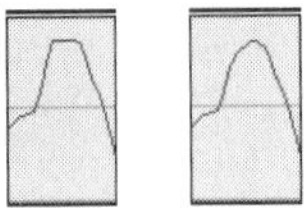

Silencing a section of your track

Many times when you record you get unwanted noises on your tracks. These can include chair squeaks, coughs, loud breathing, and other distractions during the sections where you don't play your instrument. The quick-and-easy way to get rid of these sounds is to silence them at the audio data level. This saves you from having to use the faders while you mix, and it reduces the size of the data file on your hard drive, giving you more room for other things. This process is very easy (in Pro Tools, anyway). Here's how it's done:

1. **With the Selector tool enabled, click and drag across the section of the region you want to select.**

   Note: You access the Selector tool by clicking the Selector button at the top of the Edit window.

2. **Choose Edit➪Insert Silence or press Shift+⌘+E (on a Mac) or Shift+Ctrl+E (on a PC).**

   The selected section is silenced.

Exploring other editing operations

The two preceding editing sections give you a good idea how easy it is to do some pretty useful editing operations by using a computer-based audio recording program. I'd love to walk you through how to perform a bunch of other operations, but I have to pass due to space limitations. (What? No 700-page book?)

I encourage you to look closely at the audio recording software you're considering for your studio to see what types of audio editing it can do. Most programs available can do a lot (probably more than you're going to do regularly). I cover the basics of the editing capabilities of the most popular programs in Chapter 7 insofar as how well they do compared to other programs out there, so check out that chapter for more insight into this area.

Chapter 11

Using MIDI

*M*IDI (Musical Instrument Digital Interface) is a digital communication protocol that allows your MIDI-equipped gear to send information back and forth through your system. MIDI handles the transmission of performance and system data; you, in conjunction with your recording program, can then record, edit, and transform this data into the music you hear in your head.

In this chapter, I introduce you to MIDI recording and editing within a computer program. I offer some basic information about MIDI ports and channels and help you get your system configured so that you can record MIDI in your computer. I also walk you through the process of recording your tracks, over-dubbing, and editing your data. Finally, this chapter offers a brief discussion of some of the many ways you can manipulate your MIDI data when it's in your computer.

Not all recording programs are equal in their implementation of MIDI. Some programs, such as Logic, are MIDI powerhouses; others, such as Pro Tools, are of the more minimalist variety. If MIDI recording and editing is important to you, make sure that you get a program that can do what you want it to do. Check out Chapter 8 for a look at many of the popular recording programs available and how they do MIDI.

Making Sense of MIDI

MIDI has been around for a while (about 20 years) and, even though it's considered old technology by today's standards, it's still employed a lot in music-making. This section gets you up to speed on the basic concepts of MIDI.

Perusing MIDI ports

Three types of MIDI ports exist: In, Out, and Thru. The In port receives incoming messages, and the Out port sends those messages further on their way. You use the Thru port when you create a *daisy chain,* which means you connect more than two MIDI devices together. The Thru port sends the messages that one device receives directly to the In port of another instrument.

You can connect MIDI gear in various ways by using these three ports, but for most recordists recording into a computer, a MIDI configuration usually consists of an external keyboard or controller (Chapter 4 details these pieces of hardware) connected to a MIDI interface attached to your computer. Depending on which type of device you use, you make the physical connection one of two ways:

- ✔ **By using an external keyboard/synthesizer:** An external keyboard is a keyboard that has MIDI ports in it and produces its own sounds. In this case, you make the connection by using a MIDI cable plugged into the Out port of your keyboard which is then plugged into the In port of your MIDI interface. Your interface is then connected to your computer. How that connection actually gets made depends on the type of MIDI device it is. For example, a USB MIDI interface attaches to one of the USB ports in your computer.

  This connection does get the MIDI data into your computer, but if you want the computer to actually *play* the sounds located in your keyboard — what a concept — you need to make sure that you have a MIDI cable going from your MIDI interface's Out port to the In port of your keyboard.

  Also, in order to hear the sound of your keyboard in your computer, you need to connect the analog outputs from your keyboard to the analog inputs of your audio interface.

- ✔ **By using a MIDI controller:** Unlike an external keyboard, a MIDI controller doesn't contain its own sounds. Instead, you use the controller to trigger (play) the sounds of software synthesizers in your computer. (Chapter 13 has more on soft-synths.) The connection you make depends on the type of controller you have. Most external controllers use either USB connections or MIDI Out ports (many have both). If you use the USB connection, just plug a USB cable from your controller to your computer. You don't need a MIDI cable or other hardware. If you use the MIDI Out port, though, you do need a MIDI cable and some sort of external MIDI interface.

Understanding MIDI channels

MIDI protocol allows you to have a bunch of different MIDI devices hooked up at the same time using the same MIDI cables and have them play only the data that you want each device to play. To accomplish this stunning feat, MIDI uses 16 different channels, where each device is assigned a different channel and responds only to MIDI messages that are sent along that channel.

If you have an external keyboard and use it to play back more than one MIDI track at a time, you need to assign a MIDI channel to each track in your song. I describe this procedure in the "Setting inputs, outputs, and MIDI channels" section later in this chapter.

Setting Up MIDI in Your Computer

The process of setting up your MIDI device varies according to whether you use a Mac or a PC. Either way, though, setting up a MIDI device takes only a couple minutes. This section walks you through the process.

Enabling MIDI devices in Mac OS X

Before you can record MIDI in Mac OS X, you need to do three separate things: a) set up your MIDI devices in OS X, b) enable the MIDI channels so you can choose the MIDI channels that each device receives and sends data on, and c) enable the input devices in your recording software so that you can use those devices in your computer.

To configure your MIDI devices in OS X, follow these steps:

1. **Use your MIDI cables to connect the devices you want to use with your computer to your MIDI Interface.**

   Chapter 4 has more on the different types of MIDI interfaces.

 2. **Click the Audio MIDI Setup icon (see margin) in the Dock.**

   The Audio MIDI Setup window opens.

3. **Click the MIDI Devices tab of the Audio MIDI Setup window.**

   A message appears telling you that your system is being scanned. After the scan is complete, your MIDI interface should appear in the tab's window, along with any devices connected to it, as shown in Figure 11-1.

4. **If any of your devices don't appear, double-check your cables to make sure they're properly connected and then click the Rescan MIDI icon.**

5. **If your device still doesn't appear, click the Add Device button.**

6. **In the dialog box that appears, enter the name, manufacturer, and model number of the device in the appropriate fields, and then click OK.**

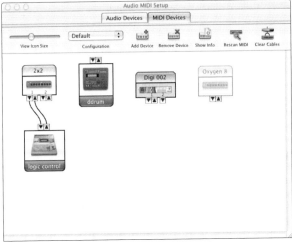

Figure 11-1:
The Audio
MIDI Setup
window
shows the
MIDI
devices
connected
to your MIDI
interface.

7. **After your devices appear on the MIDI Devices tab of the Audio MIDI Setup window, close the window by choosing Audio MIDI Setup➪ Quit Audio MIDI Setup.**

   You can also close this window by pressing ⌘+Q or clicking the red X in the upper-left corner.

After configuring your MIDI devices, you still need to enable their MIDI channels. The following list shows you how:

1. **Click the Audio MIDI Setup icon (see margin) in the Dock.**

   The Audio MIDI Setup window opens. (Refer to Figure 11-1.)

2. **Click the MIDI Devices tab of the Audio MIDI Setup window.**

   All MIDI devices connected to your MIDI interface should appear in the tab's window.

3. **In the MIDI Devices tab of the Audio MIDI Setup window, double-click the device for which you want to activate MIDI channels.**

   The device window appears.

4. **Click the More Properties tab to expand the window.**

   The window expands to include Basic and Expert tabs containing a broad range of settings for your device.

5. **Click the Basic Tab.**

6. **In the Transmits and Receives section of the Basics tab, click the channel number(s) that you want to be able to transmit and receive data through.**

Blue-highlighted channels are active.

7. Click OK to close the device window.

8. Close the Audio MIDI Setup window by clicking the red X in the upper-left corner or by pressing ⌘+Q.

Some recording programs — Pro Tools, for example — add a few steps to this process because you need to enable the devices in your system within the program. Here's how you do it in Pro Tools:

1. Choose MIDI⇨Input Devices.

The MIDI Input Enable dialog box opens, as shown in Figure 11-2, displaying all the MIDI ports in your system.

2. Select the check boxes for the devices you want to use.

3. Click OK.

Figure 11-2:
The MIDI
Input Enable
dialog box
lets you
select your
MIDI
devices.

Enabling MIDI devices in Windows XP

Enabling MIDI devices is as easy as adding a printer to your system.

To configure MIDI devices in Windows XP:

1. Install the drivers for your MIDI device as the device's manual describes.

If your audio interface has MIDI ports (such as the Digidesign 002), this step was already done when you installed the software, as I describe in Chapter 8.

2. **Use your MIDI cables to connect the devices you want to use with your software to your MIDI interface.**

3. **Turn on the power for the device.**

   At this point, your device should show up in your MIDI tracks' Input and Output selector pop-up menus. If not, restart your computer. If this still doesn't work you, you might need to go into the Device Driver menu and manually move the driver for your device into the Device Driver folder.

Some programs, such as Pro Tools, require that you enable your input devices before you can use them in your program. This process is the same for Windows XP as it is for a Mac. To wit:

1. **Choose MIDI⇨Input devices.**

   The MIDI Input Enable dialog box opens, showing the MIDI ports in your system.

2. **Select the check boxes for the devices you want to use.**

3. **Click OK.**

Getting Ready to Record

Setting up MIDI tracks involves first creating the tracks for your session and then setting the inputs, outputs, and MIDI channels for the tracks you created. This section spells out how to do all these tasks.

Creating MIDI tracks

Of course, before you can manipulate a MIDI track, you've got to have one. Creating a MIDI track is a pretty easy task in most recording programs. In Pro Tools, for example, you just do the following:

1. **Choose File⇨New Track.**

   The New Track dialog box appears, as shown in Figure 11-3.

2. **Enter the number of tracks you want to create.**

3. **Select MIDI Track from the middle drop-down list.**

4. **Click Create.**

   Your new track(s) appear in both the Edit and the Mix windows.

New Track	
Create 1 new	MIDI Track
Cancel	Create

When you create a new track in Pro Tools, the track receives a default name —
something not entirely useful (like MIDI 1). You can rename this track by following these steps:

1. **Double-click the track name in the Pro Tools Edit window.**

   The Name Track dialog box appears.

2. **Type in the new name and add any comments about the track in the
   appropriate places.**

3. **Click OK to close the window.**

   Your track gets a — hopefully more helpful — new name.

Some programs — Logic, for example — open with a bunch of MIDI tracks
already created so you don't have to go through these steps before recording
your MIDI performances.

Setting inputs, outputs, and MIDI channels

For MIDI tracks, like with audio tracks, you need to select the input and outputs sources for your MIDI data in order to be able to record and play back
your tracks. MIDI tracks differ from audio tracks in that, depending on your
recording program, you might also need to set the MIDI channel(s) through
which the MIDI data for each track travels. Here's how you do it in a program
like Pro Tools:

1. **Choose Display⇨Edit Window Shows⇨I/O View to open the I/O section of the Edit window.**

   The I/O section shows the inputs and outputs for each track.

2. **Within the I/O section of your track in the Edit window, click and hold on the Input selector until the Input contextual menu pops up.**

3. **While still holding down your mouse button, move the mouse over the Input menu until it rests on the MIDI port and channel you want, as shown in Figure 11-4.**

4. **Release the mouse button to select your choice.**

   The Input contextual menu closes your selection appears in the Input selector.

Choosing your outputs requires pretty much the same procedure, although to do that you start things off by clicking the Output selector in Step 2 instead.

Figure 11-4:
Assigning an input (or output) in Pro Tools is done by clicking and holding the Input or Output selector to open a contextual menu.

Logic offers a variety of ways to assign your inputs and outputs. Here's the one I use:

1. **In the Arrange window, click the track whose inputs and outputs you want to set.**

   The track becomes highlighted, and its channel strip appears on the left side of the window.

2. **Within the Subchannel section of the track's channel strip (located on the leftmost side of the Arrange window) click and hold on the Port selector until the MIDI Port menu pops up.**

3. **While still holding down your mouse button, move the mouse over the MIDI Port menu until it rests on the MIDI port that you want, as shown in Figure 11-5.**

4. Release the mouse button to select your choice.

The menu closes, and your selection appears in the input selector.

Assigning your track's output follows the same basic procedure, although you click and hold the Output selector in Step 2.

You use the output of the MIDI track only if you want to send the MIDI data back out of the computer again to use the sounds contained on an external keyboard. If you use a software synthesizer, follow the procedures listed in Chapter 13.

Figure 11-5:
Assign a
MIDI port in
Logic by
clicking and
holding
the Port
selector in
the Arrange
window's
track
channel
strip.

Recording MIDI Performances

Chapter 10 pretty much tells you the basics about recording MIDI performances — the process is very similar to recording audio tracks. The only significant difference is that you can set your system to wait until it receives MIDI data before starting to record. (This keeps you from having to press the Record button in the Transport window.) You also have to go through a few steps so that you can actually hear the sound from your MIDI device while you record.

Enabling recording for MIDI tracks

You can record-enable your MIDI tracks the same way you enable recording for audio tracks. This process is simple: Just click the Record Enable button (labeled R) for that track. Figure 11-6 shows the Record Enable button in Pro Tools (left) and Logic (right). After you click it, the button glows red.

Figure 11-6:
Click the track's Record Enable button (in Pro Tools, left, and Logic, right) to enable the track for recording.

As I describe in Chapter 10, how your enabled tracks act when you enable another track to record depends on your particular recording program. For example, in Logic your track stays enabled for recording when you click another track's Record Enable button, and in Pro Tools the default is that it doesn't remain enabled (enable turns off) when you click the Record Enable button on another track.

This is an important aspect of your recording program to understand. Check your application's manual to see how it treats this process. I can't tell you how depressing it is to think you've recorded a track when, in fact, it wasn't record enabled. I've lost some really good takes (performances) this way.

Monitoring MIDI inputs

Some recording programs contain internal sounds that allow you to hear your MIDI performances without having to plug in your external sound source, such as your synthesizer keyboard. I cover the steps to get sound from this approach in Chapter 14. Some programs, such as Pro Tools, require that you connect your external keyboard's analog outputs to your computer in order to hear what you're playing. You do this by connecting your keyboard to an analog input in your audio interface and routing the input to an audio track in your recording program. Here's the process for Pro Tools:

1. **Connect the analog output of your MIDI device to one of the analog inputs in your Digidesign hardware.**

2. **Choose File➪New Track.**

   The New Track dialog box appears.

3. **Use the drop-down lists of the dialog box to enter the number of tracks you want (1), the type (Audio), and whether you want your track in mono or stereo.**

4. **Using the new track's Input selector, select the analog input that your device is connected to in your Digidesign interface.**

5. **Using the new track's Output selector, select the main outputs for your session.**

   See the "Setting inputs, outputs, and MIDI channels" section earlier in this chapter for more on Steps 4 and 5.

6. **Record-enable this track by clicking the Record Enable button in either the track's channel strip (Mix window) or the track menu (Edit window).**

   Now you should hear the sound coming out of your MIDI device as you play your MIDI performance. Yes, it's an extra track, and it is being recorded at the same time as your MIDI track. But this I've-got-to-hear-what-I'm-playing track is separate; you can erase it without fear after you're done recording the take.

Recording MIDI tracks

After you've record-enabled your MIDI track(s) (see the "Enabling recording for MIDI tracks" section, earlier in this chapter), you can begin recording. Follow these steps to record one or more MIDI tracks:

1. **Click the Record Enable button located in either the track channel strip (Mix window) or track menu (Edit window) to record-enable the track(s).**

2. **To make sure you'll hear your music the way you want to hear it, set the level of the instruments in your session by using the fader for each audio track associated with your MIDI devices.**

   The faders are found in the Channel strip located in the Mix window.

3. **Enable the click track and the pre-roll if you're using them.**

   See Chapter 10 for more on click tracks and pre-rolls.

 4. **Click the Return to Zero button in the Transport section of the Transport window.**

   Doing so ensures that you start recording at the beginning of the session.

 5. **Click the Record button in the Transport section of the Transport window.**

   This step gets you ready to record; it doesn't start the actual recording process.

6. **Click the Play button in the Transport section of the Transport window.**

   Pro Tools starts recording.

7. **When you're done recording, click the Stop button in the Transport section of the Transport window or press the spacebar.**

   The finished take appears in the MIDI Regions list as a new region.

Playing Back Your Tracks

After you record a track, most likely you'll want to listen to it to make sure that it sounds the way you want it to sound. You do this by toggling off the Record Enable button on your MIDI tracks — click it to make the red light disappear — and then clicking the Play button. If you routed your external keyboard to an audio track in order to hear yourself, leave the audio tracks associated with the MIDI devices in Record-Enable mode. Doing so allows you to hear the playback of the MIDI device from the recorded MIDI data instead of hearing the audio that you recorded as a result of monitoring the analog output of your external keyboard. You can adjust the volume by moving the fader in the channel strip for the audio track associated with your MIDI device up and down.

Overdubbing MIDI Performances

After you record some MIDI performances, you can easily add to or change them. The time-honored name for this kind of recording is *overdubbing*. Overdubbing MIDI performance data is similar to overdubbing your audio data. Most programs allow you to overdub in several ways: manually punching in and out, punching automatically, and loop punching. In addition, because MIDI is strictly performance information without any actual sound, most recording programs offer you the ability to either replace or merge existing MIDI data when you overdub.

Using MIDI Merge/Replace

When you overdub to a MIDI track, many recording programs offer you the option to either replace existing material or add new data to it. For example, in Pro Tools you make this selection by using the MIDI Merge/Replace button. This button is located in the Transport window, as shown in Figure 11-7. Here's how it works:

✔ When the Merge/Replace button is engaged (MIDI Merge mode), new material is merged with any existing MIDI data on the record-enabled track(s).

✔ When the Merge/Replace button is disengaged (MIDI Replace mode), new MIDI data replaces any existing information on record-enabled track(s).

To engage MIDI Merge in Pro Tools, do the following:

1. **Open the MIDI controls section of the Transport window by choosing Display⇨Transport Window Shows⇨MIDI Controls.**

   The Transport window expands to include the MIDI controls section.

2. **Click the MIDI Merge button.**

   The button becomes highlighted.

Figure 11-7:
Add new data without erasing what's there.

Logic has a similar function, but by default any overdubs you do are placed in a new sequence — leaving the original intact. You do have the choice, however, of having your overdub replace or merge with existing material. To merge your overdub, follow these steps:

1. **Choose File⇨Song Settings⇨Recording Options to open the Recording Options toolbar.**

2. **Select the Merge New Recording With Selected Sequences option at the top of the Recording Options toolbar, as shown in Figure 11-8.**

3. **Click OK to accept the setting and close the window.**

   Now when you record, your new data is merged with the old.

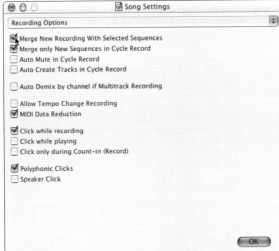

Figure 11-8:
Choosing
the Merge
New
Recording
With
Selected
Sequences
option lets
you add to
an existing
track in
Logic.

To replace existing data, follow these steps:

1. **Click and hold the arrow at the bottom-right corner of the Transport window and select either All Elements Horizontal or All Elements Normal from the pop-up menu that appears.**

   The Recording Options toolbar appears in the Transport window.

2. **Click the Replace button on the Recording Options toolbar to engage the Replace function, as shown in Figure 11-9.**

Figure 11-9:
Replace
existing
MIDI data
with new
data.

Punching in and out

If you like some of your initial take and want to record over only part of it, you can set points at which to start and stop recording within the session. This is called *punching in and out,* a process that I cover in some detail in Chapter 10 — although there I spell out how to punch in and out of audio tracks.

As is this case with audio tracks, most programs allow you to punch in to MIDI tracks in several ways. These include punching in and out *manually, automatically,* and *repeatedly* (looping).With the exception of being able to choose to merge your punched data with your original performance or being able to replace it, punching into and out of MIDI tracks is the same as punching into and out of audio tracks. I detail the exact procedures for performing these punches in Chapter 10.

Editing MIDI Data

MIDI editing has two basic types of functions: You can edit the notes manually or you can perform certain MIDI operations/functions, such as quantizing and transposing. This section offers an overview of these different functions.

Manual MIDI editing

Editing your MIDI data manually is a great way to go if you want to do any of the following tasks:

- ✔ Add notes or controller data.
- ✔ Delete notes or controller data.
- ✔ Change pitch.
- ✔ Change duration.
- ✔ Change velocity (volume).
- ✔ Change time location.

Depending on your recording program, you can make these edits a number of ways. I describe a simple way to do this in Pro Tools — one of the more basic MIDI applications — later in this section. Aside from the simple way, many programs offer a variety of different editing windows to help you work the way you want. For example, Logic — one of the more powerful MIDI programs out there — offers several windows. These include:

✔ **Matrix:** No, not that Matrix. This Matrix is the basic window that shows MIDI data in a piano roll format. (See Figure 11-10.) The MIDI notes show up as blocks in a timeline that rolls across the screen as your song plays. This is a standard format for MIDI editing; you find it in most recording programs.

✔ **Score:** The Score window shows your MIDI data in the form of a musical score. You see the notes laid out as if they were written on paper. The window is great for people who like to see their music in written form, but this window isn't available on all recording programs. (Pro Tools, for instance, doesn't yet offer this window in version 6.) Figure 11-11 shows Logic's version of this window.

✔ **Hyper Edit:** The Hyper Edit window shows your MIDI data in separate rows, making it easy to adjust parameters such as velocity, modulation, pan, and others. This window — see Figure 11-12 — is handy for making more involved changes to your MIDI data — changes other than those involving pitch, duration, or location. Not all programs have a window like this.

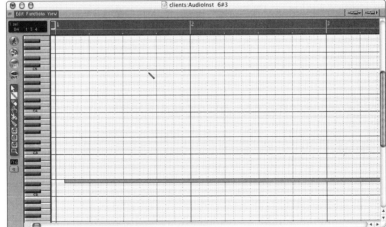

Figure 11-10:
The Matrix window in Logic shows MIDI data in the piano roll format.

Adding MIDI events

You can add MIDI notes or controller data (collectively called MIDI events) to a MIDI track by using one of your program's editing tools. In Pro Tools, for example, the editing tool of choice is called the Pencil tool.

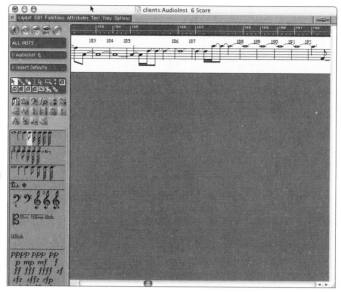

Figure 11-11:
The Score
window
looks like a
sheet of
music.

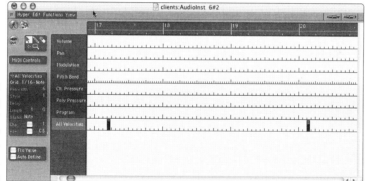

Figure 11-12:
The Hyper
Edit window
is actually
pretty calm.

To insert a note using the handy Pro Tools Pencil, do the following:

1. **Click and hold the Track View button in the Track Controls section of the Edit Window to access the pop-up menu and then drag to the Notes view. Release your mouse button to accept this view.**

2. **Click and hold the Pencil button, and then select the Freehand Pencil tool from the Pencil Tool pop-up menu that appears.**

3. **Locate the place in the track's playlist area where you want to add your MIDI note.**

4. **By using the Pencil tool that you selected in Step 2, click and drag in the playlist to insert a note.**

   You determine the pitch of this note by where you place it (from top to bottom). You can use the small keyboard display on the left side of the playlist to see what pitch relates to which location in the playlist. To determine the note's duration, drag to the right as you draw it. The velocity of the note defaults to the maximum of 127. (You can change the velocity later if you choose.)

Because MIDI performance data has no sound, most MIDI-capable recording programs allow you to add MIDI program change information, which tells your MIDI instrument to change the sound that it plays. This is called inserting a MIDI program change. Here's how you do it in a program like Pro Tools:

1. **Click and hold the Track View button and select Program Change view from the menu that appears.**

2. **Click and hold the Pencil button, and then select the Freehand Pencil tool from the menu that appears.**

3. **Click in the track's playlist at the location you want the change to occur.**

   The Patch Select dialog box opens. This dialog box lets you select the sound (called the *patch*) that your MIDI data plays in your sound module (soft-synth or external keyboard).

4. **Select the patch number or name in the main section of the dialog box.**

5. **Click Done.**

   The program change is inserted, as shown in Figure 11-13.

Figure 11-13:
View
Program
Changes for
your track.

Deleting a MIDI note

To delete a MIDI note in Pro Tools, do the following:

1. **Click and hold the Track View button and select Notes from the menu that appears.**

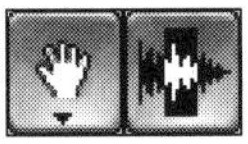

2. **Using either the Grabber tool or the Selector tool, select the note in the playlist you want to delete.**

3. Press Delete on your keyboard or choose Edit⇨Clear.

Instead of Steps 2 and 3 in the preceding list, start out with the Pencil tool. Then press Alt (on a PC) or Option (on a Mac) to change the pencil into an eraser, and then click the note to delete it.

Changing a note's pitch

To change a note's pitch in Pro Tools, do the following:

1. Click and hold the Track View button and select Notes from the menu that appears.

2. Select the Pencil or Grabber tool.

3. Press Shift to keep the note's start point from changing as you move it.

4. Click the note and drag it up (higher pitch) or down (lower pitch) in the playlist.

5. Release the mouse button when the note is where you want it.

Changing a note's duration

To change a note's duration — its Start or End points — in Pro Tools do the following:

1. Click and hold the Track View pop-up menu and select Notes from the menu that appears.

2. Select the Shuffle edit mode by clicking the Shuffle button on the upper-left side of the Edit window.

3. Select the Pencil tool.

4. Using the Pencil tool, click the note you want to change.

Press Shift as you click to select more than one note.

5. Click the Start or End point of the note and drag it left or right.

6. Release the mouse button when the note is where you want it.

Changing a note's velocity

In the MIDI world, velocity means volume. To change a note's velocity in Pro Tools, do the following:

1. Click and hold the Track View pop-up menu and select Velocity from the menu that appears.

2. Select the Grabber tool.

3. **Click the diamond-shaped icon at the top of the velocity stalk (the vertical line with a diamond at the top representing the velocity level) in the track's playlist and drag it up or down.**

4. **Release the mouse button when the velocity is where you want it.**

Changing time locations

Time locations are where the start points of your notes are placed within your session. To change a note's time location in Pro Tools, do the following:

1. **Click and hold the Track View pop-up menu and select Notes from the menu that appears.**

2. **Select the Slip edit mode by clicking the Slip button on the upper-left side of the Edit window.**

3. **Select the Pencil or Grabber tool.**

4. **Press Shift to keep the note's pitch from changing as you move it.**

5. **Click the note and drag it left or right.**

6. **Release the mouse button when the note is where you want it.**

Performing MIDI operations/ editing functions

Most recording programs offer a host of operations you can perform on your MIDI data to make it sound the way you want it to sound. These functions vary from program to program, and I can't list them all here. As an example, though, a program with arguably the slimmest MIDI capabilities (Pro Tools) offers the following MIDI operations (Figure 11-14 shows the MIDI Operations window in Pro Tools):

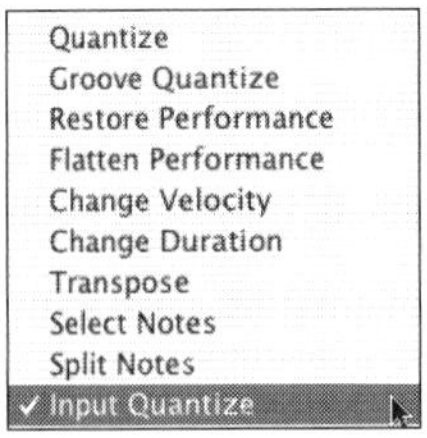

Figure 11-14:
This pop-up menu lets you select your MIDI operation.

Quantize
Groove Quantize
Restore Performance
Flatten Performance
Change Velocity
Change Duration
Transpose
Select Notes
Split Notes
✓ Input Quantize

✔ **Quantize:** Lets you adjust the timing of your selected notes.

✔ **Groove Quantize:** Similar to the Quantize operation, except you use a *groove template* (a file that contains timing data with a specific feel) to create a grid to quantize to.

✔ **Restore Performance:** Lets you return to previously saved performance settings.

✔ **Flatten Performance:** Lets you tweak performance data and lock it in before you do any more tweaking.

✔ **Change Velocity:** Lets you adjust the volume of the attack or the release of selected MIDI notes.

✔ **Change Duration:** Lets you alter the length of recorded MIDI notes.

✔ **Transpose:** Lets you change the pitch of selected notes.

✔ **Select Notes:** Lets you choose specific MIDI notes or a range of notes in a selection.

✔ **Split Notes:** Lets you select a note or range of notes — but also lets you copy or cut the selected notes.

✔ **Input Quantize:** Lets you set a Quantize value that your recorded performance is adjusted to automatically as you record it.

Chapter 12

Using Loops

In This Chapter

▶ Understanding loops

▶ Incorporating loops in your music

▶ Creating loops

▶ Finding loop libraries

*L*oops are pre-recorded musical snippets that you can put in your song and manipulate to create your music. Looping has become very popular because it makes composing music easy and saves you from having to learn to play an instrument well or hire a professional to play for you. (Purists take note: Looping is here to stay.)

In this chapter, you discover the role of loops in composing music and find out how to get decent loops to work with. This chapter also shows you how to create your own unique loops.

Not all recording programs have looping capabilities, and not all those that do have them offer ways to manipulate the loops in your program the way you might want. If this function is important to you, make sure that the program you buy has the capabilities that you want. Chapter 6 has more about how programs work with loops, and Chapter 7 looks at the looping capabilities of some of the major recording programs out there.

Understanding Loops

Loops really aren't that complicated. Think of them as short musical snippets that you can line up in various ways, and then you have them play in your song. A typical loop is a drum pattern that plays during the verse of your song or serves as the bass line of your chorus. In the simplest form of looping, you assemble your loops — one after another — to fill up the section you want them to play in. And you can often change the tempo and pitch of your loops to fit your vision of your song.

On a more sophisticated level, you can manipulate, edit, and create loops in a variety of ways, depending on the capabilities of your particular recording program (another reason to investigate the looping capabilities of your program before buying).

Loops come in two formats:

- **MIDI-based loops** are recorded as MIDI data by using soft-synths or general MIDI instruments. These loops appear as MIDI data in your track and can be edited like any other MIDI performance. (Chapter 4 has more on general MIDI stuff, and Chapter 11 has more about actually editing MIDI data.)

- **Audio-based loops** are created from audio files and are seen as waveform displays of the audio data. They act just like any other audio file except that they have a tempo grid and a key signature attached to them. This means that when you place them in a song, they conform to the song's tempo as well as to the designated key signature (if your song has one).

Not all looping programs can handle MIDI-based loops as MIDI data. Instead, these loops are treated as audio-based loops. If you're working with such a program, you'll find that the editing capabilities of the loops conform to the audio format — you can't change the pitch of individual notes that are part of a group of notes (a chord, for instance).

Using Loops in Your Song

Using loops is easy — which is why they're so commonly used. This section describes how to use them in your song.

Creating a loop track

The type of track you create for your loops depends on the type of loop you want to use. If you want to use a MIDI-based loop, you need a MIDI track (or audio instrument track if you use Logic). If you intend to use an audio-based track, you need to create an audio track. This section describes how to set up each of these track types.

Making a MIDI-based loop track

In Logic — one of the more robust recording programs in terms of looping capabilities — the easiest way to make a MIDI-based loop track is to use an audio instrument track. This way you can use a soft-synth to play the loop and not have to hook up an external MIDI sound module. This is how you make one:

1. **Choose Functions⇨Track⇨Create from the menu at the top of the Arrange window, as shown in Figure 12-1. (If the Arrange window isn't showing, choose Windows⇨Open Arrange.)**

   A new track appears in your song in the same format (and with the same name) as the track directly before it.

2. **To distinguish the new track from the track above it, assign an audio instrument to the new track by first clicking and holding the track name in the Arrange window.**

   A pop-up menu appears, as shown in Figure 12-2.

3. **Drag your mouse to one of the audio instruments in the list.**

4. **Release the mouse.**

   Your new track is assigned to the selected audio instrument.

You now have a track for your MIDI-based loops.

In Logic, you can drag a MIDI-based loop into an audio track. If you take this route, it acts like an audio-based loop instead of a MIDI-based loop. That is, you aren't able to edit the individual notes as MIDI data.

Figure 12-1:
Creating a
track for
your MIDI-
based loop
in Logic
starts in the
Arrange
window.

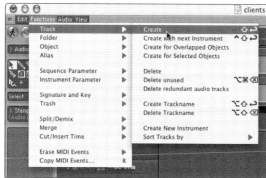

Adding an audio-based loop track

The process for creating a new audio track in Logic is the same as for creating a new audio instrument, except you choose an audio track instead of an audio instrument (duh).

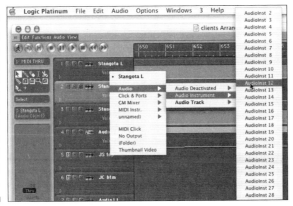

Figure 12-2:
Assign an
audio
instrument
to your new
track from
the pop-up
menu
located
under the
Track name.

If all your available audio objects are used in your song, you need to create a new one. Creating a new track adds an extra step to the process of creating an audio-based loop track. Here's how you do it:

1. **In the Environment's local menu (see Figure 12-3), choose New⇨ Audio Object. (If the Environment window isn't open, open it by choosing Windows⇨Environment.)**

   The Settings Parameter dialog box appears, displaying settings for Icon, Device, and Channel, to name a few.

2. **In the Settings Parameter box, click and hold the arrow in the Channel Parameter field to open the drop-down menu and select Track⇨ Track *x*. (*x* is any one of the unbolded tracks that appear in the list.)**

3. **Release your mouse to accept this selection.**

   Your new audio object now appears in the Audio Track submenu; you can choose this new object from the submenu when you create your new track.

Choosing loops

Most loop-capable programs have a special loop browser function to help you find the loops you want to use in your song. In Logic, the browser lets you choose from categories that include the instrument type, musical genre, and mood. (Figure 12-4 shows the Loop browser in Logic.) Browsers like this make it easy (or at least easier) to find the loop you want. This is especially important because most people end up with tons of loops in their libraries.

Figure 12-3:
The Environment's local menu lets you create a new audio object for your song.

Figure 12-4:
The loop browser helps you choose the loops for your song.

Follow these steps to choose a loop to insert in your song:

1. **Click the instrument category you want.**

   The instrument becomes highlighted, and a list of loops featuring that instrument appears on the right side of the window. (Figure 12-4 shows the Drums category selected.)

2. **You can narrow your list down a bit further by clicking buttons associated with the genre, mood, or style you want.**

   In Figure 12-4, your options include Rock/Blues, Acoustic, and Dark, to name a few. The more you specialize your categories, the narrower your list of loops becomes.

3. **Click one of the loops in the list on the right to select it.**

   In Logic, your chosen loop automatically starts playing, but some programs require you to click an Audition button (it might look like a speaker or a play button) to play the loop. To stop the audition, press the spacebar once. Pressing the spacebar a second time restarts the loop.

When you know which loop you want in your song, follow the steps in the next section to actually place the loop in your track.

Assembling loops in your song

When you insert a loop in your track, it automatically conforms to the tempo and key of your song. This means that you need to assign a key (if your program allows this), a time signature, and a tempo for your song before you start adding loops to it. I explain the process of setting a tempo and time signature in detail in the click track section in Chapter 10. In Logic, you assign a key signature to your song by using the Signature/Key Change List Editor. Here's how you do it:

1. **Choose Options⇨Signature/Key Change List Editor.**

   The Signature/Key Change List Editor window opens, as shown in Figure 12-5.

2. **Double-click in the Key section of the list to highlight it.**

3. **Type in the key signature you want.**

4. **Click Return to accept the entry.**

5. **Close the window by clicking the red button in the top-left corner of the window.**

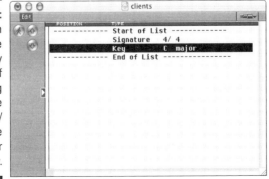

Figure 12-5: You can designate the key signature of your song in the Signature/ Key Change List Editor window.

You don't have to maintain a constant key and time signature for the entire song. You can enter any key and time signature changes for a song in this list by leaving the window open and adding them. (Repeat Steps 2 through 4.) Just be sure to include the position for the start of the change in the Position field. To enter data in this field, click the row of the time or key signature to highlight it and then double-click that row under the Position column to open the Position Indicator field.

After you set up your time and key signature parameters, you can start putting loops into your track. This process is often as simple as dragging loops from the loop browser into your track. You can then arrange them by shuffling them around in your song's Arrange window.

Editing loops

Editing loops involves the same basic procedures as editing any audio or MIDI file. Chapters 10 and 11 provide the specifics on these basic editing procedures, so if you want to get hardcore and chop up your loops, you can find out how to do it in those chapters.

Aside from the hardcore-chopping type of editing, you can make simple adjustments in your loops by dragging the Start and End points with your mouse. Here's how you do this in GarageBand (arguably one of the simplest-to-use loop programs):

1. **Open GarageBand by double-clicking the GarageBand icon in the Application folder.**

2. **Drag the loop you want to edit into your song.**

    A new track is created, and the loop is placed in the track.

3. **Select the loop you want to edit by clicking it in your song.**

    The loop becomes highlighted.

4. **To alter the Start point, position your cursor over the beginning edge of the loop. To alter the End point, position your cursor over the end of the loop.**

    An Edit icon appears.

5. **Click and drag the Start point to the right to have playback begin later in the loop sequence. Or click and drag the End point to the left to have playback end before the loop's actual ending.**

   6. **Release the mouse when you have the Start point (or End point) where you want it.**

This operation is non-destructive — meaning it doesn't change your original loop in any way. You can adjust the Start or End point again by clicking and dragging the point back and forth at will.

Creating Your Own Loops

Most looping programs let you create your own loops from your audio files. The difference between loops and simple snippets of audio data is that loops contain *metadata* (basically, data about data) that identify the key and time signature of the loop as well as categorical data — instrument type, musical style, mood, and so on — that helps you find it in your loop browser. (Check out the "Choosing loops" section, earlier in this chapter, for more on loop browsers.)

Your first step in creating a loop is to edit your audio file to the point where it contains the musical selection that you want to use. (You can find more details for this in Chapter 10 and in your program's manual.) When you have your musical snippet, you turn it into a loop by adding the metadata to the file. This process varies (of course) according to the program you use, but in Logic you do it this way:

   1. **Select an audio region (for example, your snippet) in the Arrange window by clicking it with the Selector tool (the little arrow located in the upper-left corner of the Arrange window).**

   The audio region becomes highlighted.

   2. **Choose Audio⇨Soundtrack Loop Utility⇨Open to open the Soundtrack Loop Utility window.**

   The window makes an appearance, as shown in Figure 12-6.

   3. **Enter your data in the appropriate text boxes in the window.**

   Typically, this would include the number of beats as well as the key and time signatures, among other things.

   4. **Click OK to accept your settings and close the window.**

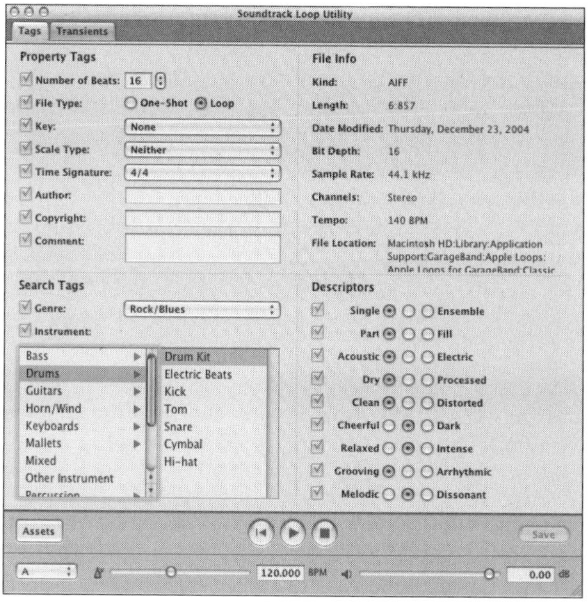

Figure 12-6:
The
Soundtrack
Loops Utility
window
lets you
transform
your audio
snippet into
a loop.

Finding Loop Libraries

You can find an almost mind-boggling number of good — even great — loop libraries that you can buy for your compositions. Although I'm a self-admitted skeptic of looping, I have had a chance to use a variety of different loop libraries over the years and have created a library of over 500 loops of my own (don't ask). As a result, I have a few (ahem) strong opinions about some of the available loop libraries. This section lists a bunch of the better/more unusual ones I've found.

✔ **Dirt Keeps the Funk, by Primesounds:** This CD contains a ton of great funk grooves with drums, Fender Rhodes, bass, and other instruments. You can find it at `www.bigfishaudio.com/4DCGI/detail.html?914`.

✔ **Metamorphosis, by Spectrasonics:** Spectrasonics makes great sample and loop libraries (not to mention some awesome soft-synths — check out Chapter 13). Metamorphosis is perfect for electronic, techno, or house music. Describing this CD is difficult, so check out `www.spectra sonics.net/libraries/metamorphosis.html` and you can download some samples to hear it for yourself.

✔ **Mick Fleetwood: Total Drumming, by Sony Media Software:** Good rock drums can make a song. This library has some great classic rock drumming by one of the best rock drummers around. If you need good drums, this is one of my favorites. You can find it at http://mediasoftware. sonypictures.com/loop_libraries/default.asp?cid=62.

So many loop libraries exist that narrowing it down here is impossible, and this list could get huge, so here are a couple places where you can find loop libraries on the Internet:

✔ www.bigfishaudio.com: This site has tons of loops and samples that you can download or buy.

✔ www.mi7libraries.com/main/samples: Another site just chock full of loops and samples worth looking into. Be careful, though: Once you start checking out the samples, you might never get any real work done.

Chapter 13

Exploring Software Synthesizers

Computer-based recording allows your computer's processing power to take the place of racks full of equipment. The world of software synthesizers is an area where this ability has fully blossomed. Just a few years ago you needed a rack (or a keyboard stand) full of hardware to get just a sampling (ahem) of the types of synthesizers and samplers that you now can store in even a small hard drive on your computer.

In this chapter, I introduce you to the wonderful world of software synthesizers (soft-synths), and help you get started using them in your music. I detail the steps of installing them in your system, show you how to create tracks in which to use soft-synths, walk you through recording your performance, and share with you how to change the sound to suit your needs. If that's not enough, I also offer some suggestions for good soft-synths that you can buy and add to your system.

Understanding Software Synthesizers

Software synthesizers, known as soft-synths, are sound modules that live in your computer. You can plug soft-synths into your songs and then trigger them with MIDI performance data that you've added to your song.

Soft-synths are plug-ins, and as with other types of plug-ins (see Chapter 15), soft-synths come in different formats. These include

▸ **Audio Units:** Audio Units (AU) is a format developed by Apple for OS X. This format is just beginning to gain a wider share of available third-party plug-ins and is used in programs that run on Mac OS X, such as Logic and Digital Performer.

✔ **Direct X:** Direct X (DX) is a format developed by Microsoft for Windows systems. The DX format is one of the most common plug-in formats, and DX plug-ins are employed in programs such as ACID and SONAR, among others.

✔ **MAS:** The MAS format was developed by MOTU for Digital Performer. This plug-in format isn't as common as many of the others — even Digital Performer now uses Audio Units in its program.

✔ **RTAS:** Real Time Audio Suite is Digidesign's proprietary plug-in format. Pro Tools software uses this format.

✔ **VST:** Developed by Steinberg (the maker of Cubase and Nuendo, among other programs), VST plug-ins are used on both Mac and Windows computers. This is by far the most popular plug-in format and as such you find a plethora of options.

Most soft-synths are available in several different formats, so you should be able to use the one you want in whatever audio recording program you have. If you have to have a particular soft-synth and it isn't supported by the plug-in format that your system uses, you can get a wrapper to act as a bridge between your recording program's supported format and that of the soft-synth. Chapter 15 has more on plug-in wrappers, including a list of the most common ones.

Using Soft-Synths

If you want to use soft-synths in your songs, you can't just wave your magic wand and wish it so — you need to follow a few steps to use them. You start by installing them in your system, and then you insert them into your tracks. This section details both steps.

To use soft-synths in your songs, you need two things: an audio recording program that supports MIDI sequencing, and a soft-synth program installed in your computer.

Installing soft-synths

Your audio recording program likely comes with some plug-ins. The quality of these included plug-ins ranges from merely okay to exceptional. If you want to buy or download additional plug-ins to use in your program, you need to install them so that your audio recording program can recognize and use them. This process is usually as easy as clicking the Install icon that pops up on-screen after inserting the CD you bought or double-clicking the folder of the plug-in that you just downloaded.

There might come a time, however, when you'll want to install these plug-ins by hand. This situation could arise, for example, if you have more than one audio recording program in your computer and you want to use the plug-ins on all of them. (An automatic install might circle in on just one program and ignore the others.) To avoid such a partial success, you need to do a custom install so that you can designate which applications should be targeted. Check your manual for details.

Recording soft-synths in your song

Soft-synths record like any MIDI instrument — the only difference here is that the sound you hear is created within your computer, rather than originating in a separate sound module like your external synthesizer or keyboard. To use a soft-synth in your song, you need to follow a few steps. This section describes the process.

Creating a track for your soft-synth

First things first. To record with a soft-synth, you need to create a track in which to insert the synthesizer plug-in. Regardless of the program you use, the process remains basically the same. The difference lies in the type of track you create, but the basic steps — at least in Logic — look like this:

1. **Choose Functions➪Track➪Create the top of the Arrange window, as shown in Figure 13-1. (If the Arrange window isn't showing, choose Windows➪Open Arrange.)**

   A new track appears in your song in the same format (and with the same name) as the track directly before it.

2. **Assign an audio instrument to your new track to separate it from the track above it by first clicking and holding the track name in the Arrange window.**

   A pop-up menu appears. (See Figure 13-2.)

3. **Drag your mouse to one of the audio instruments in the list.**

4. **Release the mouse.**

   Your new track is assigned to the selected audio instrument.

You now have a track for your soft-synth.

Connecting a keyboard controller

To record with a soft-synth, you need to have a way to trigger the sound. You'll usually want to do trigger the sound by using an external keyboard. If you've set up your system for MIDI devices, all you need to do is plug in your keyboard controller and assign it to your instrument track.

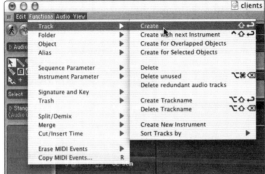

Figure 13-1:
Creating a track for your soft-synth in Logic starts in the Arrange window.

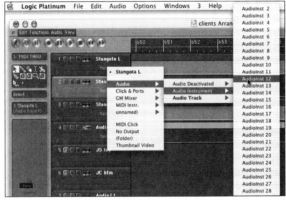

Figure 13-2:
Assign an audio instrument to your new track from the pop-up menu located under the Track name.

Chapter 11 explains the process of setting up your MIDI devices in both Windows XP and Mac OS X. If you haven't set up a MIDI device yet, take a few minutes to do so. Then follow the steps in the rest of this section to assign the device to your track.

1. **Click your soft-synth's track in the Arrange window to highlight it.**

   The track's channel strip appears on the left side of the window.

2. **Within the Subchannel section of the track (located on the leftmost side of the Arrange window) double-click the MIDI Channel selector.**

   The MIDI Channel selector becomes highlighted, as shown in Figure 13-3.

3. **Type the MIDI channel you want to use.**

4. **Press Return to accept this MIDI channel.**

Make sure that your MIDI device is set to the same MIDI channel — or set to all MIDI channels — otherwise the MIDI device won't trigger the track.

Figure 13-3:
You assign
a MIDI
channel in
Logic by
clicking and
holding
the MIDI
Channel
selector in
the Arrange
window's
track
channel
strip.

Assigning a soft-synth to your track

Inserting a soft-synth into a track is as simple as inserting an effect. Depending on your audio recording program, where you do the actual inserting varies. For example, in Logic, you set the input of your audio instrument track to the soft-synth, and in Pro Tools you insert the soft-synth into a MIDI track from the plug-in Insert menu.

The steps involved are as follows:

✔ **In Logic,** click and hold over the track's Input selector (see the left side of Figure 13-4) in the Arrange, Environment, or Global Mixer window and drag your cursor to the soft-synth you want from the pop-up menu. Release the mouse to accept this selection.

✔ **In Pro Tools,** click and hold over the track's Insert selector (see the right side of Figure 13-4) in either the Edit or Mix window, and then drag to the soft-synth you want from the contextual menu. Release the mouse to accept the soft-synth.

Recording your performance

With your MIDI device set up and your soft-synth assigned, recording is easy. Simply click the Record Enable button for the track and click the Record button to start the process. (At least that's how it works in Logic; in Pro Tools you need to click Play after clicking Record.) Click Stop to stop recording.

To hear what you're playing, all you have to do is turn up the Volume fader located at the bottom of the track's channel strip in the Mix window (Pro Tools) or in the Environment or Global Mixer window (Logic).

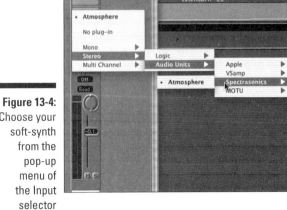
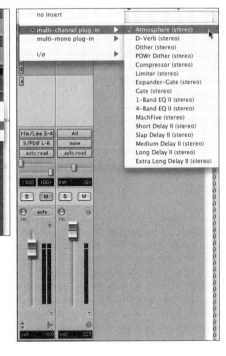

Figure 13-4:
Choose your soft-synth from the pop-up menu of the Input selector (Logic, left) or the Insert selector (Pro Tools, right).

I explain the recording process in more detail in Chapters 10 and 11. So if you want to know the specifics of adding click tracks, doing overdubs, and punching in and out, check out those chapters.

Playing back a recorded track

When you're done recording, you can hear your performance by following these steps:

1. **Disable your track by toggling off the Record Enable button.**

2. **Click either Zero (Pro Tools) or Stop (Logic) in the Transport window to return your song to the Start position.**

3. **Click Play in the Transport window.**

   Your song starts playing.

4. **Press Stop to stop your song when you're done listening.**

Changing sounds

When your soft-synth is plugged in, you can edit the sound much as you would adjust the parameters of any plug-in. Because the performance data for your soft-synth is MIDI, you can make the decision for your final sound after you've recorded your part. (I rarely do this because the sound of the instrument dictates to a large extent the way I play my part, but you might work differently.)

Anyway, to change the parameters of your soft-synth

1. **Double-click the name of your soft-synth in the Input section of the track that it's plugged in to.**

   The soft-synth's window opens. Figure 13-5 shows a typical soft-synth window in Logic.

2. **Make your adjustments.**

   For example, twirl the knobs or slide the sliders or whatever to adjust the modulation pitch or the filter.

   The sound change might be immediate, depending on your computer's speed and whether your song is playing while you make the change.

3. **Click OK to accept the new parameters and close the window.**

If you think you're going to make a lot of adjustments, you may want to keep the window open as the song plays and simultaneously make your adjustments. If you do this, though, keep in mind that it does put stress on your processor, so your changes might take a while to go into effect.

Figure 13-5:
You can change the sounds in your soft-synth by opening the soft-synth's interface window.

Finding Soft-Synths

Lots of great soft-synths are available on the market. This is one of the most exciting aspects of a computer-based recording. Instead of having to spend $2,000 on a hardware synthesizer with limited sounds, you can buy a hard drive full of soft-synths and end up with a huge variety of sounds at your disposal for about the same amount of money.

I offer a short list of free, downloadable soft-synths in Chapter 21 to get you started. The following list includes my favorite for-purchase options.

✔ **Atmosphere, by Spectrasonics:** If you want ambient synthesizer pads — background sounds that create a soundscape — these are the best I've found. You can find them at `www.spectrasonics.net/instruments/atmosphere.html`.

✔ **MachFive, by MOTU:** MachFive is one of the best software samplers around. A soft-sampler lets you use pre-recorded audio sample libraries or use your own. You can find out more at `www.motu.com/products/software/machfive/body.html/en`.

✔ **ReBirth, by Propellerhead:** ReBirth is a soft-synth of old analog hardware devices that are used in electronic music, including the TB-303, TR-808, and TR-909 synthesizers. ReBirth is great for classic bass synth lines and drum parts. You can find out more at `www.propellerheads.se`.

✔ **Absynth, by Native Instruments:** Absynth is a fun and immensely powerful soft-synth. Absynth helps you to create some innovative sounds. Check out `www.nativeinstruments.de/index.php?absynth3_us` for more information.

Chapter 14

Mixing and Mastering Your Music

· ·

In This Chapter

▶ Understanding the mixing process

▶ Setting up a mix using automation

▶ Mixing your music

▶ Mastering your finished song

· ·

*T*he mixing and mastering stages are where all your tracks are finally turned into an honest-to-goodness song. This process involves blending (mixing) all your individual musical ideas into the song that you hear in your head and then mastering that final mix — the last stage in the recording process — so that your song is transformed into something worth sharing with the world. These parts of music-making aren't rocket science (what is, though, except maybe rocket science), but both processes do have a set of objectives and common steps that you can follow.

In this chapter, I walk you through the basics of mixing your tracks. More importantly, I show you how you can do it all by using the automation features found in computer-based recording systems. I also give a step-by-step guide through the *bounce procedure* — the actual process of taking all your tracks and turning them into a single stereo file. Finally, this chapter takes you into the often-misunderstood world of audio mastering. Here, I first show you what mastering is supposed to do to your music, and then I lay out the steps to do it in your audio recording program.

Mixing and mastering are art forms. As such, no one way to do them exists; you probably need to take some time to get a feel for each process. Don't be afraid to make mistakes. One of the benefits of computer-based recording is that, as you strive for just the right mix, you can make as many mixes of your music as your hard drive space allows and not degrade the music's sound. (This isn't the case with tape-based recording, where you can hear the sound degrade as you make your way one more time — and then one more time — through the tape.)

Understanding Mixing

The goal of mixing is to make sure each instrument can be heard in the *mix* — the recorded whole that results from blending all your recorded parts together — without covering up something else or sounding out of place. You can pull this off in several ways:

- ✔ **Think about the emotion of the song.** Choose the recorded parts that add to the emotional impact of the music and build intensity throughout the song. By necessity, this also means choosing *not* to use parts that are unnecessary, or which clash with parts that have a greater impact. This involves muting the track, dropping its level, or editing out the parts you don't like. I cover editing in Chapter 10.

- ✔ **Create volume balance.** Set the *level* (volume) of each instrument relative to the others so that nothing is buried so far back in the mix that you can't hear it — and no instrument is so loud that it overpowers the other instruments. Be aware that your levels often change throughout the song, so settings that you've made for the ending of the first verse might not be appropriate for the fourth chorus. You can, however, set up your audio recording program so that it automatically deals with such variations. I discuss this process later in this chapter.

  Another way to affect the levels of your tracks is to use dynamics processing to even out inconsistent performances. Essentially, dynamics processing lets you control the difference between the loudest and quietest parts of your recording so that you end up with a more interesting or even performance. I talk about dynamics processing in Chapter 18.

- ✔ **Create tonal clarity.** Adjust the *equalization* (also called *EQ* or *frequency response*) of each instrument so that each one leaves room for the other instruments in the mix. This means getting rid of any frequencies of an instrument that clash with those of another, or emphasizing certain frequencies that define the sound of an instrument so it can be heard clearly in the mix. I cover equalization in detail in Chapter 16.

- ✔ **Put instruments in their places.** Take advantage of stereo *panning* (movement from left to right) to put each instrument in its proper place in the stereo field — toward the left or right — where it can either sound as natural as possible or produce a desired effect. Also, stereo panning allows you to make room for each instrument in the mix, especially those with similar frequency ranges.

- ✔ **Use effects effectively.** Add effects (such as reverb or delay) and dynamics processors (such as compression) to the instruments in the mix to either place them "in front" or "in back" relative to other instruments or to create a desired sound. Chapter 17 covers effects in detail, and you discover dynamics processors in Chapter 18.

The mixing process is where you can get really creative in crafting your song. The stress of capturing great performances is over — all that's left for you to do is to massage all the parts of your song into a cohesive whole. Don't be afraid to try new things. Experiment with different EQ, panning, and effect settings. Take your time and have fun. The great thing about mixing is that you can make as many versions as you want — and you can always go back and try again.

Mixing with Automation

One of the great assets of computer-based recording is the ability to make a mix that you can then perform without any mistakes and repeat as many times as you want. This involves using the automation features included in your audio-recording program. All audio recording programs have some sort of automation, so the basics I outline in this section apply to all programs even though the specific steps and vocabulary used by each program may be slightly different.

Unless you have an external controller such as a digital mixer or MIDI-based DAW controller (like the Mackie Control or the Digi 002 control surface) you have no choice but to use some automation when you mix more than a couple tracks within your computer. This is because your mouse can control only one thing at a time. So if you want to fade out your guitar lead while you bring in the backup vocals, you need to program these changes into your computer.

Knowing what you can automate

Most audio recording programs let you automate quite a few parts of your mix. For example, when working with audio tracks in Pro Tools you can automate the following:

- **Volume:** This parameter controls the overall volume of the track.
- **Pan:** This lets you set the left/right balance of the track in the stereo field. This allows you to place your instrument where you want on the virtual soundstage, giving your music a sense of spaciousness or dimension.
- **Mute:** This allows you to turn the track on and off.
- **Send:** This includes volume, mute, and panning settings for the *send* — the routing section that lets you send part of your track's signal to an effect. Chapter 18 has more about Sends and effects.
- **Plug-in parameters:** You adjust these parameters within the Plug-In window. Chapter 15 has all the details about plug-ins.

Automation data for each of these parameters resides in a playlist that's separate from the regions that contain your edits for that track. This allows you to move the regions in and out of the track's playlist without changing the automation data for that track.

MIDI tracks are equally amenable to automation. Pro Tools, for example, lets you automate the following parameters:

- ✔ **Volume:** This parameter sets the overall volume of the MIDI data.

- ✔ **Pan:** You can place your tracks anywhere from left to right in the stereo field to give your music a sense of dimension.

- ✔ **Mute:** This allows you to turn the track on and off.

- ✔ **Controller data:** This includes a number of MIDI settings, including options such as the modulation wheel, breath controller, and sustain.

Pro Tools stores the automation data for MIDI tracks — with the exception of Mute settings — within the MIDI region for that track. So when you move a region within a track's playlist, the automation data (except for any mute settings) moves along with the region.

Getting to know automation modes

Most audio recording programs offer several different automation modes. These allow you to record, play back, and change your automation data so that you get the "performance" that you want from each track. Here's a look at some of the typical automation modes you'll find in most audio recording software:

- ✔ **Auto Off mode** turns off all automation data for the selected track.

- ✔ **Auto Read mode** plays back the automation data for the selected track.

- ✔ **Auto Write mode** writes automation data for the selected parameter(s) while the session plays — overwriting any pre-existing automation data in the process. When you stop playback after writing automation in this mode, most programs (such as Pro Tools) automatically switch the automation mode to Auto Touch (see next bullet) so you don't accidentally erase this data next time you play back the session.

- ✔ **Auto Touch mode** writes automation data only when you click a parameter with your mouse; it stops writing when you release the mouse button.

At this point, your automated parameter returns to any previously auto-mated position. By using Auto Touch, you can fix parts of your previously recorded automation data without erasing the stuff you want to keep.

✔ **Auto Latch mode** works much like Auto Touch mode (see previous bullet) — when you touch or move a parameter, new automation data is written. The difference is that Auto Latch mode continues to write new automation data *until you stop playback*.

Recording your automation data

Recording your automation moves is a simple process and is the same regard-less of the parameter you want to automate. This process involves selecting the parameter you want to automate, choosing the proper automation mode to record your data, and letting the song play as you record your automation data. These steps are outlined in this section.

When I work on my mixes, I always start setting up some basic level and panning settings. After I have a rough mix with these settings, I move on to adjusting EQ and then adding effects and dynamics processing. After *these* settings are recorded, I go back to the level and panning settings and adjust them some more. Next it's back to the EQ, effects, and dynamics processing. This circular process continues until I have everything just the way I want it.

Enabling automation

The first steps in recording your automation moves is choosing the automa-tion you want and enabling it for the track you want to record. This process is simple. For example, here's how you enable automation in Logic:

1. **Make sure the Arrange window is open. (If it isn't open, choose Windows➪Open Arrange to open it.)**

2. **Click and hold over the automation mode selector in the track and drag your cursor to the mode that you want, as shown in Figure 14-1.**

   For a reminder of the different automation modes and how they work, check out the "Getting to know automation modes" section, earlier in this chapter.

3. **Release the mouse button to make your selection.**

   The automation mode that you selected is listed in your track's display.

Recording your mix performance

Most audio recording programs offer you several ways to record and edit your automation moves. These often include the following:

- **Mousing:** Mousing involves using your mouse to adjust your chosen parameter (fader level, pan, send level, and so on) as your song plays. This method has the disadvantage of allowing you to make only a single automation move at a time.

- **Drawing:** This approach is where you "draw" the automation data right in your track. As you can see in Figure 14-2, this process is as simple as drawing with the appropriate tool in the track you want to automate. (In Pro Tools, for example, you use the Pencil tool.) For this to work, you need to have the parameter you want to automate displayed in the track. (In Pro Tools, click and hold the Track Display menu and drag to your selection to have that selection displayed in your track.)

  As was the case with mousing, you can adjust only one parameter at a time. This isn't that much of a drawback, however, because it's more than likely that you'll want to do your automation drawing while your song isn't playing. Here, you most likely want to draw in order to edit existing automation data. (You do this by drawing over the existing data in your track.)

- **Controlling:** If you have an external controller, such as the Logic Control for Logic, you can use it to write your automation data. With a controller that's well-integrated with your software, you can write a large variety of parameters by using the controller, and you can write as many at the same time as your hands and fingers (and brain) allow. This can significantly speed up the mixing process, especially if you have a lot of tracks to mix.

I tend to write my automation in stages. I start with volume and panning for all tracks, then move on to the extras such as plug-in parameters and send levels. As you work, don't worry about how your automation looks on the screen. Use your ears instead. This seems like a logical thing, but I have to tell ya, with all the fancy graphics on-screen you might end up having to put a towel over your computer's monitor while you work (that is, if you use a controller or your mouse — it's kind of hard to draw automation when you can't see it).

Figure 14-2:
Drawing automation is as simple as drawing with your mouse along a track.

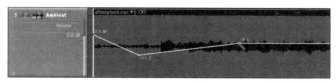

Making Your Mix

You have a couple options when you actually create your mix with a computer-based recording system: You can mix in-the-box (within the computer) or you can mix to an external recorder. Mixing in-the-box involves performing a bounce procedure. This is a simple process regardless of the audio recording software that you use. Mixing to an external recorder is also relatively straightforward, but it does require that you have some sort of external recording device — a tape deck, for example, or a digital recorder such as an Alesis Masterlink. This section lays out the process for making your mix either way.

Mixing in-the-box

Mixing in-the-box refers to using the Bounce feature in your audio recording program to create your final mix. (*Bounce* is the term Logic and many other audio recording programs use, but you'll find that Pro Tools refers to it as "Bounce to Disk.") The Bounce feature processes your audio tracks into one stereo track. Essentially, this means that your computer creates a new file with the settings you choose in the Bounce dialog box. This gives you a stereo file that you can then master or burn onto a CD.

When you use the Bounce feature in your recording program, all the mixing and routing instructions that you designate by using the steps I describe earlier in the chapter are followed to create your final mix. This includes any EQ or effects that you have plugged in and turned on in your tracks, any fader levels (volume) you have for each track, and all automation settings you assigned to your tracks (and have turned on).

Examining bounce options

Although each program is a little different, the process of making a bounce is fairly similar and involves choosing settings such as the bounce source, file type, format, bit depth, and sample rate. For example, when you select the bounce procedure in Pro Tools (choose File⇨Bounce), a dialog box opens so that you can make these selections. (Check out Figure 14-3.) Here's a look at the Pro Tools options you have to choose from:

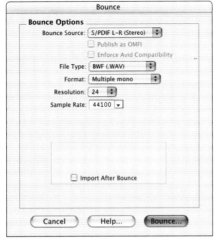

Figure 14-3:
The Bounce dialog box lets you select several bounce options.

✔ **Source:** You can use the Bounce Source drop-down list to select any output or bus path as your source for the bounce. (Figure 14-4 gives you a peek at some of the choices.)

✔ **File Type:** This drop-down list sets the file type for the bounced file. You have many choices, but for your final mix the following common file types are the ones to choose from:

• **BWF (WAV):** This file type is the standard for older, PC-based Pro Tools systems — and it's currently the most commonly used file type. (One reason: BWF files are compatible with both Macs and PCs.) This is the type I generally choose because it increases that chances that my files are compatible with other systems.

• **AIFF:** This stands for Audio Interchange File Format and used to be native to Macs. AIFF files can be imported into any Pro Tools session without any prior converting — including sessions on a PC — but because BWF is becoming the standard I skip this type. If you use a Mac and you plan to do your mastering on your Mac with Pro Tools, this file type is a fine choice.

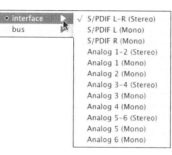

Figure 14-4:
The Bounce
Source
drop-down
list shows
you your
choices.

You get the same sound quality in BWF and AIFF files. Choose based on your computer platform and whether you intend to send your music out to a mastering house or do it yourself.

If you intend to have your music professionally mastered, make sure that you contact the folks at the mastering studio ahead of time to see what file type they prefer.

✔ **Format:** This drop-down list determines whether your bounced file is in Mono, Multiple Mono, or Stereo Interleaved. These formats do have some differences that are good to know:

• **Mono (Summed):** Selecting this option creates a single audio file that contains all the material without any panning information.

Because any stereo information is summed when using this option, it's easy to get too high of a combined signal. This might result in clipping (distortion) depending on your software and your overall summed levels. If you want to record with this format, I recommend that you reduce your levels so that the left and right channels peak at no more than –3dB, although –6dB is better. This reduces the chances of creating distortion. You can make this level up during the mastering stage if you feel your mix isn't loud enough.

• **Multiple Mono:** This format puts the left and right channels of your stereo mix in separate files, labeling the files with (respectively) the .L and .R filename extensions.

Multiple mono is the file format supported by most audio recording programs — which makes it the one to use if you intend to master your music yourself in a different program from the one you recorded it in. If you plan to use a professional mastering engineer, call him or her to see what file format works with the mastering equipment. (It will either be multiple mono or stereo interleaved.)

• **Stereo Interleaved:** This format contains all stereo information in a single stereo file. Panning information is retained. Any tracks set to even-numbered outputs end up on the right side of the stereo file;

tracks set to odd-numbered outputs go to the left side of the stereo field. This is the file format to use when you make your final master to 16 bit because stereo interleaved files are required to burn a CD.

✔ **Resolution:** This setting lets you choose one of three bit rates for your bounced files: 8, 16, or 24. (Chapter 4 has more on resolution.) For your final mix, choose 24 bit (maximum resolution). You can reduce the resolution as needed later on when you master your music yourself or when you have a professional do it for you.

✔ **Sample Rate:** You can save your file with any of several sample rates, but I recommend saving it with the same rate as the files in your session. Check out Chapter 4 for all the details about sample rates.

If you intend to have your music mastered by a professional, make sure to ask her what she prefers. Some mastering engineers want the files at the highest sample rate possible, but others would rather you not change the rate.

✔ **Conversion Quality:** If you select a sample rate different from the files in your session — which I don't recommend — you're prompted to choose a level of quality for the conversion. Choose the highest quality possible for your mix material, but keep in mind that the higher the quality you choose, the longer it takes to do the conversion process.

Performing the bounce

To use the Bounce feature in any program, first make sure that all your tracks are the way you want them. Check all routing, automation, effects, and EQ settings to make sure they're right.

When it comes to actual bouncing in Pro Tools, do the following:

1. **Choose File⇨Bounce to Disk.**

   The Bounce dialog box appears. (Refer to Figure 14-3.)

2. **Set your Bounce options to the settings you want.**

   Check out the "Examining bounce options" section earlier in this chapter for the scoop on these options.

3. **Click the Bounce button.**

   The Save Bounce As dialog box opens.

4. **In the dialog box, select a destination point for this file, enter the name of this mix, and then click Save.**

   The session plays while the bounce happens.

When bouncing in Logic, follow these steps:

1. **Click the Bounce button in the lower-right corner of the channel strip of the output that you want to bounce.**

   The Bounce dialog box appears, as shown in Figure 14-5.

2. **Make your selections for the bounce settings you want.**

   For a general introduction to possible bounce settings, check out the "Examining bounce options" section earlier in this chapter.

3. **Click the Bounce button.**

   The Save Bounce As dialog box opens.

4. **Using the dialog box, select a name and destination point for this file and then click Save.**

   You have a choice of having the session play while the bounce happens (online) or skipping the whole playing business (offline). If you choose offline bouncing, your bounce will take less time than if you choose online, but you obviously won't hear your song as it bounces.

Bounce "Output 9–10"

Start Position	End Position
1 1 1 1	560 1 1 1

Requires 325,6 MB of free disk space (Time 21:17)

File Format:	AIFF
Resolution:	24 Bit
Stereo File Type:	Interleaved
Surround Bounce:	Off
Dithering:	None
Bounce Mode:	Offline

Cancel   Bounce & Add   Bounce

Figure 14-5: The Bounce dialog box in Logic is where you select your bounce settings.

Mixing to an external recorder

You can mix to an external device instead of mixing solely within your computer. This section explains how to mix to both analog and digital recorders.

Before you make your mix, you need to have all your mix settings created in your song. Even though you're mixing to an external device you can still automate your mix in the same way you would for mixing in-the-box. The "Mixing with Automation" section earlier in this chapter explains the process.

You can mix to an external digital device such as a DAT (Digital Audio Tape) deck — or, for you classic technology fans, to an analog device such as a reel-to-reel tape recorder — by following these steps:

1. **Connect your device to your audio interface.**

   For digital recorders, run a cable from the digital outputs of the interface to the digital inputs of your device. You need to use an optical or coaxial connection, depending on the interface.

   For analog recorders, run cables from two of the analog outputs of the interface to the inputs of your device.

2. **If you want to be able to monitor this device as it records, connect the device's outputs to your monitor speakers or plug your headphones into the headphone jack (if your device has one).**

3. **Using the Output selectors, set the outputs of your tracks, auxiliary inputs, and master fader to the physical outputs of your interface.**

   These must correspond to the outputs you connected your device to.

4. **Enable recording in your external device.**

   This usually involves clicking the Record Enable button for the track that you want to record to and then clicking the Record button.

5. **Click the Play button in the Transport window of your song.**

6. **Adjust your input levels on your external device.**

   The level you set depends on your type of device. For example, if you use an analog tape deck, you can get away with a level that runs into the red if you want to fully saturate the tape. For a digital device, keep your levels from hitting digital zero (0dB); otherwise you'll end up with digital distortion. I usually set my mix level so that it peaks at between –6dB and –3dB when I mix to an external digital recorder. You can make up the volume a little when you master your song. The following section, "Mastering Your Music," details this process.

7. **Rewind the session.**

8. **Start recording on the external device and immediately press the spacebar or click the Play button in the Transport window.**

   The session plays, and you record it into your external device.

9. **Click the Stop button in the Transport window or press the spacebar when the music is done.**

   You now have a mix recorded into your external device.

Mastering Your Music

The final step in recording your music is to master it. Mastering involves taking your stereo mix and tweaking it so that it sounds the best it can. Mastering isn't a mysterious process — it's pretty simple, really. But it does require certain skills. That's where this section comes in.

The mastering steps I present in this chapter use the Bounce feature in your audio recording program. You don't necessarily have to go this route. If you want, you can also send your mastered tracks out to a digital device by following the steps in this section — and *then* use the steps that describe mixing to an external digital device (found earlier in this chapter).

Demystifying mastering

The *mastering* process of recording involves preparing your music for duplication. Five basic steps are involved in this process:

1. **Optimize the dynamics.**

   This doesn't mean making your music as loud as possible. Instead, this step in the mastering process consists of finding the best volume and dynamic range for your music. This is the most critical part of the mastering process and the one that is abused the most.

2. **Perfect the tonal balance.**

   Because your songs were probably recorded and mixed over a long period of time, they're unlikely to have the same tonal characteristics. This is a good thing, but for a group of songs to be an effective CD, you want the tones of your songs to be similar enough that your listener doesn't have to make adjustments to his stereo's EQ as he listens. This step involves using parametric EQs to get all your tunes to sound good together.

3. **Match the volume of your songs.**

   Having consistent levels from song to song helps with the cohesiveness and flow of a CD and keeps your listener from having to adjust her player's volume from song to song. You do this with simple gain adjustments, compressors, and/or limiters — and by making those processes consistent, audio recording programs give us mere mortals a crack at doing it right.

4. **Select the order of your songs.**

   This is called sequencing and involves putting your songs in the order that you want on your duplicated CD and setting the blank space between each song so that the CD flows well from one song to another. Because a CD is supposed to represent a cohesive body of work, this is one of the most important aspects of mastering.

5. **Put it on CD.**

This is the process of burning an audio CD so that you can listen to your song in any stereo or create multiple copies to give away or sell.

Following these steps isn't a linear process. Most of the time you need to go back and forth between a few steps — optimizing the dynamics, matching the volume, and perfecting the tonal balance — before you get everything the way you want it. Take your time in the mastering process and take a second listen after you think you have it right to make sure it's the best you can do. I recommend taking a first crack at the mastering and then re-evaluating it again after a few days have passed.

If you have to do a lot to master your song to make it work, you might want to consider going back to the mixing stage and tweaking it instead. You should have to make only minor adjustments during mastering — if you do more than that, your time is best served remixing your music first. Every adjustment you make during mastering is a compromise. Adding a bit of high-end (frequencies above 10 kHz) to your vocal adds high-end to everything and what might be just enough to make the vocals sound right might make the bass guitar too twangy (a highly technical term). In this case, go back to your mix and add the high-end to only your vocal track before you master the whole song.

Setting up a mastering session

The first step in mastering your music in your computer is to set up a mastering session. This involves creating a new song in your audio recording program and importing the mixed tracks from each song you want on your CD. This section details that process.

In Pro Tools, you start by creating a new session for mastering:

1. **Choose File⊏▷New Session.**

The New Session dialog box appears.

2. **Type in the name of the file in the Save As text box.**

I usually call the file mastering and include the name of the CD project that I'm working on.

3. **Using the File browser, navigate to the location where you want to place the new session, and then select the location.**

   I usually create a new folder called Mastered Mixes so I can easily find the files later when I burn them to CD.

4. **Select the session parameters that match the mixed files for your songs.**

   You set audio file type, sample rate, I/O settings, and bit depth here. Chapter 10 has more on the basics of setting up a new session.

5. **Click Save.**

   Your new session opens.

Okay, at this point you have a general "same place" to put the songs. Next, create tracks to import the mixed song files into:

1. **Choose File⇨New Track.**

   The New Track dialog box appears.

2. **In the Create text box, enter a number corresponding to the number of songs you want on your CD.**

3. **Choose Stereo and Audio Track from the drop-down lists.**

4. **Click the Create button.**

   Your session now has the necessary tracks for importing your audio.

With tracks created, you can now import your mixed tracks into this session:

1. **Click and hold the Audio title in the Audio Regions list located on the right side of the Edit window.**

   If the Audio Regions list isn't visible, click the double arrow at the bottom-right corner of the Edit window.

2. **Choose Import Audio from the menu that appears or press Shift+⌘+I (on a Mac) or Shift+Ctrl+I (on a PC).**

   The Import Audio dialog box opens.

3. **Using the Look In text box, navigate through your folder structure to find and select the song file you want to import.**

4. **Click Done.**

   The file appears as a region in the Audio Regions list.

5. **Repeat Steps 1 through 4 for each song you want to master in this session.**

Using a mastering pro

Mastering your music is no mystery, but often the fresh perspective and top-notch gear that a professional mastering engineer has can take your final product from good to truly stellar. If you want to hire a pro to master your music, here are some suggestions that can help the process along:

✔ **Ask around for referrals.** If you know local bands or musicians whose music you like and whose CDs sound great, ask them who mastered their music. Call local studios and find out whom they recommend for mastering in your area. Also check out resources on the Internet. Two great Internet forums are www.musicplayer.com/cgi-bin/ultimatebb.cgi and http://recforums.prosoundweb.com. In a forum, do a search for the term *mastering* or post a new topic and ask your question. Try to get referrals from people who work with your type of music.

✔ **Listen to other recordings that the mastering house has done in a style of music similar to yours.** If you're entrusting your artistic vision to someone else, make sure that this person is the right person for the job. If you like what the prospective mastering engineer has done on other people's music, you'll probably like what he or she does with yours. If this person has never worked with music similar to yours — or has mastered someone else's music but you don't like the way it came out — you'd probably better keep looking.

✔ **Clarify the fee for your project before you actually start working together.** Most mastering engineers charge by the hour and can give you a pretty good estimate of how many hours they'll need to do the job. You'll also be expected to pay for materials (reference CDs, for example).

Tip: Many mastering engineers will do a demo for you, tooling up one or two songs so you can hear what kind of job they can do for your music before you hire them. Ask whether the mastering engineer you're interested in offers this service. This simple step can save both you and the engineer a lot of time and energy if he or she isn't right for the job. It can also help you determine whether your mixed music is ready for mastering — if you need to go back and make adjustments, now's the time to find out.

After you choose the mastering engineer that you think will work well for you and your music, you can make the process much easier and less stressful (for both you and the engineer) if you follow a few guidelines:

✔ **Discuss your expectations and desires.** This is the best way to ensure that your mastered music turns out the way you want. People who are unhappy with the job that the mastering engineer does usually aren't clear about what they want or don't understand what is possible in the mastering process.

✔ **Take a few CDs whose sound you like with you to the mastering session.** Talk with the engineer about how you can get your music to sound similar. A skilled engineer can let you know right away whether the sound you want is possible.

✔ **Try to be present at the mastering session.** Many people send their music to a mastering engineer and expect him or her to do the job without their presence in the studio. Try to go to the studio, but if you can't, be sure that the engineer clearly understands your desires and expectations.

Finally, place your audio regions into the tracks in the session:

1. **Click and drag the region from the Audio Regions list into the playlist of the track you want the song in.**

2. **Repeat Step 1 for each of your songs.**

   You end up with only one song in each of the available tracks.

You now have a session that contains all the songs for your project. Having them all in one session allows you to switch from one song to the next as you master your tunes and makes it easy to check loudness levels and EQ balancing as you work. (See the "Perfecting tonal balance" and "Balancing levels" sections later in this chapter.)

Optimizing dynamics

Okay, this is where the magic in mastering happens. This is where you can make your music shine or where you can royally mess it up. (How's that for adding a little pressure?) Before you get tense (okay, breathe), remember that you can always go back and try again. Oh, did I mention that you should make backup copies of your individual tracks and your final mix? Well, if you haven't already done the backing up business, now would be a good time to do that. I'll wait.

You done? Okay, now to the job at hand — getting your music to be as loud as possible. (I'm just kidding; see the sidebar "Turn it up!" to see why.) Seriously, optimizing the dynamics of your songs doesn't mean getting it loud enough to level a city block, but rather getting it to have life and emotion. And, yes, this *also* means getting it to be loud *enough* to sound good.

The style of your music and the arrangements that you use determine how you optimize the dynamics of your music. For example, classical music has a much broader dynamic range than rock music, and the infamous "wall of sound" type of arrangement (producer Phil Spector's approach to mixing) has a narrower dynamic range than a song with sparse verses and thicker choruses.

When you're optimizing the dynamics of your music, be sensitive to the song and try not to get sucked into the idea that you need to get the most volume out of your music. I know I'm beating this volume thing into the ground, but you'd be surprised how seductive the lure of Big Volume can be. ("C'mon, let's get just a *few* more decibels out of the song . . ." Trust me, you'll soon find out.)

You have two main types of tools to use when you work on the dynamics during mastering in your computer — compressor plug-ins and limiter plug-ins — and each has its purpose. For the most part, if you're trying to add punch or smoothness to your music, a compressor plug-in does the job nicely. On the other hand, if you're trying to squeeze a *little* more volume out of a song and you don't want to change the song's sound quality, a limiter plug-in is your best choice.

Here are suggestions that might help you to use compression and limiting most effectively during mastering:

- ✓ **Use a low ratio.** A compression ratio between 1.1:1 and 2:1 keeps you from over-compressing your music. Too high of a ratio increases the chances that you'll end up with artifacts that will mess with the sound of your pristine music.

- ✓ **Go easy.** Apply only 1 or 2dB of compression or limiting at one time. If you need more than that, chain more than one compressor together by inserting more than one compressor plug-in in your track and use these small amounts on each. If you compress or limit more than 1 or 2dB at a time, you end up with *artifacts* (audible changes to your music caused by the compressor or limiter).

- ✓ **Spend time tweaking.** Work with your attack and release times. An attack that's too short takes the punch out of your music by cutting off the initial transients. Likewise, a release time that's too long doesn't recover quickly enough, and the dynamics of the vocal disappear. In contrast, if the release time is too short, you hear distortion.

- ✓ **Make your meters dance.** Set the threshold so your compressor's meters dance (bounce) to the rhythm of the music. The meter you want to watch in your compressor plug-in is the one labeled "reduction" located below the input and output meters. Only the loudest notes (snare drum or lead vocal accents, for example) should trigger the meters — and then only by 1 or 2dB.

- ✓ **Split the frequency spectrum.** Use a multiband compressor to apply different amounts of compression to specific frequency ranges to bring out individual instruments in the mix. For example, if the bass drum seems to be getting lost, you can apply mild compression to the lower frequencies (around 80 to 100 Hz). This brings the instrument forward in the mix slightly.

  Some audio recording programs, such as Pro Tools LE, come with a multiband compressor plug-in. If you want to use one on your music and your audio recording program doesn't come with such a plug-in, you'll need to go the third-party route. A quick search on the Internet for "multiband compressor plug-in" should give you some options.

- ✓ **Lay off.** When you're not sure whether what you're doing actually sounds better, don't use the processor. Any dynamics processing is going to affect the quality of your song's sound to some extent. If adding this processing doesn't improve the overall sound, you're better off not using it.

You can find out more about compression and limiting in Chapter 18.

Turn it up!

Everyone wants his or her music to be as loud as possible. Louder sounds better. In fact, test after test has shown that when people listen to two versions of a song, they nearly always prefer the louder one (whether or not it actually sounds better).

Musicians, producers, and engineers seem to be in the middle of a competition to see who can make the loudest CD. If you compare a CD made about ten years ago with one made this year, you'll notice that the newer one is much louder. Give them both a good listen, though. Does the louder one *really* sound better?

You can test this by setting them both to play at the same volume and switching back and forth. (You need to turn the volume up a bit on the older CD to match the volume of the newer one.)

One way to do this is to record both songs into your audio recording program and set the levels of each so that they're the same. At the same volume, which song sounds better to you? I'm willing to bet that, nine out of ten times, you'll prefer the older song. This is because older recordings have more dynamic range than newer ones. The variety is pleasing to listen to, whereas the song with only a small dynamic range quickly becomes tiring.

Do yourself and your listeners a favor and resist the temptation to compress the dynamic variability out of your music. It will be much easier to listen to and have a lot more life and excitement. You can always turn the volume up on your stereo if it's not loud enough, but you can't add dynamic range after you've squashed it out.

When you're testing your compressor plug-in or limiter plug-in settings (you do this by comparing the processed and unprocessed versions), be sure to have the volume of both versions exactly the same. Any difference in volume defeats the purpose of a side-by-side comparison because you're going to think that the louder one sounds better even if it doesn't. (See the "Turn it up!" sidebar.)

Perfecting tonal balance

The *tonal balance* of a song is how the various frequencies of the music relate to one another. You're not concerned with how each individual instrument sounds in the mix (that's the job for the mixing stage); instead, what you're looking for is an overall balance of frequencies within the hearing spectrum.

For the most part, a tonal balance consists of an even distribution of frequencies from 20 to 10 kHz with a slight drop-off (1 or 2dB) from 10 to 20 kHz or higher. "That's great," you say, "but what does that sound like?" Well, listen to any number of great CDs, and you'll hear it.

When you master your music, you want to constantly compare what your song sounds like to other CDs whose sound you like. Do this by switching between your song and someone else's while you work. The easiest way to do this is to import the song you want to compare your music to into your audio recording program along with your songs.

When you work on adjusting the overall tonal balance of your songs, listen carefully for any frequencies that seem too loud or too soft. You can find these by listening to particular instruments in the mix or by using the parametric EQ plug-in and sweeping the frequency spectrum. To do this, set your Q fairly wide (0.6, for instance) and move the Gain slider all the way to the right. Start with the lowest frequency and slowly raise the frequency as the song plays by moving the Freq slider from left to right. Adjust any annoying frequencies by cutting them by a couple decibels to see whether your overall mix improves.

As far as general EQ guidelines go, try these suggestions:

✔ If your mix sounds muddy, add high frequencies (above 10 kHz) or cut low ones (200 to 400 Hz). Likewise, if your mix is too bright (common with digital recording), try reducing the frequencies above 10 kHz by using a shelf EQ or a Baxandall curve.

(To use a *Baxandall curve,* use a parametric EQ and set the threshold at 20 kHz with a Q setting around 1. This gradually cuts frequencies above around 10 kHz. You can adjust the Q to reach as far down as you want. Your EQ graph shows you what's happening.)

✔ Use the same EQ adjustments for both the right and left channels because this keeps the stereo balance intact and doesn't alter the relative phase between the channels. For example, if you add some bass frequencies (100 Hz, for example) to the one channel and not the other, you might hear a wavering or pulsating sound around this frequency go back and forth between the speakers.

✔ If you used a multiband compressor on any specific frequencies, you might need to adjust the EQ for those frequencies; compression tends to mess with frequency response.

✔ If you need to adjust the EQ of certain instruments in the mix (the snare drum is buried, for example), be careful and notice the overall effect of your adjustments on the rest of the mix. If your adjustments aren't fixing the problem, go back to the mixing process and make your adjustments there. You'll be glad you took the time to do that.

Any adjustments you make to the EQ during mastering impact more than just those frequencies. Such adjustments alter the entire frequency spectrum — and the relationship between all the instruments. So listen carefully as you make adjustments and back off on the additional EQ if you don't like what you hear.

For more specific information on EQ and inserting EQ in your tracks, go to Chapter 16.

Some people employ some pretty sophisticated technology to check the tonal balance of their songs against that of their favorite CDs. They do this by recording a song into their mastering program and taking a look at its frequency response by using a spectral analyzer. Not all audio recording programs come with a spectral analyzer. For example, Logic comes with one in their Channel EQ plug-in but Pro Tools doesn't — you need to find a third-party plug-in in this case. (Chapter 15 has more about finding third-party plug-ins.) Then do an analysis of your song and compare it to the spectral analysis of a CD you like. This technique seems to work for many people. (Not me — I like using my ears instead — but alas, I'm old-fashioned.)

Balancing levels

For a truly professional-sounding CD, you want all your songs to be at nearly the same relative level so your listeners (I *hope* you have more than one) don't have to adjust the volume on their stereos from song to song.

Balancing the levels of your songs to one another is pretty easy. In fact, in most cases, you have very little to do after you EQ and optimize the dynamics of each song. You balance the levels from one song to the next in your audio recording program by putting each track's fader up to 0dB — this puts them at the level you mixed them to — and then *soloing* (silencing all other tracks in your song) Track 1 and comparing the level to Track 2 by soloing back and forth.

If you use a mouse to mix, this can be kinda tricky because you can't press more than one button at a time. The best way I've found to deal with this situation — at least the best way in Pro Tools — is to follow these steps:

1. **In the Track Controls section of Track 1, click the Solo button to solo the track.**

   You hear only Track 1 in your monitors.

2. **In the Track Controls section of Track 1, click the Mute button so both the Solo and Mute buttons for Track 1 are engaged.**

   Track 1 is silent.

3. **In the Track Controls section of Track 2, quickly click the Solo button.**

   You now hear Track 2.

4. **To switch back to hearing Track 1, click Track 2's Solo button (disengage it) and — as quickly as possible — click Track 1's Mute button (disengaging the Mute button and engaging the Solo button).**

   You hear Track 1 again.

You get a short bit of silence when following this procedure, but you can still hear the relative volumes of the two.

Do this procedure for each of the tracks (Track 1 to Track 2, Track 2 to Track 3, and so on) until you've checked all the tracks in your mastering session.

If you miss one of the buttons while you're doing this quick-switch procedure, you might end up with both tracks playing at the same time. This will be very loud because the tracks are summed together in the mix bus. To avoid damaging your speakers — and ears — keep your monitoring (speaker) volume down pretty low.

If you notice any differences, just raise (or better yet, *lower*) the levels until they are all roughly the same. Don't get too finicky. Some variation from song to song is okay. In fact, minor differences can help to make your CD more interesting to listen to. When you're balancing levels, just make sure that any differences aren't enough to make the listener run to his or her stereo to adjust the volume knob. If one or two songs seem much lower in volume than the rest, you might want to go back to the volume-optimizing stage and raise those songs up a bit to make them more consistent with the rest of the songs on the CD. That way you don't lower the volume *of the entire CD* because one or two songs are too quiet.

Mastering your mix

When you have all your songs dynamically optimized, EQed, and level-balanced (see the preceding sections) you're ready to record your final master. This process is essentially the same as making your final mix, so check out the "Making Your Mix" section earlier in this chapter for details on how to do this. You need to do one more thing when mastering, however — this involves getting your songs to the CD format.

Most likely, your session's songs are recorded at 24 bits, using any number of possible sample rates (44.1, 48, 88.2, or 96 kHz) — and your final master should be 16 bit at 44.1 kHz. Making this change can reduce the sound quality of your music if it's not done right. This section details how to change the sample rate and bit depth as you create a final master version of your music.

Making the most of your bits

Getting your music from 24 bit to 16 bit means *dithering* or *truncating* your files. This section explains how these processes differ, and gives you pointers on which one to use so your music sounds as good as possible.

Dithering is the process of adding random noise to your music when 8 bits get cut from your pristine 24-bit files. This random noise helps keep the quiet sections of your song (fade-outs, for instance) from sounding grainy when those 8 bits are removed. Several types of dithering exist — each produces a slightly different result in a piece of music.

The process of dithering is done differently in each audio recording program. For example, in Logic you can choose the Dither option within the Bounce dialog box when you make your bounce. Pro Tools, on the other hand, requires that you use a dithering plug-in and insert it into the master fader for your song. You do this by inserting one of the two dithering plug-ins into one of the inserts in your master fader, and then following the steps for mixing your music (which I detail in the "Making Your Mix" section earlier in this chapter). The dithering happens automatically as your song is mixed (or, in this case, mastered).

Truncation involves simply cutting off the last 8 bits of information. This option works well for material that doesn't have quiet sections (for example, hard rock with punchy endings that don't fade out).

To master your music using truncation in Pro Tools, for example, follow the steps in the "Making Your Mix" section earlier in this chapter for mixing your song and choose 16-bit as your Bounce to Disk resolution. This cuts off the last 8 bits without otherwise processing the signal (which makes this process different from dithering).

To dither or not to dither (and which dithering option to use)? That is the question. No universal answer exists. The only way to know which sounds better on your music is to try mastering with dithering and without it (in which case your file is truncated instead). For the most part, songs with quiet passages and fade-outs often sound better if you dither 'em.

Mastering to 16 bits

When you master — regardless of whether you're using the dithering or the truncating approach — make sure you select the 16-bit option under the Resolution drop-down list. (In Pro Tools, for example, it's located in the Bounce dialog box, as shown in Figure 14-6.) If you have a dithering plug-in inserted into your master fader, your music is dithered while it's being bounced; if you don't use a dithering plug-in, your music is truncated.

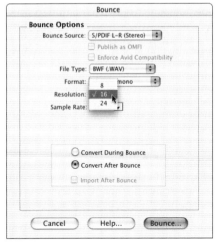

Figure 14-6:
Select 16
in the
Resolution
drop-down
list to
bounce to
16 bits.

Settling on a sample rate

If you recorded at any sample rate other than 44.1 kHz, you need to do a *sample rate conversion* (SRC) process. SRC can change the sound of your song (and not for the better). Your best bet when bouncing from one sample rate to another is to set the conversion quality as high as possible if your audio recording program offers you the choice. The following steps show how to do this in Pro Tools:

1. **Choose Setups⇨Preferences.**

   The Preferences dialog box appears.

2. **Click the Edit tab of the Preferences dialog box.**

3. **Click the Conversion Quality drop-down list in the center of the Edit tab, as shown in Figure 14-7, and select TweakHead if you want the highest quality possible.**

   It takes a while to process (go get a cup of coffee or read your favorite gear magazine while you wait), but I think it's worth it.

Figure 14-7:
You can
select the
quality of
your sample
rate
conversion.

You have several options for sample rate conversion quality. Don't take my anal-retentive word for which works best for your music. Do some experimenting on your own. One of the lower-quality conversion settings might work just fine (and you won't have to wait so long while your song is being processed).

When you actually bounce your song to disk, you need to choose 44.1 kHz from the Sample Rate drop-down list. In Pro Tools, it's located in the center of the Bounce dialog box, as shown in Figure 14-8.

Figure 14-8:
You select your final sample rate from the Sample Rate drop-down list in the Bounce dialog box.

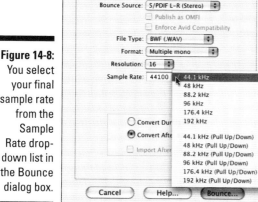

I might sound a bit old-fashioned here, but I'm a big fan of recording all my music to 44.1 kHz so I don't have to do a sample rate conversion when I master my music (assuming I'm mastering for CD release). To my ears, the loss in quality is significant. The only time I ever record at a higher rate is if I know I'll be sending my music to be mastered by a professional. Most top-notch mastering houses have top-notch sample rate conversion gear.

Burning Your CD Master

When you have your mastered mixes all done (see the mastering sections earlier in this chapter), your last step in the process is burning all your songs on a CD so that you can make the number of copies that you need. This process involves sequencing your songs and burning them onto a blank CD in the proper format. The following sections show you the way.

I don't go into detail about having mass quantities of your music made in this book because there just isn't enough room for it. You can find info on CD duplication and replication in my *Home Recording For Musicians For Dummies* book or you can do an Internet search using "CD duplication" or "CD replication" as keywords. A ton of places perform these services. Many offer lots of information about the process.

Getting what you need

You need to own a couple things in order to burn your final master onto a CD. These include

- ✓ **A CD burner in your computer:** Chances are you have one on your computer. If you don't, you need to get one. My recommendation is to get the fastest burner you can find (and afford). You'll likely be burning a lot of CDs — various mix options for each of your songs to play in your home stereo, boombox, or car, for example — and a fast burner will save you a ton of time.

- ✓ **CD-burning software that can burn Red Book CDs:** Red Book CDs are the industry standard protocol for audio CDs. Most CD-burning software can handle burning audio CDs, but some software isn't Red Book compliant. They can burn a CD just fine for you to play in your various CD players, some data might be missing that your CD replicator (the people who make mass quantities that you can sell) needs, such as PQ subcodes. (*PQ subcodes* are data imbedded in the CD that provides time code information on each track on the CD.)

- ✓ **High-quality CDs that record well in your burner:** Not all CD-Rs are created equal. Some have flimsy reflective surfaces and are prone to getting scratches that affect their playback, but others are much more durable. Some CD-Rs also have a higher error rate in some CD burners. (I don't know why this is, it just is.) The best thing you can do is look for high-quality CD-Rs (you can find "Gold" or "archive quality" discs that are rated to last 20+ years) and try a few brands out in your burner. Just don't buy the cheapest CD-Rs you can find — they might not hold up for the long run. If you find a brand that works for you, stick with it, and if you find a brand that produces a high rate of coasters, skip it.

Sequencing your songs

Sequencing your songs consists of choosing the order of the songs on the CD as well as the amount of silence between songs. Chances are that when you wrote and recorded your songs, you had an idea about the order in which you wanted them to appear on your final CD. If you don't know how you want to arrange your songs, here are some things to consider:

✔ Consider each song's tempo in the sequencing equation. Some CDs work well if songs with a similar tempo are grouped together, but others work best when contrasting songs follow one another.

✔ Think about a song's lyrics and how they relate to the lyrics from the other songs on your CD. If you want to tell your listener a story, consider how the order of the songs can best tell that story.

✔ Think about the chords that you used in each song and how they relate to another song you might want to place before or after it in the sequence. The ending chord of one song might conflict with the beginning chord of another — or lead right in.

For most recordists, sequencing has more to do with the actual process of placing each song in its proper place on the CD than with trying to decide where that proper place might actually *be*. I cover the placement process in detail in this section.

Most of the sequencing process involves deciding how much time to place between the songs on your CD. No set amount of time has to be placed between songs. Choose what seems right for the two songs you're working with. Sometimes you might want just a second or two; other times four or five seconds is more appropriate. For example, if you have a mellow ballad followed by an upbeat song, you might want to leave a little more time between these two songs so the listener is prepared for the faster song. (Try leaving a space that lasts about 4 to 6 beats at the slower song's tempo, for instance.) On the other hand, if you want two tunes to flow together, you can leave less time in between. Use your ears and think about how you want your listener to respond when the music moves from one song to another.

Making a CD for mass production

If you intend to send your CD-R to a duplication or replication company to have it mass-produced, you need to do certain things. Here are a few things to keep in mind:

✔ **Check for physical defects to the CD-R before you try to burn to it.** Scratches, fingerprints, smudges, and other imperfections on the mirror side (bottom) of the CD-R can cause errors in the data. Be sure to use a clean and unblemished CD-R for burning your master. After all, CD-Rs are cheap.

✔ **Always write your master CD by using the Disc at Once or Write Disk mode.** This allows the CD to be read as a Red Book audio CD. Your other option when recording a CD is Track at Once. Track at Once burns one song (track) at a time and produces more errors than Disc at Once, which burns the entire CD at one time. Because of the errors present on CDs burned with Track at Once, mass producer's equipment can't read — and therefore summarily reject — CDs that people produce with this method. (In fact, many older CD players for homes and cars can't read these CDs either.) So be sure that you use Disc at Once whenever you make a CD of your mastered music.

✔ **If you can, use an error-detection software program to check for errors in your recorded CD.** If you don't have access to an error-detection program, check the back of the CD for any blemishes (just like you did before recording onto it).

✔ **Listen carefully to your entire CD after you record it.** Compare it with your original file and make sure that the CD is perfect. Also, spend time reevaluating the order of the songs. Make sure that they flow well together.

✔ **Use a felt-tip marker to label your finished CD master, not a ballpoint pen or an adhesive label (paper or plastic).** A ballpoint pen can damage the surface of the CD. Adhesive labels can slow the rotation speed of the CD and can cause errors in the duplication or replication process. They have also been known to come off inside a duplication machine, clogging the works.

✔ **Label the CD master with the name of your album and all your contact info.** Use a felt-tip marker, of course, and write on the top of the disc. Your contact information should include your name (or your band's name), your phone number, and the date the master was made.

✔ **Make three CD-Rs of your mastered music.** Keep one safe in your studio and send two to the duplication or replication company. This ensures that, if one of the two CDs that you send off for mass production has an error, you don't waste any time sending the company a replacement.

✔ **Prepare a PQ subcode log.** PQ subcodes are additional information written on the CD that provides time code information, such as track numbers and start and stop times of each track. If your CD burner software doesn't support PQ subcodes, make a list of the start and stop time of each track (referenced from the start of the CD) on a separate piece of paper — as well as the track number and length of each track — and send it along with your CD masters. If your software program can generate a PQ subcode log, print it and send it with your CD master.

If you're burning a CD for a major record label, first of all congratulations, and secondly you need to supply ISRC codes with your CD. ISRC stands for *International Standard Recording Code,* and it contains information about the CD, such as the owner of the song, the country of origin, year of release, and serial number. You enter ISRC codes into a dialog box on most CD-burning programs, and the information is placed within the PQ subcodes.

Protecting your rights

Before you put your music out into the world, get it copyrighted. Getting a copyright on your music is easy and relatively inexpensive, so there's no reason not to do it. If you're a United States citizen, all you have to do is fill out an SR (sound recording) form and send it into the copyright office at the Library of Congress. You can find the form at www.loc.gov/copyright/forms, or you can call the copyright office at 202-707-9100 to have it mailed to you. Choose (or ask for) the *Form SR with Instructions.* The current cost for filing the form is $30, but double-check this fee before you send it in, because it's been known to go up. (Hey, it's the government.) You can fill out one form for each CD, so the cost per song isn't very high. (Citizens of other countries need to check with the copyright offices of their respective countries on how to do this, but the drill is not going to be much different wherever you are.)

The U.S. form is pretty easy to fill out, but if you find that you have difficulty, you can call an information specialist to help you out. The number is 202-707-3000. Be prepared to wait on hold for a little while. (Hey, it's the government.)

Send your completed form, the fee, and a copy of your CD to the address listed on the form. You'll receive a certificate in the mail, but you can consider your music copyrighted as soon as you mail it in (as long as you sent it to the correct address). If you're especially protective of your music (paranoid?), wait until your check clears your bank. At this point, you can be almost certain that your form is being processed. If you can't sleep at night unless your music is copyrighted, you're best off waiting until your certificate arrives in the mail before you start selling or distributing your CD. (This is a good reason to file for your copyright early.)

Burning the CD

Okay, with all the sequencing and CD preparation steps done you're ready to burn your CD. This process is simple: Put the CD-R in your CD burner, assemble your songs in your CD-burning software, click the Burn option, and play FreeCell, DOOMIII, your trombone, or whatever until the disc is done.

Part V
Playing with Plug-Ins

The 5th Wave   By Rich Tennant

"It's bad enough he fell asleep waiting for a huge music file to download into his music folder, but wait until he finds out he hit the 'SEND' button instead of selecting 'DOWNLOAD'."

In this part . . .

Part V introduces you to one of the most powerful tools in the computer-recording world: plug-ins. *Plug-ins* are software processors that you plug in to your instrument tracks. Chapter 15 provides the basics on these these powerful tools and shows you how to (er . . .) plug them in to your songs. Chapter 16 examines equalizer plug-ins that you can use to sculpt the frequency characteristics of your tracks. Chapter 17 shows you how to add effects — including reverb and delay — to make your tracks shine. Chapter 18 digs into the role of dynamics processors and shows you how to use them to improve the sound of your tracks.

Chapter 15

Understanding Plug-Ins

. . . .

. . . .

*A*udio recording programs — nice programs that they are — let you use plug-ins to alter the sound of your audio data. *Plug-ins* are digital signal processing (DSP) tools that you can run your tracks through — as a send or line effect or as an offline processor. Typical plug-ins include equalizers, compressors, reverbs, and delays — all of which can be important parts of the mixing process in multi-track recording. Such tools allow you to get all your tracks to sound the way you want and help you get them to blend together in a pleasing way.

In this chapter, I introduce you to plug-ins. I describe the role of plug-ins in mixing your music and describe the many ways you can use them. I also shed light on the many types of plug-in formats and processing approaches. This chapter ends with a look at the differences between native and third-party plug-ins and also steers you to some places where you can find third-party plug-ins to fit your audio recording software.

Recognizing the Role of Plug-Ins

Plug-ins are an important part of your computer-based system and one of the things that sets it apart from your old tape deck. Plug-ins allow you to process the sound of your instrument in an almost unlimited variety of ways. These can range from basic effects — stuff such as reverb or delay — to tricks such as raising the overall volume of your track (called *normalizing* your track) or changing the pitch of an instrument.

By using plug-ins, you can process your tracks in one of two ways:

- **Real time:** Real-time processing means that your audio is processed as your song plays. This approach puts a load on your computer, so the number of plug-ins you can run at one time depends on how powerful your computer is. This is the approach you use when you actually mix songs and you want to add effects to your tracks.

- **Offline:** Using plug-ins offline means you process the audio when your song isn't playing; you end up with a new audio file that includes your newly processed audio. This is common for some usual processing chores, such as normalizing, quantizing, transposing, and other new-fangled audio processing approaches. The ways you can process your audio offline depend on your audio recording program and the plug-ins you have loaded into your system.

Some audio recording programs, such as Apple's Logic, have a freeze function that lets you apply your effect plug-ins (reverb, compression, and others) in a manner similar to that of the offline approach. The difference is that you can unfreeze your track, adjust your effect parameters, and freeze it again. This offers the advantage of leaving your processor unburdened by the weight of your effect as your song plays, thus allowing you to run more plug-ins in your song without having to get a faster computer.

Taking a Look at Plug-In Types

Plug-ins come in many formats but follow only two different processing approaches. These facets of plug-ins are covered in this section.

Figuring out formats

When audio recording software programs were first developed, they each used their own formats for their plug-ins. Because originally no plug-ins were made by third-party manufacturers, this wasn't a problem. As recording programs became popular, third-party plug-ins starting becoming available, and these third-party makers needed to make some decisions — including which format to develop their programs in. (Figuring out a catchy name for marketing purposes was also high on their To-Do lists.)

The most popular plug-in formats are

- **Audio Units:** Audio Units (AU) is a format developed by Apple for OS X. This format is just beginning to gain a wider share of available third-party plug-ins; it's used in programs that run on Mac OS X, such as Logic and Digital Performer.

✔ **Direct X:** Direct X (DX) is a format developed by Microsoft for Windows systems (sorry Mac users, you can't use these plug-ins) and is employed in programs such as SONAR and other Cakewalk products. The DX format is one of the most common plug-in formats.

✔ **MAS:** The MAS format was developed by MOTU for Digital Performer. This plug-in format isn't as common as many of the others, and Digital Performer now uses Audio Units in its program.

✔ **RTAS:** Real Time Audio Suite is Digidesign's proprietary plug-in format used on Pro Tools LE software (and sometimes Pro Tools TDM). Numerous RTAS plug-ins are available.

✔ **TDM:** TDM plug-ins are Digidesign's DSP-based plug-ins for the Pro Tools TDM system. (DSP stands for digital signal processing.) These plug-ins are *host-based* plug-ins, which means they run off of the DSP chips for Pro Tools instead of from the processor in your computer. This has a couple advantages:

- Your system isn't stressed by these plug-ins. This is less of an issue now than it was, say, a couple years ago, because computer-processing power has improved a lot.

- The makers are insured against piracy. Because these plug-ins require a computer chip to run, they can't be copied. This has resulted in some very high-end plug-ins being developed in this format.

The problem is that you need a Pro Tools TDM system (which is expensive), and these plug-ins are much more expensive than their non-host-based counterparts.

✔ **VST:** Developed by Steinberg (the maker of Cubase and Nuendo, among other programs), VST plug-ins are used on both Mac and Windows computers. This is by far the most popular plug-in format and as such you find lots and lots of options.

You can find special adapters known as *wrappers* that allow you to use one format of plug-in in a program that runs on another format. For instance, many people who used Logic or Digital Performer before OS X (myself included) collected a huge array of VST or MAS plug-ins for their work. When making the switch to OS X, these plug-ins suddenly became useless. That is until the FXpansion VST to AU wrapper was introduced (`www.fxpansion.com/product-auadapter-main.php`). Now all you have to do is install the wrapper and you can run your VST plug-ins in a program that requires an AU plug-in. This relatively inexpensive option saved many people from having to throw away their old plug-in collections.

Peeking into processing approaches

Plug-ins come in two varieties: those that run off your computer's processor (native) and those that have their own DSP chip to run from (host-based). This section details the difference.

Native plug-ins

Native plug-ins are those plug-ins included in your audio recording program and those that you get when you download or buy them as software. *Native plug-ins* run off the processing power of your main computer. This used to limit both the quality of the plug-in and the number of plug-ins you could run at one time. Because computers are getting more powerful, this isn't much of limitation anymore.

Host-based plug-ins

Host-based plug-ins are plug-ins that run off a dedicated processor. Until recently, unless you had a Pro Tools TDM system you couldn't take advantage of plug-ins that ran on their own processor chips. Now, with the help of some savvy third-party manufacturers, no matter what types of audio recording software you use, you can use plug-ins that don't put stress on your computer. Currently, two options are available:

- ✔ **TC Powercore:** The TC Powercore is available as a PCI card that you put into one of the PCI slots in your computer or as a FireWire unit that you plug in to a FireWire port in your computer. (The latter approach lets you use the Powercore with a laptop.) This unit has lots of good plug-ins. The reverbs stand out as some of the best available. You can find out more about TC Powercore at www.tcelectronic.com/powercoreconcept.

- ✔ **Universal Audio UAD 1:** The UAD 1 is available only as a PCI card at this time, so this option can't be used unless you have a free PCI slot in your computer. The UAD 1 is known for having some dynamite dynamics processors, including a great limiter and compressor. Check out www.uaudio.com for more information.

Host-based plug-ins are always sold with some sort of processor chip and can't be used without the host processor. These plug-ins often sound very good, but you pay more for them because you're buying hardware as well as software. After you have the hardware in place, though, you can often buy more plug-ins to run on your host's processor, making this option expandable.

Using Plug-Ins in Your Songs

Plug-ins are easy to use. All you have to do is install them and route your track into the one of your choice. This section lays out the process.

Installing plug-ins

Your audio recording program already comes with some plug-ins pre-installed. The included plug-ins range from merely okay to exceptional. If you want to buy or download additional plug-ins to use in your program, you need to install them so that your audio recording program can recognize and use them. This process is usually as easy as clicking the Install icon that pops up on-screen after inserting the software CD — or appears when you double-click the plug-in folder that you downloaded. At times, however, you might have to install your plug-ins by hand. For example, if you have more than one audio recording program in your computer — and you want to use these plug-ins on all of them — you'll have to make sure that all your recording programs get clued in to the presence of the plug-ins. (An automatic Install might circle in on just one program and ignore the others.)

This process involves putting your plug-ins in the proper folder on your system hard drive by dragging them there with your mouse. Here's where you put them:

- ✔ **In Windows XP:** The location depends on the plug-in format your program uses. Check with your plug-in manufacturer for details. Here are some examples:

    - • **VST plug-ins in Cubase:** Place these in `C:\ProgramFiles\ Steinberg\Vstplugins`.

    - • **MAS plug-ins in SONAR:** You can put these in any folder, such as `C:\ProgramFiles\plugins\`.

- ✔ **In Mac OS X:** Place your plug-ins in *Main User*/Library/Application Support/*audio program folder such as Logic*/Plug-ins.

If you use more than one audio recording program, you need to put copies of your plug-ins in the Plug-ins folder of each of your programs. If the plug-ins aren't in the application's Plug-ins folder, it won't be able to find them.

Plugging in plug-ins

For the most part, you can plug the plug-ins into your track one of two ways: by inserting them or by using a send. In case you aren't familiar with these approaches, here's the lowdown.

Inserting

Inserting a plug-in involves placing the plug-in in line with your track. This means that all of the signal from your track is sent through the plug-in, altering all of its sound. This is common for certain effects, such as dynamics processors (see Chapter 18) and equalizers (see Chapter 16).

You insert a plug-in into a track the following way (in Logic):

1. **Choose Windows⇨Show Arrange to make sure the Arrange window is showing.**

2. **In the Arrange window, click the name of the track you want to insert a plug-in into.**

   The track becomes highlighted, and a channel strip for the track appears on the left side of the Arrange window.

3. **Click one of the Insert bars in the Inserts section of the track's channel strip.**

   The Insert pop-up menu appears, as shown in Figure 15-1.

4. **Choose your desired plug-in type — EQ, Compressor, Delay, whatever.**

5. **Choose the plug-in from the expanded pop-up menu (Channel EQ in the case of Figure 15-1).**

6. **Release the mouse to choose the plug-in.**

   The Plug-In window opens, as shown in Figure 15-2; here's where you set your parameters, such as frequency, gain/slope, and Q.

7. **Play your track by clicking the Play button in the Transport window.**

   Your session plays, and you hear the effect of your plug-in on your track. You can then tweak the parameters as your song plays.

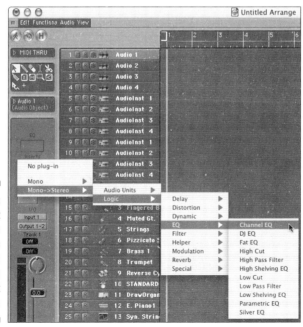

Figure 15-1: The Insert pop-up menu opens when you press the Insert input selector.

You can use the Bypass button located in the upper-left corner of the plug-in window to test the sound of your plug-in. Toggle (click with your mouse) the Bypass button to turn the plug-in off and on. Toggling lets you compare the unaffected and effected track. If the effected sound isn't better than the unaffected sound, you're better off not using the plug-in for that track (or it might be time to try some different settings).

Figure 15-2: The Plug-In window opens when you select your effect from the Insert menu.

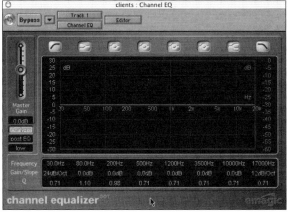

Using a Send

A Send is a mixer-routing function that lets you apply an effect to only part of the sound of a track and not to an entire signal as with an Insert. You do this through a *bus* (audio terminology for the path that a send takes). Using a Send to add the plug-in to your track's sound lets you alter the sound sent through the Send and then mix it with your original unaffected sound. This is a common approach for plug-in effects such as reverb.

Follow these steps to use a Send for your plug-in (again, in Logic):

1. **Select one of the buses from the Send selector in each track's channel strip that you want to route to the effect.**

   You can view a track's channel strip in the Environment window (choose Windows➪Environment if the window isn't open) or in the Arrange window. To open a track's channel strip in the Arrange window, click the track name in the Arrange window to highlight it. The channel strip appears on the left.

   When you release your mouse after selecting the bus, the bus is listed, and a trim pot (knob) appears next to the bus number, as shown in Figure 15-3.

2. **Adjust the trim pot to a moderate level.**

   I usually start with about –15dB.

3. **Double-click the bus number.**

   You're taken to the Bus Channel strip in the Environment window, where you can choose the effect to insert into the bus.

4. **By using the Insert selector pop-up menu in the Bus Channel strip, select the effects plug-in you want to use from the Inserts pop-up menu.**

   The Effect Plug-In window opens. Here you can set your parameters. (For instance, if you're working with a reverb plug-in, you can set the pre-delay, reverb time, and room type.)

5. **Play your track by clicking the Play button in the Transport window.**

   Your session plays, and you hear the effect of your plug-in on your track. You can then tweak the plug-in parameters or the Send level for your track as your song plays.

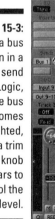

Figure 15-3:
With a bus chosen in a track's send in Logic, the bus becomes highlighted, and a trim knob appears to control the send level.

Processing your audio

In addition to plugging in processors directly into your tracks, many programs let you process your audio data by using a plug-in offline. This means that you select your audio data from a track and process it while your song isn't playing.

Processing your audio this way generally (depending on your audio recording program, of course) alters your original file permanently. If you want to keep your original file intact, you need to make a copy of your original data from which to work. This process is pretty simple. In Pro Tools, for example, just do the following:

1. **Select the audio you want to duplicate in one of your tracks.**

   You do this by using the Selector tool and clicking and dragging over your selection to highlight it.

2. **Choose AudioSuite⇨Duplicate.**

   The Duplicate menu opens.

3. **Click Process to duplicate your track's audio file.**

   This process might take a few minutes depending on the length of the file and the power of your computer.

When the duplication is complete, you can work with this new file and not have to worry about losing your original data.

Finding Good Plug-Ins

Finding quality plug-ins for any audio recording program is pretty easy. The most difficult part is sifting between the decent ones and the garbage. The following is a list of the most common third-party effects (Chapter 21 lists some free or really cheap — as in inexpensive — plug-ins):

- ✔ **Sonalksis:** Sonalksis makes some nice EQ and compression plug-ins. Check out www.sonalksis.com/index.php?section_id=17&area_id=8 for more information.

- ✔ **PSP Audioware:** PSP makes quite a few great plug-ins. I've been using its Vintage Warmer tape saturation emulator for several years. This is a great-sounding plug-in (as long as you don't use too much, anyway) for adding a nice approximation of the *glue* (the pleasing harmonic distortion that can make sounds blend better) that analog tape imparts to audio tracks when driven hard. You can find out more at www.pspaudioware.com.

- ✔ **Voxengo:** These are some really decent plug-ins. The only problem is that they're for Windows PCs only. I've used (and liked) its EQ plug-ins — it has several. You can find out more about Voxengo at www.voxengo.com.

- ✔ **Waves Audio Ltd.:** The Waves plug-ins are some of the most popular, and many people I know and respect use its compressors and reverbs daily. They're expensive, but for many users they're worth it. You can find out more at www.waves.com.

Chapter 16

Using Equalization

In This Chapter

▶ Understanding equalization

▶ Inserting EQ in a track

▶ Getting to know EQ options

▶ Equalizing your tracks

*E*qualization (EQ) is the process of changing the frequency response of the data in the session's track to make the track sound the way you want it to sound. The main goal when EQing during the mix process is to get the instruments in your song to smoothly blend together.

In this chapter, you discover the types of equalizers used in multi track recording. Most audio recording programs handle their EQ tasks similarly so, I use Pro Tools and Logic as examples, but they should be close to the program you use. I also provide some basic EQ settings for a variety of instruments to get you started EQing your songs.

Exploring Equalization

The most useful tool you have for mixing is equalization (EQ). You use equalizers to adjust the various frequencies of your instruments so that there's enough "room" for each instrument in your stereo mix. Basically, you want to carve out a reserved space for each instrument in the sonic landscape you're creating so that there's room for each instrument to get its point across without stepping on the toes of the other instruments.

Audio recoding programs typically offer three types of equalizers — *parametric, low-shelf/high-shelf,* and *low-pass/high-pass.* I outline these types of EQ in the following sections. (The graphic equalizers I discuss in Chapter 1 are not available as plug-ins; you'll only find them as standalone units.)

Parametric

The *parametric equalizer* (the Pro Tools icon for this EQ is shown in the margin) allows you to choose the frequency that you want to change as well as the range of frequencies around that frequency. With a parametric EQ, you dial in the frequency that you want to change and then set the range itself (referred to as the *Q*) that you want to affect.

The Q is a number that signifies the range of frequencies that the EQ affects — traditionally between 0.5 and 2 octaves, but recently programs have been offering more. Pro Tools offers settings from 0.33 to 12, whereas Logic offers a range between 0.10 and 100. The lower numbers universally allow larger ranges of frequencies to be EQed, and the higher numbers affect smaller ranges of frequencies. Unfortunately, no set formula exists for determining what these numbers represent in octaves — you have to adjust each of them based on your ears instead of the actual numbers.

You choose your Q setting based on what you hear in the mix. Just as you can experiment with different frequencies to adjust in the mix, you can also try different Q settings to find the best possible frequency range to use.

The beauty of a parametric EQ is that you can take a small band (range) of frequencies and boost (increase) or cut (decrease) them. This enables you to get the various instruments in a mix to fit in with one another. (Audio geeks call this *carving out* frequencies.) When you're mixing, the parametric EQ is the most useful equalizer because you can adjust the frequency response of each instrument so that you can clearly hear the other instruments in the mix. The only downside to parametric EQs is that they need processing power to run. If you have a lot of EQing to do, you might end up stressing your system pretty hard — yet another reason to have a powerful computer.

Low-shelf/high-shelf

A shelf equalizer affects a range of frequencies above (high-shelf) or below (low-shelf) the target frequency. Shelf EQs are generally used to roll off the top or bottom end of the frequency spectrum. For example, you can set a low-shelf EQ to roll off the frequencies below 250 hertz (Hz), which reduces the amount of rumble (low-frequency noise) in a recording. You generally use the shelf EQ to adjust the lowest and highest frequencies and the parametric EQ to adjust any in-between frequencies when you mix.

In most audio recording programs, the low- and high-shelf EQs are designated with the icons that you see here in the margin.

Low-pass/high-pass

Believe it or not, sometimes your track just sounds better if you eliminate a few carefully chosen frequencies. You just need to know which ones to target. That's where a couple computer-based audio recording program capabilities can help with the needed audio acrobatics: *low-pass* (ducking the high frequencies you don't want) and *high-pass* (jumping over the low frequencies you don't want).

 This type of EQ is actually called a *filter* — it filters out frequencies either higher (low-pass) or lower (high-pass) than the target frequency. The high-pass filter is useful for getting rid of unwanted low frequencies, and the low-pass filter is used for eliminating unwanted high frequencies. In most audio recording programs, the low- and high-pass filters are designated with the icons that you see here in the margin.

Dialing In EQ

Before you start EQing your tracks, you need to know how to insert the EQ plug-in into a track and how to actually make any adjustments by using the EQ plug-ins in your recording program. Each program is going to do this a bit differently, but they all follow the same basic idea. I'm hoping that if I show how to do these tasks in two programs — the ever-popular Pro Tools and Logic Pro programs — you'll have something to go on when EQing in whatever program you're working with.

Inserting an EQ plug-in in a track

To EQ a track, you first need to insert the plug-in into the track. To do this in Pro Tools, follow these steps:

1. **Choose Display⇨Mix Window Shows⇨Inserts to make sure that the Inserts section is showing in the Mix window.**

   The Inserts section appears at the top of each track's channel strip.

2. **Click the top arrow on the left side of the Inserts section of the track's channel strip.**

   The Insert pop-up menu appears, as shown in Figure 16-1.

3. **Choose either the Multi-Channel Plug-In or the Multi-Mono Plug-In option, depending on what type of track you have.**

   If your track is stereo, use Multi-Channel; if it's mono, use Multi-Mono.

4. Choose either the 1-Band EQ II or 4-Band EQ II option.

Your chosen EQ plug-in window opens. (The 1-Band EQ II option lets you set one EQ parameter, whereas the 4-Band EQ II option lets you work with four parameters. For more on which option would work best for you, check out the following section.)

5. Adjust the parameters that you want to EQ.

You can find the particulars for each kind of EQ — parametric, low-shelf/ high-shelf, and low-pass/high-pass — later in the chapter.

Figure 16-1:
Open the Inserts pop-up menu and choose the EQ plug-in to insert into your track.

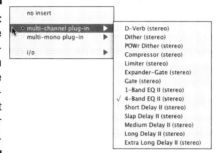

If you want to EQ a bunch of tracks in Pro Tools at the same time and use the same settings (submixes, for example), you can do this the following way:

1. Select one of the buses (the path that the Sends use to route a signal) from the Output selector in each track that you want to submix.

2. Choose File⇨New Track.

The New Track dialog box appears.

3. Use the drop-down lists to enter the number of tracks that you want (1), the type (Auxiliary Input), and whether you want your track in stereo.

4. Use your new track's Input selector to select the bus that you used for the output of the submix tracks as the input for this auxiliary track.

5. Insert one of the EQ plug-ins from the Insert pop-up menu in this auxiliary track.

The EQ Plug-In window opens.

6. Adjust the EQ settings to get the sound that you want.

You can find the particulars for each kind of EQ — parametric, low-shelf/ high-shelf, and low-pass/high-pass — later in the chapter.

Examining EQ options

Using an EQ in computer-based audio recording programs consists of selecting one of the plug-ins, inserting it into the track that you want to affect, and then setting your parameters. Most programs come with a nice selection of EQ plug-in options. The most useful are multiband EQ, such as the 4-band EQ in Pro Tools (see Figure 16-2) and the Channel EQ in Logic (shown in Figure 16-3). As its name suggests, multiband EQ lets you apply different levels of equalization to specific frequencies, and is really great if you have to tweak your bass guitar so that it doesn't get lost behind the kick drum, for example.

All audio programs allow you to use third-party EQ plug-ins as long as they are in the supported format (Pro Tools uses RTAS, and Logic uses AU; Chapter 15 has more on these format types), but any such plug-ins have to be purchased separately. If you do an Internet search with the keywords *RTAS plug-ins* (Pro Tools) or *AU Plug-ins* (Logic), you're sure to find tons to choose from.

Pro Tools' 4-band EQ

The 4-band EQ in Pro Tools, shown in Figure 16-2, lets you adjust up to four EQ filters to a track. This type of EQ is useful when you have to do some major EQing to a track. You can choose from a low-shelf, a high-shelf, and two parametric (Peak) EQs.

In the 4-Band EQ Plug-In window, the high-shelf is located at the top of the window and the low-shelf at the bottom. The two parametric EQs are located between the two shelf EQs.

Parametric

High-Shelf

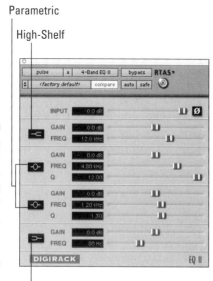

Figure 16-2:
The 4-band EQ in Pro Tools lets you apply four EQ filters to a track.

Low-Shelf

Logic's Channel EQ

Logic's Channel EQ is an 8-band EQ with four parametric bands, one high-shelf EQ, one low-shelf EQ, one high-pass filter, and one low-pass filter. As you can see in Figure 16-3, the EQ types are listed at the top of the graph, but the adjustments for these bands are located under the main graph.

Logic's EQ has a really great feature where you can see the frequency response of your track. This function is engaged by clicking the Analyzer button on the left side of the plug-in window. This is handy because, with the Analyzer button engaged, you can actually see the changes you're making to your track as you make them. This is also a potential problem because many people rely on their eyes instead of their ears. Be careful not to let what you see affect what you hear.

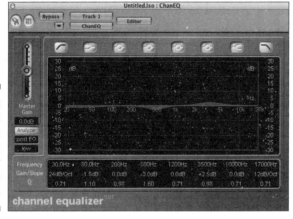

Figure 16-3:
The Channel
EQ in Logic
lets you
apply four
EQ filters to
a track.

Using parametric EQ

To use the parametric EQ, click the Peak EQ button in the EQ plug-in window you have open. You have three settings to adjust:

- **Gain:** This is the amount of *boost* (increase) or *cut* (decrease) that you apply to the signal. In Pro Tools, you can either type in the amount in the text box next to the Peak EQ button or use the slider to the right. In Logic, to get your boost (gain) amount, you can either point your mouse over the parameter and click and drag up or down or you can click in the EQ graph above the parameter controls and drag up or down.

- **Freq:** This frequency is the center of the EQ. You select the range of frequencies above and below this point by using the Q setting (see next bullet). In Pro Tools, you can either type the frequency in the text box on the left or you can use the slider to make your adjustment. In Logic, to get the desired frequency you can either point your mouse over the parameter and click and drag up or down or you can click in the EQ graph above the parameter controls and drag left or right.

✔ **Q:** This is the range of frequencies that your EQ will affect. The higher the number, the narrower the range that gets EQed. In Pro Tools, you adjust this setting either by moving the slider or by clicking in the text box and typing a value between 0.33 and 12. In Logic, you can point your mouse over the parameter and click and drag up or down to get the Q value you want. Your settings can be anywhere from 0.10 to 100.

Using low-shelf/high-shelf EQ

 To use low-shelf/high-shelf EQ, click the Low Shelf and High Shelf buttons in the EQ plug-in window. When you use low-shelf/high-shelf EQ, you have two parameters to adjust in Pro Tools and three on Logic:

✔ **Gain:** This is the amount of boost or cut that you apply to the signal. In Pro Tools, you can either type in the amount in the text box next to the shelf button or use the slider to the right. In Logic, to set the boost (gain) you can either point your mouse over the parameter and click and drag up or down or you can click in the EQ graph above the parameter controls and drag up or down.

✔ **Freq:** This is the starting frequency for the shelf. In Pro Tools, you can either type in the frequency in the text box or use the slider to make your adjustment. In Logic, to set your desired frequency you can either point your mouse over the parameter and click and drag up or down or you can click in the EQ graph above the parameter controls and drag left or right.

✔ **Q:** This is the steepness of your EQ's shelf in Logic. (Pro Tools doesn't have this option.) The higher the number, the steeper the shelf that's applied — meaning that you have a narrower range of frequencies that are affected to create the gain change of the shelf. To adjust this parameter, you can point your mouse over the parameter and click and drag up or down to get the Q value you want. Your settings can be anywhere from 0.10 to 2.

Using low-pass/high-pass EQ

Here's where you tell your plug-in which frequencies to avoid in the course of adjusting the EQ. The low- and high-pass buttons appear in the margin.

 To use the low- or high-pass filter, click the appropriate button in the EQ window. In Pro Tools, the only option to set is Freq, which is the frequency that the filter begins filtering. Any frequency below (high-pass) or above (low-pass) the setting is removed from the track. You can either type the frequency in the text box or use the slider to make your adjustment.

In Logic, you have the same three settings — frequency, gain/slope, and Q — as the rest of the EQ types. And as with the other EQ types, you adjust the settings by pointing your mouse over the column of the setting and clicking and dragging the parameter that you want to adjust. With the high-pass and low-pass EQ (filters), the gain/slope parameter adjusts the slope of the filter — how quickly it totally cuts off the frequency.

Equalizing Your Tracks

Only so many frequencies are available for all the instruments in a mix. If multiple instruments occupy a particular frequency range, they can get in each other's way and muddy the mix. Your goals when EQing during the mixing process are to reduce the frequencies that add clutter and/or to enhance the frequencies that define an instrument's sound. To do this, make a little space for each instrument within the same general frequency range, which you can accomplish by EQing the individual tracks as you mix. The first part of this chapter shows you how to get up to the point of doing some EQing. The rest of the chapter gets your hands dirty with some real EQing experience.

Here's a good trick to use when initially trying to decide which frequencies to boost or cut: First, solo the track(s) that you're working on and set your parametric EQ to a narrow Q setting (a high number). Next, turn the boost all the way up (move the Gain slider all the way to the right) and sweep the frequency setting as you listen. (To sweep, just move the Freq slider to the left and right.) Noticing the areas where the annoying or pleasing sounds are located can help you better understand the frequencies that your instrument produces. When you find a frequency to adjust, experiment with the Q setting to find the range that produces the best sound, and then adjust the amount of boost or cut until it has the effect that you want.

After you determine the frequencies that you want to work with, do your EQing to the individual track while the instrument is in the mix (not soloed). You want to make the instrument fit as well as possible with the rest of the instruments, and to do this you need to know how your instrument sounds in relation to all the music going on around it.

Your goal when making adjustments in EQ is to make all the tracks blend together as well as possible. In some instances, you might have to make some radical EQ moves. Don't be afraid to do whatever it takes to make your mix sound good — even if it means having cuts or boosts as great as 12dB or more.

General guidelines

Although some instruments do call for specific EQ guidelines, you need to think about some general considerations when EQing, regardless of the instrument involved. When it comes to the audible frequency spectrum (which is about 20 Hz to 20 kHz), certain frequencies have special characteristics:

- Frequencies below 100 Hz can either warm up an instrument or add boominess to it.
- Frequencies between 100 and 200 Hz can be muddy for some instruments and can add fullness to others.
- Frequencies around 400 Hz can sound boxy.
- Frequencies around 800 Hz can add depth or body.
- The 1-kHz to 2-kHz frequencies can add *attack* (initial signal) or *punch* (pronounced attack) to some instruments and can create a nasally sound in others.
- Frequencies from 2 kHz to 5 kHz can increase the presence of instruments.
- Frequencies of 5 kHz to 8 kHz can sound harsh on some instruments.
- Frequencies from 8 kHz to 17 kHz add airiness or brightness to an instrument.

You're generally better off cutting a frequency than boosting one. This belief goes back to the days of analog EQs, which often added noise when boosting a signal. This can still be a factor with some digital EQs, but the issue is much less. Out of habit, I still try to cut frequencies before I boost them, and I recommend that you do the same (not out of habit, of course, but because if a noise difference exists between cutting and boosting, you might as well avoid it).

The exact frequencies that you end up cutting or boosting depend on three factors: the sound you're after, the tonal characteristic of the instrument, and the relationship between all the instruments in the song. In the following sections, I list a variety of frequencies to cut or boost for each instrument. If you don't want to follow all the suggestions, choose only the ones that fit with your goals.

Use parametric EQ when you're trying to get your tracks to fit together. Parametric EQ gives you the greatest control over the range of frequencies you can adjust. You can often successfully use the other EQ types (high-shelf, low-shelf, high-pass, low-pass) for the top or bottom frequencies that I list in the following sections.

To adjust frequencies by using Pro Tool's EQ plug-ins, use the Frequency slider to choose the frequency you want to EQ and the Gain slider to control the amount of EQ that you boost (move the slider to the right) or cut (move the slider to the left) from your track. In Logic, you can point your cursor the frequency in the graphic section of the EQ window and click and drag up or down to adjust the gain.

Vocals

For the majority of popular music, the vocals are the most important instrument in the song. You need to hear them clearly, and they should contain the character of the singer's voice and style. One of the most common mistakes in mixing vocals is to make them too loud. The next most common mistake is to make them too quiet. (The second mistake most often occurs when a shy or self-conscious vocalist is doing the mixing.) You want the lead vocals to shine through, but you don't want them to overpower the other instruments. The best way to do this is to EQ the vocal tracks so they can sit nicely in the mix and still be heard clearly. The following guidelines can help you do this.

Lead

The lead vocal can go a lot of ways, depending on the singer and the style of music. For the most part, I tend to cut a little around 200 Hz and add a couple decibels at 3 kHz and again at 10 kHz. In general, follow these guidelines:

 ✔ To add fullness, add a few decibels at 150 Hz.

 ✔ To get rid of muddiness, cut a few decibels at 200 to 250 Hz.

 ✔ To add clarity, boost a little at 3 kHz.

 ✔ For more presence, add at 5 kHz.

 ✔ To add air or to brighten, boost at 10 kHz.

 ✔ To get rid of sibilance, cut a little between 7.5 and 10 kHz.

Backup

To keep backup vocals from competing with lead vocals, cut the backup vocals a little in the low end (below 250 Hz) and at the 2.5- to 3.5-kHz range. To add clarity, boost a little around 10 kHz without letting it get in the way of the lead vocal.

Guitar

For the most part, you want to avoid getting a muddy guitar sound and make sure that the guitar attack comes through in the mix.

Electric

Electric guitars often need a little cutting below 100 Hz to get rid of muddiness. A boost between 120 and 250 Hz adds warmth. A boost in the 2.5- to 4-kHz range brings out the attack of the guitar, and a boost at 5 kHz can add some bite.

Acoustic

Acoustic guitars often do well with a little cut below 80 Hz and again around 800 Hz to 1 kHz. If you want a warmer tone and more body, try boosting a little around 150 to 250 Hz. Also, try adding a few decibels around 3 to 5 kHz if you want more attack or punch. A few decibels added at 7 kHz can add a little more brightness to the instrument.

Bass

This instrument can get muddy pretty fast. The mud generally happens in the 200- to 300-Hz range, so I either leave that alone or cut just a little if the bass lacks definition. I rarely add any frequencies below 100 Hz. If the instrument sounds flat or thin, I boost some between 100 and 200 Hz. Adding a little between 500 Hz and 1 kHz can increase the punch, and a boost between 2.5 and 5 kHz accentuates the attack, adding a little brightness to the bass.

One of the most important things to keep in mind with the bass guitar is to make sure that it and the kick drum can both be heard. You need to adjust the frequencies of these two instruments to make room for both. If you add a frequency to the kick drum, try cutting the same frequency from the bass.

Drums

The guidelines for EQing the drums depend on whether you use live acoustic drums or a drum machine. (The drum machine probably requires less EQ because the sounds were already EQed when they were created.) The type and placement of your mic or mics also affects how you EQ the drums. (You can find out more about mic placement in Chapter 9.)

Kick

You want the kick drum to blend with the bass guitar. To do this, reduce the frequencies that the bass guitar takes up. For example, if I boost a few decibels between 100 and 200 Hz for the bass guitar, I generally cut them in the kick drum (and maybe go as high as 250 Hz). To bring out the bottom end of the kick drum, I sometimes add a couple of decibels between 80 and 100 Hz. The kick drum can get boxy sounding (you know, like a cardboard box), so I often cut a little between 400 and 600 Hz to get rid of the boxiness. To bring out the click from the beater hitting the head, try adding a little between 2.5 and 5 kHz. This increases the attack of the drum and gives it more presence.

Snare

The snare drum drives the music, making it the most important drum in popular music. As such, it needs to really cut through the rest of the instruments. Although the adjustments that you make depend on the pitch and size of the drum and whether you used one mic or two during recording, you can usually boost a little at 100 to 150 Hz for added warmth. You can also try boosting at 250 Hz to add some depth. If the drum sounds too boxy, try cutting at 800 Hz to 1 kHz. A little boost at around 3 to 5 kHz increases the attack, and an increase in the 8- to 10-kHz range can add crispness to the drum.

If you used two mics during recording, you might consider dropping a few decibels on the top mic in both the 800-Hz to 1-kHz range and the 8- to 10-kHz range. Allow the bottom mic to create the crispness. I generally use a shelf EQ to roll off the bottom end of the bottom mic below, say, 250 to 300 Hz. Depending on the music (R&B and pop, for instance), I might use a shelf EQ to add a little sizzle to the bottom mic by boosting frequencies above 10 kHz.

For many recording engineers and producers, the snare drum sound is almost a signature. If you listen to different artists' songs from the same producer, you'll likely hear similarities in the songs' snare drum sound. Don't be afraid to take your time getting the snare drum to sound just right. After all, if you become a famous producer, you'll want people to recognize your distinct snare drum sound. And you want it to sound good anyway.

Tom-toms

Tom-toms come in a large range of sizes and pitches. For mounted toms, you can boost a little around 200 to 250 Hz to add depth to the drum. A boost in the 3- to 5-kHz range can add more of the sticks' attack, and for some additional presence, try adding a little in the 5- to 8-kHz range. If the drums sound too boxy, try cutting a little in the 600-Hz to 1-kHz range.

For floor toms, you can try boosting the frequency range 40 to 125 Hz if you want to add some richness and fullness. You might also find that cutting in the 400- to 800-Hz range can get rid of any boxy sound that the drum might have. To add more attack, boost the 2.5- to 5-kHz range.

Hi-hats

Most of the time, the hi-hats are pretty well represented in the rest of the mics in the drum set, but depending on which mics are picking up the hi-hats, you can use the mics to bring out their sheen or brightness. To do this, try boosting the frequencies above 10 kHz with a shelf EQ. You might also find that cutting frequencies below 200 Hz eliminates any rumble created by other drums that the hi-hat mic picked up.

Cymbals

With the cymbals, I usually cut anything below 150 to 200 Hz with a shelf EQ to get rid of any rumbling that these mics pick-up. I also drop a few decibels at 1 to 2 kHz if the cymbals sound kind of trashy or clanky. Adding a shelf EQ above 10 kHz can add a nice sheen to the mix.

Overhead mics

If you used overhead mics to pick up both the drums and the cymbals, be careful about cutting too much from the lower frequencies — doing so just sucks the life right out of your drums. Also, if the drums coming through the overhead mics sound boxy or muddy, work with the 100- to 200-Hz frequencies for the muddiness and 400-Hz to 1-kHz frequencies for the boxiness.

Percussion

High-pitched percussion instruments (shakers, for example) sound good when the higher frequencies are boosted a little bit, over 10 kHz for instance. This adds some brightness and softness to their sound. You can also roll off many of the lower frequencies, below 500 Hz, to eliminate any boxiness that might be present from miking too closely. (See Chapter 9 for more on mic placement.)

Lower-pitched percussion instruments, such as maracas, can also have the lower frequencies cut a little — use 250 Hz and lower. Try boosting frequencies between 2.5 and 5 kHz to add more of the instrument's attack. To brighten them up, add a little bit in the 8- to 10-kHz range.

Piano

For pianos, you often want to make sure that the instrument has both a nice attack and a warm-bodied tone. You can add attack in the 2.5- to 5-kHz range, and warmth can be added in the 80- to 150-Hz range. If your piano sounds boomy or muddy, try cutting a little between 200 and 400 Hz.

Chapter 17

Using Effects Effectively

*U*nless you record your songs using a live band in a perfect acoustic environment, your music is going to sound a little flat without the addition of some type of effects. Effects allow you to make your music sound like you recorded it in just about any environment possible. You can make your drums sound as if they were recorded in a cathedral or your vocals sound as if you were singing underwater. Effects also have the ability to make you sound better than the real you. For example, you can add harmony parts to your lead or backup vocals, or you can make your guitar sound like you played it through any number of great amplifiers.

In this chapter, you discover many of the most common effects processors used in recording studios. (*Signal processors* are the neat software plug-ins behind all the effects you can achieve in your computer-based studio.) You discern the difference between Insert (that is, line) effects and Send/Return effects. You also get a chance to explore ways of using these processors, and I make recommendations for using reverb, delay, and chorus. To top it off, you get a glimpse into offline effects processing, such as pitch-shifting.

The best way to find out how to use effects on your music is to experiment. The more you play around with the different settings, the more familiar you become with how each effect operates. Then you can get creative and come up with the best ways to use effects for your music.

The *Bypass* button in your effects-processor Plug-In window is your friend. With a click of the Bypass button, you can quickly turn off any effect in use with your signal. Use this button to check your effect settings against your original signal. Sometimes you'll like the original sound better.

Routing Your Effects

Effects processors can be used as either Send effects, where you send part of your track's signal through the effect, or Insert effects, where you affect the entire signal from your track. In both cases, you can work with the *dry* (unaffected) signal and the *wet* (affected) signals separately. If you use the effect in a Send/Return routing, you can adjust the wet and dry signals with two track faders: Aux Send (opened by clicking the effect's name in the Send list), and Auxiliary. If you use the effect in a line configuration, the Plug-In window displays a Mix parameter where you can adjust the wet/dry balance.

You choose whether to insert an effect in a track or to use the Send function based on what you intend to do. For example, if you *insert* the effect into a track as I describe in the next section, that effect alters only the signal that exists on the track it's inserted into. On the other hand, using an *effect send* for your effect allows you to route more than one track through that effect. (You can adjust the individual levels going to the Send at each track so you still have control over how much effect is applied to each track going to the Send.) In addition, inserting an effect always puts the effect before the fader in the track (pre-fader); if you use a Send, you can choose whether the effect does its magic before *(pre-fader)* or after *(post-fader)* the signal enters the fader that controls the track's output. If you use a Send to apply the effect to more than one track at a time, you also reduce the amount of processing power the effect has to use. (Inserting the same effect into each track you want to alter ends up using more processing power.)

Inserting effects

If you want to use an effect on only one specific track, you can insert it into the track by using the Insert function. The procedure for inserting plug-ins into a track is common among many, if not all, audio recording programs. Here are the basic steps for Pro Tools and Logic:

1. **Make sure that the Inserts section is showing in the Mixer window. In Pro Tools, you do this by choosing Display⇨Mix Window Shows⇨ Inserts. In Logic, choose Windows⇨Show Environment.**

2. **Click the top arrow on the left side of the Inserts section of the track's channel strip.**

   The Insert pop-up menu appears, as shown in Figure 17-1. Pro Tools is on the left, and Logic is on the right.

3. **Choose your desired plug-in — D-Verb, Platinum Verb, Long Delay, whatever — from the menu.**

   The Plug-In window opens, as shown in Figure 17-2. Here you can set your parameters. (My professional advice on what settings to actually tweak comes later in this chapter, when I cover the individual effects.)

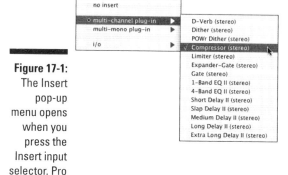

Figure 17-1: The Insert pop-up menu opens when you press the Insert input selector. Pro Tools (Left) and Logic (Right) are shown.

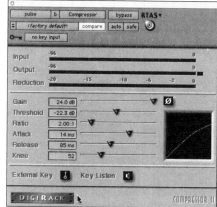

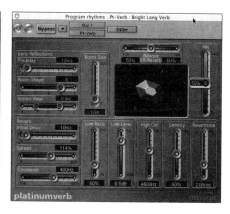

Figure 17-2: The Plug-In window (Pro Tools on the left, Logic on the right) opens when you select your effect from the Insert menu.

Sending signals to effects

Sometimes you want to route a bunch of tracks to a single effect (in the case of reverbs, for instance). This involves using the Send in your track's channel strip and routing it to an auxiliary bus. The process for doing this is pretty similar in most programs; here's how you do it in Pro Tools:

1. **Select one of the buses from the Send selector in the upper section of each track's channel strip that you want to route to the effect.**

   The Send Output window appears, as shown in Figure 17-3. The window contains a handy channel strip for controlling the signal being sent to the selected bus.

2. **Choose File⇨New Track.**

   The New Track dialog box appears.

3. **Use the drop-down lists to enter the number of tracks you want (1), the type (Auxiliary Input), and whether you want your track in mono or stereo.**

4. **Using the Input selector pop-up menu, select the bus (the pathway used for Send effects) you used for the Send of the tracks in Step 1 as the input for this auxiliary track.**

Figure 17-3:
The Send Output window in Pro Tools lets you control the signal going to the effect.

5. **Select one of the effects plug-ins from the Inserts pop-up menu and insert it into this auxiliary track.**

   The Effect Plug-In window opens.

6. **Adjust the effect settings to get the sound you want.**

Pro Tools makes it pretty easy to route a bunch of tracks to a single effect; Logic takes a slightly different approach, but it's just as easy:

1. **Select one of the buses from the Send selector in the upper section of each track's channel strip that you want to route to the effect.**

   When you release your mouse after selecting the bus, the bus is listed, and a trim pot (knob) appears next to the bus number in the track's channel strip, as shown in Figure 17-4.

2. **Adjust the trim pot to a moderate level.**

   I usually start with about –15dB.

3. **Double-click the bus number.**

   This takes you to the Bus channel strip in the Environment window, where you can choose the effect to insert into the bus.

4. **Using the Input selector pop-up menu, select the effects plug-in you want to use from the Inserts pop-up menu.**

   The Effect Plug-In window opens.

5. **Adjust the effect settings to get the sound you want.**

Figure 17-4: With a bus chosen in a track's Send in Logic, the bus becomes highlighted, and a trim knob appears to control the Send level.

The "Inserting effects" section, earlier in this chapter, gives you the gory details on inserting effects.

Chapter 16 further details plug-ins and how to route signals through your system to them.

Rolling Out the Reverb

Reverb is undoubtedly the most commonly used effects processor. *Reverb,* short for reverberation, is the natural reflection of sound, which occurs in any enclosed room and is the result of sound waves bouncing off the walls, floor, and ceiling. A small room produces reflections that start quickly and end soon; in larger rooms, halls, or cathedrals, the sound has farther to travel, so you get slower start times and a longer-lasting reverberation.

This *room* effect enables you to place your track closer to the imaginary "front" or "back" of the mix. You do this by varying how much of the affected signal you include with the unaffected one. For example, mixing a lot of reverb with the dry (unaffected) signal gives the impression of being farther away, so your instrument sounds like it's farther back in the mix.

You have a ton of reverb choices in the computer-based recording world. Every recording program comes with at least one, but to be honest, most of them don't sound very natural. This doesn't mean they aren't useful, but don't expect them to sound the same as a good room or an external reverb unit. That said, some reverbs do sound pretty darn good to my ears. But don't take my word for it — read the next two sections to bone up a bit on reverbs and then give the ones I recommend a shot.

Seeing reverb settings

Every reverb plug-in offers different parameters that you can adjust. As much as I'd like to, I can't possibly run down a comprehensive list of all the parameters you'll encounter. Instead, I've chosen a basic, fairly full-function, popular reverb plug-in from Pro Tools. As you can see in Figure 17-5, a full-function plug-in gives you quite a bit of flexibility.

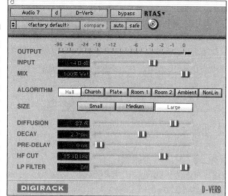

Figure 17-5:
Reverb
can add
ambience
to your
instrument,
giving it a
more
realistic
sound.

The following list explains how the parameters — most, but not all, visible in Figure 17-5 — affect the sound of the reverb:

✔ **Algorithm:** This setting lets you choose the type of room that the reverb sounds like. You have the option of a hall, church, plate (a type of reverb that uses a metal plate to create its sound), two different rooms, ambient (natural room sound), and non-linear (less natural) sound. Each choice also sets the other parameters for the reverb, but you can adjust those as you like to give your reverb a distinct sound.

✔ **Size:** This option refers to the room choices you have in the Algorithm setting. You have three setting to choose from: Small, Medium, and Large. Clicking one of these buttons adjusts the rest of parameters in the window, except for the Algorithm setting.

✔ **Diffusion:** Diffusion affects the density of the reflections in the room you've chosen. A higher diffusion setting results in a thicker sound. Think of the diffusion parameter as a way to simulate how reflective the room is. More reflective rooms produce a much higher diffusion. To simulate a less reflective room, use lower diffusion settings.

✔ **Decay:** The *decay* is the length of time that the reverb lasts. Larger or more reflective rooms produce a longer decay.

✔ **Predelay:** A sound reaches your ears before the sound's reverb does, and the *predelay* is the amount of time from the sound's beginning and the start of the reverb, which is described in milliseconds (ms). Because reverb is made up of reflections of sound within a room, the sound takes time to bounce around the room and reach your ears. By then, you've already heard the sound because it came directly to you. Predelay helps to define the initial sound signal by separating it from the reverb. This parameter is essential in making your reverb sound natural.

A small room has a shorter predelay than a large room.

✔ **HF Cut:** This setting allows you to control the rate at which the high frequencies decay. Most of the time the high frequencies decay faster, so being able to control this effect can result in a more natural-sounding reverb.

✔ **Low Pass:** This filter controls the level of the high frequencies within the reverb. Setting this frequency gives the impression of a darker (lower-frequency setting) or brighter (higher-frequency setting) room.

Getting started using reverb

Reverb is like garlic: The more you use, the less you can taste it. Just as the new chef puts garlic in everything (and lots of it), many budding engineers make the same mistake with reverb. Go easy. ***Remember:*** Less is more.

Here are some other useful tips to keep in mind:

✔ Mixes often sound better when you use reverb on only a few instruments instead of them all. For example, often just the snare drum of the drum set to have reverb on it. The rest of the drums and cymbals remain dry (unaffected).

✔ Try using reverb to glue instruments together. Routing all your drum tracks to the same reverb, for instance, can make them sound like they were all recorded in the same room. When gluing instruments together, make sure that you adjust the Send level for each instrument so that the effect sounds natural. Also, use less reverb for all the instruments than you would for just one. This keeps the sound from becoming muddy from using too much reverb.

✔ Think about how you want each instrument to sit in the mix when you choose reverb. Make sure the type and amount of reverb fit the song and the rest of the instruments.

✔ Try putting the dry (unaffected) sound on one side of the stereo field and the reverb on the other. For example, if you have a rhythm guitar part that you set at 30 degrees off to the right of the stereo field, set the reverb 30 degrees off to the left. This can be a nice effect.

✔ To keep the vocals up front in the mix, use a short reverb setting. A vocal plate is a great choice because the decay is fast. This adds a fair amount of the reverb to the vocal without making it sit way back in the mix.

✔ Experiment with room types, sizes, and decay times. Sometimes a long decay on a small room reverb sounds better than a short decay on a large room or hall reverb.

Detailing Delay

Along with reverb, delay is a natural part of sound bouncing around a room. When you speak (or sing or play) into a room, you often hear not only reverb, but also a distinct echo caused by the return of the original sound bouncing off the walls of the room to your ears. This echo might be short or long depending on the size of the room. The original sound might bounce back to you as a single echo or as multiple, progressively quieter ones. These echoes are created by a delay effect.

Digging into delay settings

Several types of delay effects exist, including a slap-back echo, tape delay, and multiple delays, and each of them is designed to add dimension to your instrument. To create these various effects, you adjust several parameters. The delay plug-ins included with audio recording programs have a lot of similarities. Figure 17-6 shows a delay plug-in that comes with Pro Tools so you can see how this type of plug-in works. This plug-in offers the following parameters:

Figure 17-6:
A Delay
plug-in
allows you
to create
various
echoes.

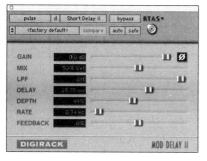

- ✔ **Gain:** This lets you set the signal level going into the delay.

- ✔ **Mix:** This parameter controls the output level of the effect. The higher you set this parameter, the louder the delayed signal is relative to the original signal.

- ✔ **LPF:** The low-pass filter (LPF) lets you filter out some of the high frequencies from the delay.

- ✔ **Delay:** This parameter controls the amount of time between the initial signal and the repeated sound. The time is listed in milliseconds (ms) and can be as short as a few milliseconds or as long as several seconds.

✔ **Depth:** This parameter lets you add modulation to the delay so that you can create a chorus effect. (See the "Creating Chorus Effects" section, later in this chapter, for more on chorus and flange effects.) The higher the level on this setting, the greater the modulation.

✔ **Rate:** This setting lets you adjust the amount of time that the modulation takes to go once through its cycle.

✔ **Feedback:** The Feedback parameter controls how many times the echo repeats. A low setting makes the echo happen just once, and higher settings produce more echoes.

Some delay plug-ins also offer the ability to set the delay to the tempo of your song. The following list covers these settings:

✔ **Tempo Match:** This option allows you to set the delay to beat in time with the music. The Tempo Match feature is referenced to the tempo map that you set for the song. You can set this parameter to any note division, from 16th notes to whole notes, if you want the delays to keep time with your song. (Quarter- and eighth-note delays are the most commonly used note divisions.)

Set that tempo map before you start to record. If you didn't bother to set a tempo map — metronome settings for each section of the song — this feature will be relatively useless to you because it won't have a reference point from which to draw. (For tips on creating and using tempo maps, see Chapter 10.)

✔ **Meter:** This lets you set the meter of the song and the subdivision of the measure, such as quarter note or eighth note, that you want the delay to follow. When you change this parameter, the Delay parameter moves, too.

✔ **Groove:** Use this parameter to adjust the rate of the delay in relation to the tempo and subdivision you chose. By changing this setting, you alter the delay (by percentages) away from the strict tempo and subdivision settings. This can be useful if you're adjusting the exact delay that you want. When you adjust this parameter, the Delay setting changes as well.

Getting started using delay

Many mix engineers and producers use delay frequently in contemporary music, and many times you don't hear it unless you listen carefully. Other times it's prominent in the mix (for example, the snare drum in some reggae music). Here are ways you can use delay in your music:

✓ **One of the most effective ways to use delay is as a slap-back echo on vocals.** A *slap-back echo* consists of one to three echoes spaced very closely together, which fattens up the sound of the vocals. You generally want to set your time parameter between 90 and 120 milliseconds. Set the level so you barely hear the first echo when your vocal is in the mix and adjust it from there until you like the sound. In pop music, a slap-back echo and a vocal plate reverb are commonly used on lead vocals. (It was *really* common in the 1950s, and shows up a lot — less subtly — in rockabilly.) A good place to start is a slap delay (Pro Tools) or a tape delay (Logic).

✓ **Use the Tempo Match feature to have your delay echo in time with the music.** This can add some depth to the mix without creating a muddy or cluttered sound. Be careful — if you use this too much, it can make your music sound annoyingly repetitive.

Creating Chorus Effects

The *chorus* effect takes the original sound and creates a copy that is very slightly out of tune with the original and which varies over time. This variance is called *modulation,* and the result is an effect that can add interest and variety to an instrument. Many recordists use chorus quite extensively to add fullness to an instrument, particularly guitars and vocals. Some programs (Pro Tools, for example) don't come with a chorus plug-in, but other programs (Logic) have several modulation effects to choose from.

If reverb is like garlic, chorus is cayenne pepper. You might get away with a little too much garlic in your food without too much trouble, but if you add too much cayenne, you run the risk of making your food inedible. Such is the case with the chorus effect. Used sparingly, it can add a lot to your music; overdone, it can wreak havoc on a good song. Keep the following tips in mind:

✓ To fill out a vocal track, try setting the rate at 2 Hz, the depth with a value of about 20 to 30, and the delay at 10 to 20 ms. Keep the Feedback level low.

✓ Use a chorus on backup vocals to make them much fuller and allow you to use fewer tracks.

✓ Pan the chorus to one side of the mix and the dry (unaffected) signal to the other. This can be especially interesting on guitars and synthesizer patches.

Chapter 18

Digging into Dynamics Processors

Dynamics processors allow you to control the dynamic range of a signal. The *dynamic range* is the difference between the softest and loudest signals that a sound source produces. The dynamic range is listed in decibels (dB). The larger the dynamic range, the more variation exists between the softest and loudest notes.

The four types of dynamics processors are *compressors, limiters, gates,* and *expanders.* This chapter gives you the lowdown on the different types and how they can help you do several important adjustments to your music. You can add punch, smooth out an instrument's sound, even out an erratic performance, eliminate noise from a track, and more.

Dynamics processors can be tricky to use. With just a minor change in settings, you can go from no noticeable change in the source sound to supreme ugliness in your track. The worst part is that you might not even notice it as you tweak the settings. The best way to ensure that you don't mess up your mix with these processors is to make it a practice to switch the effect on and off as you work by using the Bypass button in the Plug-In window. This lets you check your effect settings against your original signal, reducing the possibility that you'll use too much processing. Don't be afraid to skip the processor and go with the original sound if you don't get it to sound better.

Connecting Dynamics Processors

Dynamics processors are *Insert effects.* This means you insert them into a track so they become part of it, affecting the track's entire signal. In most computer-based recording programs, applying a dynamics processor usually involves choosing the plug-in in the Insert section of your track's Channel strip. Here's how you do it in Pro Tools and Logic:

1. **In Pro Tools, choose Display⇨Mix Window Shows⇨Inserts to make sure that the Inserts section is showing in the Mix window; In Logic, choose Windows⇨Environment to show the Mixer window.**

2. **Click the top arrow on the left side of the Inserts section of the track's channel strip (Pro Tools) or click and hold over the insert in the track's channel strip (Logic).**

   The Insert pop-up menu opens, as shown in Figure 18-1.

3. **In Pro Tools, select the Multi-Channel Plug-In if your track is a stereo track; select the Multi-Mono Plug-In option if your track is a mono track. In Logic, choose Mono⇨Logic⇨Dynamic for a mono track or choose Stereo⇨Logic⇨Dynamic for a stereo track.**

4. **In Pro Tools, select the Compressor, Limiter, Expander-Gate, or Gate option. In Logic, choose one of several dynamic processors in the drop-down list.**

   The chosen plug-in window opens, and you're now ready to create your settings. The rest of this chapter explains how and when to use the different processors. For example, you'd use a compressor to even out an erratic performance. (Later in this chapter, you can see the Compressor, Limiter, Expander-Gate, and Gate windows in Pro Tools in Figures 18-2, 18-3, 18-4, and 18-5, respectively.)

Figure 18-1:
Open the Insert pop-up menu and select the dynamics processor plug-in to insert into your track. Pro Tools (Left) and Logic (Right).

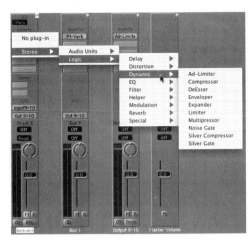

Introducing Compressors

The compressor's job is to compress (go figure) the dynamic range of the sound being affected. The compressor not only limits how loud a note can be but also reduces the difference between the loudest and softest note — which is pretty much what I mean when I say something compresses the dynamic range.

You use compressors for three main purposes (although other purposes certainly exist as well):

- ✔ They keep *transients* — the initial attack of an instrument — from creating digital distortion during tracking. This is common with drums that have a very fast *attack* (initial signal), which can easily overload the recorder (or converters or preamps).

- ✔ They even out any performance that shows signs of a high degree of unwanted dynamic variation. An example of unwanted dynamic variation is a singer who might have great energy but poor mic control — for example, jumping and dancing around in front of the mic. As a result of all that movement, some recorded passages are too loud, and others are too quiet. This type of compression is usually performed during the tracking (see Chapter 10) or mixing (see Chapter 14) stage.

- ✔ They raise the overall apparent level of the music during mastering. For example, compressing your mixed song just a couple of decibels brings up the quieter parts of music and makes your entire song louder.

I cover Purpose 1 in Chapter 9, and you can find Purpose 3 in Chapter 14. So that leaves Purpose 2 to explore (with sample settings) later in this section.

Getting to know compressor parameters

You can find hundreds of different compressor plug-ins for your computer-based system, and many of those plug-ins have unique controls. Because I can't explain all of them in this section (it would take an entire book to do that), I highlight a very common compressor setup from a very common audio recording program: Pro Tools. You insert this plug-in into a track by following the procedures in the "Connecting Dynamics Processors" section at the beginning of this chapter. This plug-in contains the following parameters (listed top to bottom as they appear in Figure 18-2):

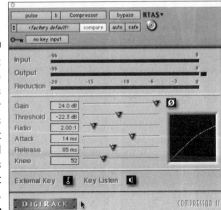

Figure 18-2:
The Pro
Tools
compressor
plug-in lets
you adjust
several
parameters
to even out
your sound.

✔ **Gain:** The Gain slider allows you to adjust the level (volume) of the signal going out of the compressor. This is listed in decibels (dB). Because adding compression generally reduces the overall level of the sound, you use this control to raise the level back up to where it was when it went in.

✔ **Threshold:** The Threshold setting dictates the decibel level at which the compressor starts to act on the signal. This setting is often listed as decibel below peak (0dB). In other words, a setting of –6dB means that the compressor starts to act when the signal is 6dB below its calibrated 0dB mark. (In digital systems, 0dB is the highest level a signal can go before clipping.)

✔ **Ratio:** The Ratio setting shows how much the compressor affects the signal. For instance, a ratio of 2:1 means that every decibel that your signal goes over the threshold setting the level of this signal is reduced by two decibels. So if a signal goes 1dB over the threshold setting, its output from the compressor will be only 0.5dB louder. With ratios above 10:1, your compressor starts to act like a limiter. (See the later section "Looking into Limiters.")

✔ **Attack:** The Attack slider controls how soon the compressor kicks in. The attack is defined in milliseconds (ms); the lower the number, the faster the attack.

✔ **Release:** The Release slider controls how long the compressor continues affecting the signal after it drops back below the Threshold setting. Like the attack, the release is defined in milliseconds. The lower the number, the faster the release time.

✔ **Knee:** The Knee slider controls how the compressor behaves as the input signal passes the threshold. The lower the Knee setting, the more gradually the compressor acts as the signal passes the threshold.

Getting started using compression

Regardless of the type of compressor or audio recording program you use, I can tell you that this particular processor is one of the most useful — and one of the most abused — pieces of gear in the recording studio. The most difficult part of using compression is that every instrument reacts differently to the same settings. In this section, I offer you some guidelines and ideas for using the compressor effectively.

The following steps show you one good way to get familiar with the compressor:

1. **Start with a high Ratio setting (between 8:1 and 10:1) and move the Threshold slider all the way to the right.**

2. **While playing your track, slowly move the Threshold slider back to the left; watch the meters and listen carefully.**

   As you reduce the threshold, notice where the meters are when you start hearing a change in the sound of the track. Also notice what happens to the sound when you have the threshold really low and the meters are peaked. (The sound is very different from where you started.)

3. **Slowly move the Threshold slider back to the right and notice how the sound changes back again.**

After you get used to how the sound changes as you adjust the Threshold setting, try using different Attack and Release settings and do this procedure again. The more you experiment and critically listen to the changes made by the different compressor settings, the better you'll understand how to get the sound that you want. The following guidelines can also help you achieve your desired sound:

✔ **Try to avoid using any compression on your 2-track mix while you mix your music.** Compression is a job for the mastering phase of your project. If you compress your stereo tracks during mixdown, you limit what you can do to your music in the mastering stage. This is true even if you master it yourself and think you know what you want during mixdown.

✔ **If you hear noise when you use your compressor, you've set it too high.** What's happening is you're compressing the loud portions enough to make the level of the softest sections of the music (including any noise) much louder in comparison. To get rid of the noise, decrease the Ratio or the Threshold settings.

✔ **To increase the punch of a track, make sure that the Attack setting isn't too quick.** Otherwise, you lose the initial transient and the punch of a track.

> ✔ **To smooth out a track, use a short Attack setting and a quick Release time.** This evens out the difference in level between the initial transient and the body of the instrument. The result is a smoother sound.

Less is more when using compression. Resist the temptation to move those sliders too much to the right — it just squashes your music. On the other hand, if that's an effect that you're going for, don't be afraid to experiment.

Looking into Limiters

The *limiter* works much like the compressor except that it limits the highest level of a sound source. Any signal above the threshold is chopped off rather than compressed. Limiters are great for raising the overall level of an instrument and keeping transients from eating up all the *headroom* (maximum level) of a track.

Understanding limiter settings

As is the case with compressor plug-ins, limiters come in many varieties. Still, many of them use a few common controls. In this section, I detail the limiter that comes standard with Pro Tools (shown in Figure 18-3). Again, you insert this plug-in into a track by following the procedures in the "Connecting Dynamics Processors" section at the beginning of this chapter. The limiter contains the following parameters:

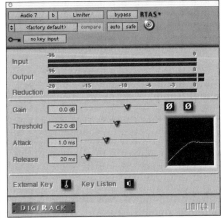

Figure 18-3: The limiter plug-in limits the maximum level of the signal passing through it.

✔ **Gain:** The Gain slider allows you to adjust the level (volume) of the signal going out of the limiter. The level is listed in decibels.

✔ **Threshold:** The Threshold setting dictates the level at which the limiter starts to act on the signal. This is listed in decibels (dB). This setting is often listed as decibels below peak (0dB). So a setting of –5dB means that the limiter kicks in when the signal is 5dB below its calibrated 0dB mark. (In digital systems, 0dB is the highest level a signal can go before clipping.)

✔ **Attack:** The Attack slider controls how soon the limiter kicks in. The attack is defined in milliseconds (ms); the lower the number, the faster the attack.

✔ **Release:** The Release slider controls how long the limiter continues limiting the signal after it drops back below the Threshold setting. The release is defined in milliseconds. The lower the number, the faster the release time.

Setting limits with the limiter

The limiter is essentially a compressor on steroids, so many of the settings that you can use for a compressor work for limiters. The only difference is that you don't have the Ratio and Knee settings. Keep in mind these two tips when using limiters on your tracks:

✔ When using limiters to raise the volume of a track or mix, limit only 2 or 3dB at a time. This way, the limiter doesn't alter the sound of your signal; it just reduces the highest peaks and raises the volume.

✔ To add grunge to a track, lower the Threshold setting so that you limit the signal 6 to 12dB. Tweak the Attack and Release parameters to get the sound you're after. This creates distortion that might work for a particular track such as the snare drum.

Introducing Gates

A *gate* is basically the opposite of the limiter: Rather than limiting how loud a note can get, the gate limits how *soft* a note can get. The gate filters out any sound below the threshold and allows any note above it to be passed through unaffected.

Gates are useful for filtering out any unwanted noise that might be present in the recording environment. A classic situation for using gates is when you record drums. You can set the gate to filter any sound (other drums, for instance) except for the sounds resulting from the hits to the particular drum that you have miked.

Getting to know gate parameters

Almost all gates use the same basic controls. Figure 18-4 shows the gate plug-in that you get when you buy Pro Tools. As you can see, the various settings that you get to play with are similar to the ones for compressors and limiters. Insert a gate into a track by following the procedures in the "Connecting Dynamics Processors" section at the beginning of this chapter and then play around with the following parameters:

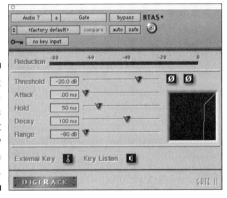

Figure 18-4:
The gate plug-in lets you filter out noise below a certain level.

- **Threshold:** The Threshold slider sets the level (in decibels) at which the gate opens (stops filtering the signal). The gate allows all signals above the Threshold setting to pass through unaffected, whereas any signals below the Threshold setting are reduced by the amount set by the Range control.

- **Attack:** Like with the compressor and limiter, the Attack slider sets the rate at which the gate opens (in milliseconds). Fast attacks work well for instruments with, well, fast attacks, such as drums, whereas slow attacks are better suited for instruments with slow attacks, like vocals.

For the most part, try to match the speed of the gate's Attack setting with the attack speed of the instrument that you're gating. If you don't do this well, you might hear a click when the signal crosses the gate's threshold. This generally happens because the attack is set too slow for the instrument. Adjust the attack until this click goes away.

- **Hold:** The Hold setting controls the amount of time that the gate stays open after the signal drops below the threshold. When the hold time is reached, the gate closes abruptly. This parameter is listed in milliseconds (ms). The Hold parameter allows you to get the gated drum sound that was so popular in the 1980s. (Phil Collins, anyone?)

✔ **Decay:** The Decay setting dictates the rate at which the gate closes after the signal hits the threshold (listed in milliseconds). Unlike the Hold feature, the Decay setting doesn't close abruptly; rather, it slowly (according to the Decay setting) closes, which produces a more natural sound. You want to try to set the release time so that it matches the natural decay time of the instrument. Otherwise you can get a clipped-off sound. (If you want the clipped-off sound, use the Hold feature.)

✔ **Range:** The Range setting is similar to the Ratio setting on the compressor except that you choose the decibels amount by which the gate attenuates (reduces) the signal. For example, a setting of 40dB drops any signal below the Threshold setting by 40dB.

Getting started using gates

Noise gates can be extremely useful for getting rid of unwanted noise. The most common use for a gate is to eliminate bleeding from drum mics. For example, you might get bleed from your snare drum into your tom-toms mics. When using noise gates, keep the following in mind:

✔ When the threshold is reached, the gate allows the signal through. If your background noise level is high enough, when the gate opens you still hear not only the intended sound but the background noise as well. This can be a problem if you're using gates to eliminate the noise of your hard drive fan or other room noise. Your best bet is to use acoustic panels (rather than gates) to eliminate the noise.

✔ When gating drums, be sure to set the attack very fast. Otherwise, the initial transient is lost, and you end up with mushy-sounding drums.

✔ When setting the release time of the gate, adjust it until it sounds natural and doesn't clip off the end of your instrument's sound.

✔ Set the range just high enough to mask any unwanted noise. If you set it too high, the sound becomes unnatural because the natural resonance of the instrument is filtered out.

Examining the Expander

The expander is the gate's diminutive cousin — instead of reducing the volume of notes below the set threshold by a specified amount, the expander reduces them by a ratio. In other words, with the gate, you set a certain decibel amount by which a signal is reduced, and with the expander, you reduce the signal by setting a ratio. The ratio changes the signal gradually, making the affected signals sound more natural.

You use an expander when you want to subtly reduce noise from a track rather than just filtering it out completely. A classic example is when you deal with breath from a singer. If you use a gate, you get an unnatural-sounding track because the breaths are filtered out completely. With the expander, you can set it to reduce the breath just enough so that it's less noticeable, but you can leave a little of the sound in to make the singer sound normal. (I mean, everyone has to breathe, right?) This is such a common use of an expander that I explain this process in detail in the "Getting started using an expander" section later in this chapter.

Playing with expander parameters

Given that Expander plug-ins usually contain similar parameters, the Expander plug-in shown in Figure 18-5 should give you a good sense of what such a plug-in looks like. (If you guessed that this expander is part of the Pro Tools package, you guessed right.) You can see pretty much the same basic controls as you find on the compressors, limiter, and gates. They are as follows:

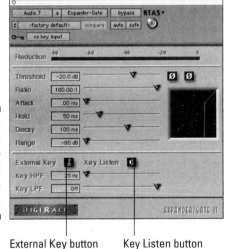

Figure 18-5:
The expander has several parameters to set.

External Key button   Key Listen button

✔ **Threshold:** The Threshold setting in an expander works the same way as with the gate — anything below the threshold is affected, and any signal above the threshold passes through unaffected.

✔ **Ratio:** The ratio dictates how much the signal is attenuated by the expander. When using a ratio of 2:1, for instance, the expander reduces any signal below the threshold by two times. In this case, a signal that is 10dB below the threshold is reduced to 20dB below it; likewise, a signal that's 2dB below the threshold is reduced to 4dB below it.

✔ **Attack:** As with the compressor and limiter, the Attack slider sets the rate at which the expander opens (in milliseconds). Fast attacks work well for instruments with fast attacks, such as an acoustic piano, whereas slow attacks are better suited for instruments with slow attacks, such as a bass guitar.

✔ **Hold:** The Hold setting controls the amount of time that the expander stays open after the signal drops below the threshold. The hold time is listed in milliseconds (ms).

✔ **Decay:** The Decay setting dictates the rate at which the expander closes after the signal hits the threshold (listed in milliseconds). Unlike the Hold feature, the Decay setting doesn't close abruptly; rather it slowly (according to the Decay setting) closes. This produces a more natural sound. I recommend setting the release time so that it matches the natural decay time of your instrument.

✔ **Range:** The Range setting is similar to the Ratio setting on the compressor except that you choose the decibel amount by which you want the expander to be attenuate (reduce) the signal. For example, a setting of 30dB drops any signal below the threshold setting by 30dB.

You also have two settings that you can make if you use an external key to trigger the expander. (I discuss external keys in the "Signing On to Side-Chains" section at the end of this chapter.) These settings include

✔ **Key HPF (High-Pass Filter):** This setting allows you to choose the lowest frequency that can affect the expander. Setting this parameter at 50 Hz, for example, keeps any frequencies lower than that from triggering the expander.

✔ **Key LPF (Low-Pass Filter):** This setting lets you determine the highest frequency that can trigger the expander when you use a key input to trigger the expander.

Getting started using an expander

Because the expander works much like a gate, you can use the same basic starting points. Choose between a gate or an expander based on the type of overall attenuation that you want of the signal. For example, the expander is a good choice if you have an instrument that contains sounds that are too loud but you don't want to get rid of them completely — you just want to reduce them a little.

Adjusting for a vocalist's breath is the perfect situation for using an expander rather than a gate. In this case, you can set the expander's threshold just below the singer's softest note and start with a low ratio (1.5:1 or 2:1, for instance). See whether the breathiness improves, and if it doesn't, slowly move the Ratio slider until you get the effect that you want. Be careful not to overdo it, though. If the breath is too quiet compared to the vocal, the vocal sounds unnatural.

If you use a high ratio in your expander (6:1 or above), the effect that you get is similar in sound to the gate, but you end up having less control over the sound because you don't have the Hold or Release settings to adjust. So if you find yourself using a high ratio on a signal, a gate might be a better choice for that situation.

Signing On to Side-Chains

A side-chain is a mixing technique where you trigger your dynamics processor with another device such as an EQ. Using a side-chain means that the signal from another track (through one of the buses) or from one of your interface inputs triggers your dynamics processor into action. The signal that you choose to do the triggering is called the *key input* in Pro Tools and a *side-chain* in Logic.

Side-chains are great for de-essing (getting rid of "s" sounds) a vocal track, making tracks fit together better in a dense mix, or letting a kick drum be heard when it plays at the same time as the bass guitar. Not sure how to do this? Don't worry; I provide some examples later in this section.

Setting up a side-chain

Setting up a side-chain in an audio recording program involves some simple steps. To illustrate, here's how you do it in Pro Tools:

1. **Using the Key Input pop-up menu (click the drop-down list located next to the little Key icon at the top of the Plug-In window to get there), choose the interface input or bus that has the signal that you want to use to trigger the dynamics processor.**

    This step routes the signal from that input or bus to the processor.

2. Click the External Key button to engage the side-chain.

The External Key button is located near the bottom-left corner of the various plug-in windows. (Refer to Figure 18-5.)

3. Click the Key Listen button — located to the right of the External Key button — to hear the signal coming through your selected key input.

The side-chain is now happily set up and minding its side-chain business.

4. Play your session and adjust the processor's parameters until you get the sound that you want.

A couple common side-chains

The uses for side-chains are numerous, and only your creativity limits how you end up using your side-chain. In the following two step lists, I give just a couple examples of using a side-chain.

The most common use for side-chains is to create more room for your instruments in the mix. You do this by EQing (see Chapter 16) the Key Input signal and letting that EQed signal trigger a compressor or limiter. To make room for a vocal in a dense mix, follow these steps (when you use Pro Tools):

1. Route all your instruments in the mix (except the vocal) to Bus 15 and 16.

2. Insert the Compressor plug-in in this bus and set the Key Input to Bus 14.

3. Make a copy of your vocal tracks and assign their outputs to Bus 14.

4. Shift the copied vocal tracks ahead (to the right) a few milliseconds.

For example, in Pro Tools, you do this by choosing the Slip edit mode from the upper-left corner of the Edit window. Then you click and drag the audio region in your track.

5. Adjust the settings on the compressor so that the volume of the instruments drops slightly whenever the vocals come in.

You can also use a special trick to make the bass guitar drop slightly in the mix whenever the kick drum is played. This helps you hear the kick drum when the bass guitar and kick drum occupy the same basic frequencies. Follow these steps:

1. Insert the compressor plug-in into the bass guitar track and set the Key Input to Bus 16.

2. **Make a copy of the kick drum track and set the output for the copied track to Bus 16.**

   The kick drum signal will trigger the compressor that's assigned to the bass guitar track.

3. **Use fast Attack and Release settings on the compressor.**

   You want the compressor to activate only when the initial strike of the kick drum happens. The bass guitar drops in volume when the kick drum plays. This means that the kick drum creates the attack, and the bass guitar produces the sustain.

This trick works really well for music that has a kick drum and bass guitar that play similar patterns.

Part VI
The Part of Tens

The 5th Wave   By Rich Tennant

"It's my homage to the 'Limp Korn Chilies' rock group. I have recordings of all their performances in concert halls, hotel rooms, and airport terminals."

In this part . . .

Part VI contains some chapters to help you add to your knowledge-base (and hard drive). Chapter 19 contains ten terrific tips to help you improve the performance of your system and keep it running smoothly. Chapter 20 has a handful of great Internet resources that can help you discover new techniques and tools. Chapter 21 finishes this book off with a awesome list of free (or really cheap) software that can add to your music without subtracting from your bank account (too much anyway).

Chapter 19

Ten Tips for Improving the Performance of Your System

Computer-based recording systems can be finicky. If you're not diligent about taking some basic precautions, your system will get sluggish and eventually become unstable. This gradual slow-down doesn't have to happen, however. With some simple housekeeping tasks and system tweaks, you can keep your computer running without a hitch. (Okay, so it actually runs without as many hitches as you might otherwise encounter — how's that for a disclaimer?)

This chapter contains ten simple tasks that you can do to make and keep your system running as smoothly as possible, regardless of the platform — Mac or Windows — that you use.

Keep Your Drives Clean

Hard drives can get sluggish after you've recorded heaps of data on them, erased some of it, edited still other parts, and recorded more. Over time, as you write and rewrite, your system writes the new data on the drive inefficiently, and your system might slow down a bit, or you might experience audio problems such as dropouts, clicks, or pops.

The best and easiest solution is to occasionally wipe your drives clean. You can do this in several ways. Here's one:

1. **Back up all your files.**

   You should be doing this regularly anyway.

2. **Reformat your audio drive.**

Windows XP. *Note:* These steps assume that your hard drive file format is set to FAT32. See your manual to find out how to check your hard drive file format.

   a. Open the Windows Recovery Console by using the Windows Setup floppy disks or the Windows CD-ROM that came with Windows XP to start your computer.

   b. Press F10 or press R when the Welcome to Setup screen appears. The Windows Recovery Console opens.

   c. Type your Windows application number. (It's usually 1.)

   d. Enter your administrator password to log in to your computer. (If you didn't set up an administration account when you installed Windows XP, your password is probably blank. Simply press Enter.)

   e. Type **map** and press Enter.

   f. Type **format d** and press Enter to reformat your D drive. This assumes that your audio drive is your D drive. If it isn't, enter the letter for the drive in place of the d in the prompt for this step.

   g. Type **y** and press Enter. This starts the formatting process. Go ahead and read a novel for a few minutes while your system erases and reformats your hard drive.

   h. When the formatting is finished, type **exit** and press Enter. Your computer restarts, and your drive is reformatted.

Mac OS X.

   a. Open the Disk Utility application by choosing Macintosh HD⇨ Applications⇨Disk Utility from the Finder menu.

   b. Click the Erase tab to open the Disk Erase window.

   c. Choose your audio drive from the list by clicking it.

   Be sure not to choose your system drive — that will erase your operating system and all your application files.

   d. In the Disk Erase window, choose Mac OS Extended (Journaled) from the Volume Format drop-down menu.

   e. Enter a name for your drive, such as Audio Files, in the Name text box.

   f. Click the Erase button to erase and format your drive. Because this process takes a few minutes, I usually take this time to glance through one of my favorite gear catalogs. (Of course this always leads me to spend more money, so maybe this isn't the best idea.)

3. **Reload your files.**

I suggest performing this procedure every month or so and definitely whenever you start hearing dropouts, pops, or clicks coming from your audio.

Keep Your Hard Drive Free of Unnecessary Applications

Using your computer for tasks other than recording and adjusting audio can clutter up your hard drives and slow down your system. This saps resources that could go toward an extra plug-in or audio track. Some particularly sneaky software programs, such as appointment calendars, run in the background and drain power even when they're not launched.

If you do use a computer with other programs on it, put all the data from the other programs on a separate hard drive from your audio files and try to avoid installing programs such as calendars, Internet programs (both browsers and e-mail — getting a virus is as easy as clicking a Download button), or any program that constantly runs in the background.

You basically have two solutions for this dilemma:

✔ Get a computer and use it only for audio.

✔ Get a super powerful computer and accept the hit you'll take by having these applications on your system.

Keep an Eye on Buffer Settings

Low buffer settings put a huge burden on your computer — especially if you use a lot of plug-ins. Here's what I recommend:

✔ **When you record, use as few plug-ins as possible so that you can keep your buffer settings as low as you can.** Using a low buffer setting minimizes your latency when tracking, making it easier to play along with previously recorded tracks and have everything line up within your single file.

✔ **When you mix, raise the buffer setting so that your processor doesn't have to work as hard.** Changing your buffer setting from 128 samples (common for recording) to 512 or 1,024 samples when you mix might even allow you to add a couple extra plug-ins when mixing.

Adjusting your buffer settings depending on your needs can make your recording process go much smoother. I cover the steps for making buffer setting adjustments in Chapter 8.

Use the Freeze Function

Some programs have a function that lets you render your effects to a track, thus taking the load off your processor for that track. In Logic, this function is called *freeze*. This freezes the effect settings in your designated track. With this function, you can use as many plug-ins as you want without choking your processor. To change the plug-in setting for a frozen track, you have to unfreeze it first. This puts your track's effects back on the processor's workload, so after you change the setting you need to refreeze the track.

If your program doesn't have the freeze function or something similar (Pro Tools version 6, for example, has no equivalent), you can approximate the Freeze function by creating a submix of your track with the effects plugged in and then using the submix in your mix. To change any effects setting, you have to submix the raw track and effects again after you make your adjustments.

Keep Other Programs Turned Off

This almost goes without saying. Running other programs while you record is asking for trouble. These programs use up RAM and bog down your processor. Running these programs while you work with audio increases the likelihood that you'll encounter some glitches. The most common glitches are:

- **Program or system crashes:** Your audio application or the other programs might freeze up. If anything freezes, your computer might try to do an impression of road kill.

- **Audio clicks, pops, or dropouts:** Having your RAM used up by another active program can cause access problems with your audio hard drive.

- **Slow graphics:** One of the first places you can see stress on your computer is with the graphic redraw in your recording program. (The graphic redraw is the refreshing of the visual images on your screen.) If the visuals start getting jerky, you need to be careful because other problems will likely appear soon after this.

- **Errors in accessing your audio or MIDI hardware:** Aside from audio problems such as pops, clicks, and dropouts, hardware errors are the most common result of an over-stressed computer. These interruption errors can cause the audio problems, but most often they abort recording or playback.

The best way to avoid these problems is to keep other applications turned off while you work with audio.

Exercise Some Discipline

A lot of the pop songs that you hear on the radio use over 100 tracks. And you know what? They often don't sound that good. Exercise some discipline and keep your songs to a minimum on track counts. You don't need 24 tracks of backup vocals or 12 tracks of guitars, or 16 tracks of a 5-piece drum set. The only reason to have this many tracks is that you're unable to make a decision on what to use in your mix. No way will 100 or more tracks of audio sound good. There just isn't enough auditory real estate available in the human hearing spectrum. (Trust me on this; I research this stuff for my day job.)

If you have a clear vision of your music, you don't need 100 tracks of material to get your message across. Record and use only those tracks that you absolutely need in order to make your song fit the sound you have in your head. Chances are that you'll be topping at 24 to 32 tracks for most songs. Having fewer tracks stresses your system less and improves its performance.

Use Submixes

If you do have more tracks than your computer can play back without hiccupping, your best bet is to submix groups into stereo tracks. For example, take the four or five tracks (I hope you didn't use more) that you used to record your drums, add effects to each drum or group of drums, and then mix all this down to two tracks. This can reduce your total track count, which in turn reduces the work your computer has to do.

If you use lots of plug-ins in your music, your computer is even more likely to start hiccupping. By submixing, you bounce your grouped tracks (including the plug-ins for them) into a set of tracks that have no plug-ins. This takes even more stress off your computer, leaving it relaxed enough to achieve a state of audio Zen.

Clean Up Your Tracks

The problem: As you cut up your takes and assemble them together, your computer plays your assembled data from the original files. This means that it often reads from various parts of the hard drive at the same time (well, not exactly the same time — it can't multitask). This puts extra stress on your hard drive and, if you have tracks with lots of chopped-up parts, it can slow your system down or limit the number of tracks you can play back before causing drop-outs, clicks, or pops.

The solution: Consolidate your parts into one continuous audio file after you finish making your edits to the individual tracks. This way your hard drive has all the data for your track in one place, making it easier to play back.

Turn Off Unused Tracks

Some programs, such as Pro Tools, use processing power in tracks even if no data is playing. These programs also usually offer the option of being able to turn off the tracks. In Pro Tools, this is called deactivating them. By deactivating your tracks, you might be able to free up some processing resources, depending on your program.

Bypass Plug-Ins

Plug-ins use resources when they are inserted into a track even if no data is flowing through them. Granted, they don't use as much of the resources as when data is going through them, but they do use some resources, nonetheless. When you mix, automate your plug-in bypass (simply click the Bypass button to send your audio past the plug-in) for times when no signal is being sent to it. This reduces the work your processor has to do and might allow you to add another plug-in somewhere or include an extra audio or MIDI track playing back during your mix.

Chapter 20

Ten Great Internet Recording Resources

In This Chapter

▶ Finding online forums

▶ Getting to know gear reviews

▶ Discovering online educational resources

*T*he Internet is a home recordist's dream: It has tons of great information and plenty of support to help you make the best music you can. The only problem with the Internet is weeding through all the garbage (and there's a lot of garbage out there) to find the places that provide quality resources and information.

In this chapter, I list ten (more, actually) of my favorite places to go on the Internet for recording information and resources. These include forums, educational sites, and entertainment to inspire my creativity. These sites are just a small sampling of what's available on the Internet, but they can get you started and give you some ideas for digging deeper.

Checking Out Online Chats

Being able to talk with other musicians and home recordists is one of the biggest assets of the Internet. Tons of great online forums focus on music and recording. Here are two of the most popular:

```
www.musicplayer.com/cgi-bin/ultimatebb.cgi
```

```
www.homerecording.com
```

Gearing Up for GAS

One thing that almost all home recordists (or any recordist for that matter) can't stop talking about is gear, and because of this, many develop a bad case of GAS. Gear Acquisition Syndrome (GAS) is a prevalent problem, and the best way to deal with it is to talk to other people who have it and to feed your need to know about all the gear out there. Here are some Web sites that cater to (or create) people with GAS:

```
www.gearslutz.com/board
```

```
www.musicplayer.com
```

```
www.harmony-central.com
```

Getting Help with Mastering

Mastering music is often misunderstood. I cover the basics of this process in Chapter 14, but I don't have enough space in this book to go into more advanced details. Fortunately, a couple Web sites can help you make sense out of this process and even find a good mastering engineer to help you with your music.

For a great source of information from one of the legends of mastering, check out Bob Katz's Web site at:

```
www.digido.com
```

If you have specific questions and don't know who to ask, mastering engineer Brad Blackwood has a great forum dedicated to mastering at:

```
http://recforums.prosoundweb.com/index.php?t=thread&SQ=0&foru
           m_redr=1&frm_id=31
```

Finding Support for Setting Up Your Studio

Some Web sites offer great pictures and designs of recording studios. For a home recordist who doesn't have a million dollars to spend setting up a

studio, most photos of commercial studios are depressing and not at all helpful. So, to counteract this and to offer you some inspiring ideas, here's a great
Web site run by studio designer John Sayers:

```
http://johnlsayers.com
```

You can find photos of various studio construction projects as well as tons of
information about studio design and construction. The site even includes a
forum where you can post your questions.

You can also find some other forums for information about building a studio
on the Internet. One of the most informative is Ethan Winer's forum. Here's
the address:

```
www.musicplayer.com/ubb/ultimatebb.php?ubb=forum;f=26
```

Discovering CD Duplicating

If you want to get your music out to other people and even sell some copies
of your finished CD, your computer isn't the best option for burning the
discs. Instead, you're better off going to a company that can make them
"retail ready" (professional printing and graphics, shrink wrap, even a UPC
code so you can sell it in retail stores such as Amazon.com or your local
record store). The company does this in two ways:

- **Duplication** is copying your CD-R onto multiple CD-Rs. This approach is
  great for runs under 500 (sometimes even under 300) because the initial
  setup costs are lower than with replication.

- **Replication** involves making a special master CD (called a *glass master*)
  of your CD-R and creating mass quantities of CDs from the glass master.
  Replication is the best choice for amounts of 500 or more CDs. Thanks to
  the replication process, you can produce CDs that look just like the major
  or indie labels — with high-quality, direct-to-CD printing (no paper labels).

Most companies that create retail-ready CDs can offer either duplication or
replication, depending on the number of copies that you want (and can
afford). Here are some Web sites with info on this process:

```
www.discmakers.com
```

```
www.groovehouse.com
```

```
www.oasisduplication.com
```

Finding Industry Connections

Indie musicians need connections. Whether you need to find other musicians to work with, get feedback from professionals on your music, or discover ideas for promoting yourself, several Web sites can help you further your career. These include

```
http://marsh.prosoundweb.com/index.php?t=thread&SQ=0&forum_re
        dr=1&frm_id=2&frm_goto=Go
```

```
www.taxi.com
```

Discovering Inspiring Indie Music

Most creative people need inspiration from which to draw. I find that listening to as much music as possible inspires me to try new tricks and improve my old ones. As far as I'm concerned, the major record labels by and large put out less-than-inspiring music. So I seek out independent musicians and small labels to feed my muse. Here are some places to start looking:

```
www.mp3.com
```

```
www.cdbaby.com
```

Chapter 21

Ten (Or So) Free or Really Cheap Software Programs

In This Chapter

▶ Getting your hands on low-cost recording software

▶ Finding free plug-ins

▶ Introducing inexpensive MIDI programs

▶ Discovering free MP3 software

$\mathcal{B}$ecause you're recording into a computer, you need software to do any work. This can get expensive, especially if you want to use lots of plug-ins or make your music available in a variety of formats, such as CD or MP3. This chapter lists several software titles that you can use for free or for just a few bucks. Some of these programs don't have the features that a more costly program has, but many offer enough power to do the basics until you can afford to buy something else. Also, you can find tons of shareware plug-ins floating around that sound pretty good even compared to the ones you have to pay for. This chapter puts them at your fingertips.

Creating high-quality software takes a lot of time and energy, and the people who go through all this effort need to be compensated for their work. Although you might find *cracked* (pirated/illegally copied) copies of almost all programs that you can download, I implore you not to do this: It's illegal, but worse, it devalues intellectual property (including your music). If people don't get paid for their work, eventually you'll see the good programs disappear because the creators can't keep giving it away for free. Another reason to avoid cracked software is that it's inherently buggy, and if you put it on your computer, I almost guarantee you that your system will crash. Please avoid cracked software — your computer will be happier, and your conscience will be clean.

On the Web, freeware, shareware, and demo programs are as common as flies. The best place I've found for many of these options is Shareware Music Machine (`www.hitsquad.com/smm`). This Web site has an easy search function that can help you find the titles or applications you want. Much of the software I link to in this chapter can be found on this site (among others).

Recording Programs

When you buy an audio interface — almost any interface — it comes with some software. This is often your best free option because these programs are often simplified versions of very powerful products. You can get to know the approach that the designers used in all their products, and when you outgrow it you can upgrade without having to figure out a new application. When you look for an audio interface, I recommend that you consider the software that is included as well as the cost to upgrade to the full version later.

That said, you can cheaply acquire some other recording software programs to start you out. These include

- ✔ **n-Track Studio:** This is a really inexpensive program for audio and MIDI recording. It's for Windows computers only, but for a mere $75 you get lots of features and an easy-to-use interface. You can download a demo version for free from `www.fasoft.com`.

- ✔ **Tracktion:** This program is free with the Mackie USB audio interface but can be purchased separately for $80. This program is really easy to use and is available for both Windows and Mac computers. You can download a free demo from `www.mackie.com/products/tracktion`.

- ✔ **GarageBand:** GarageBand is free with all new Apple computers. (You can get it as part of iLife for $49 if you have an older Mac.) This program is great for composing with loops. The only downside is that it doesn't work on Windows computers.

Audio Editing Programs

Many programs are designed with audio editing in mind. Depending on the program that you use for day-to-day recording, you might find that having a program specifically for your occasional tough edit can come in handy. Here are some free versions:

✔ **Audacity:** This is a great audio editor that's easy to use. It's available for both Windows and Mac computers. You can download it at `http://audacity.sourceforge.net`.

✔ **soundhack:** This is a audio spectrum editor that you can use to create some bizarre effects. This is freeware and for Mac only. It's definitely worth a look. It's available here: `www.soundhack.com/freeware.php`.

MP3 Programs

If you want to put your music on the Internet, you need to be able to convert it to MP3 format. Before you get your checkbook ready or pull out the plastic, be aware that plenty of free programs can get the job done. These include:

✔ **BladeEnc:** This is a free encoder for Macs. You can download it here: `www.mp3machine.com/software/BladeEnc_mac`.

✔ **iTunes-LAME Encoder:** This is a Mac program only and is free. You can download it at `www.mp3machine.com/software/iTunesLAMEEncoder`.

✔ **001 MP3 Encoder:** This encoder is for Windows computers. It's free and really easy to use. You can find it at `www.mp3machine.com/software/001MP3Encoder`.

✔ **Power MP3 Cutter:** This program encodes MP3s from WAV files like the other programs, but it also allows you to cut sections from MP3 or WAV files if you want to create short snippets. This program costs $20 and is for Windows only. You can download it at `www.mp3machine.com/software/MP3Cutter`.

When you have your MP3s, you might want to mix some together and create something new. A great program for this is Acoustica MP3 Audio Mixer. This program is a simple mixer for MP3s. It's not free but it's pretty cheap (it costs $25). It's for Windows only. Here's where you can download a demo of it: `www.acoustica.com/mp3-audio-mixer/download.htm`.

MP3 programs are bountiful on the Internet. You can find more at `www.mp3machine.com`.

Plug-Ins

There's an old saying in computer-based audio: You can never have too many plug-ins. (Okay maybe it's not that old, but I have to tell ya that even the worst-sounding plug-in has its uses — for something.) Buying plug-ins can get expensive, but as surprising as it might sound, some decent-sounding free plug-ins are available. Here are a few that stand out:

- ✔ **The fish fillets:** These are dynamics processor plug-ins that rival the ones you pay for. I find myself using these a lot. You can download them at `www.digitalfishphones.com/main.php?item=2&subItem=5`.

- ✔ **SimulAnalog Guitar Suite:** This is an analog guitar amp simulator. It's available only for PC users, but it's free and sounds good. You can get it at `www.simulanalog.org/guitarsuite.htm`.

- ✔ **RoomMachine 844 and RubyTube:** These are free plug-ins from Silverspike software. RoomMachine is a room simulator and reverb plug-in, and RubyTube is a tube preamp simulator. These are both really good plug-ins, especially for the price. They're available for both Mac and Windows computers. You can download them at `www.silverspike.com/download.html`.

Tons more good plug-ins are available, so check out Shareware Music Machine for more options.

MIDI Programs

Recordists use MIDI a lot for music composition. MIDI can be handy if you want to sketch out some ideas without buying a powerful computer or expensive software. Most audio recording programs come with some sort of MIDI implementation, but if yours doesn't or if you want to be able to do some nifty things such as convert a MIDI file into a WAV file without hassle, here are some options:

- ✔ **Audio Compositor:** This program creates audio WAV files from your MIDI files. (Remember, MIDI files don't contain any sound — only performance information.) This software is $40 and is for Windows only, but if you need to convert your MIDI into WAV, this is great way to do it. You can download it at `www.sonicspot.com/audiocompositor/audiocompositor.html`.

- ✔ **MID Converter 3.3:** Here's another program that converts MIDI files to audio WAV files. You can download a free demo, which you can register for unlimited use for $25. Here's a link to download from: `www.mp3machine.com/software/MIDConverter`.

Software Synthesizers

Soft-synths are becoming about as commonplace as all the other types of plug-ins used in recording. These make playing back MIDI data exciting because you can create an almost unlimited variety of sounds. You can pay a lot for great soft-synths, but the following are free ones to get you started:

- **Delay Lama:** This soft-synth is a riot. Its interface is a singing monk, and it creates some really cool sound. It's definitely worth checking out. It's for both Macs and Windows PCs. This program is free. You can download it at www.audionerdz.com/index2.htm.

- **Crystal:** This is one of the most popular free soft-synths available. Mac and Windows versions are both available, but it does use quite a bit of power to run. Still, it sounds great. You can download it at www.green oak.com/crystal/download.html.

Index

USINESS, CAREERS & PERSONAL FINANCE

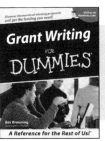

0-7645-5307-0

0-7645-5331-3 *†

Also available:

- Accounting For Dummies †
  0-7645-5314-3
- Business Plans Kit For Dummies †
  0-7645-5365-8
- Cover Letters For Dummies
  0-7645-5224-4
- Frugal Living For Dummies
  0-7645-5403-4
- Leadership For Dummies
  0-7645-5176-0
- Managing For Dummies
  0-7645-1771-6

- Marketing For Dummies
  0-7645-5600-2
- Personal Finance For Dummies *
  0-7645-2590-5
- Project Management For Dummies
  0-7645-5283-X
- Resumes For Dummies †
  0-7645-5471-9
- Selling For Dummies
  0-7645-5363-1
- Small Business Kit For Dummies *†
  0-7645-5093-4

OME & BUSINESS COMPUTER BASICS

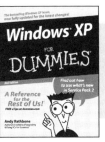

0-7645-4074-2

0-7645-3758-X

Also available:

- ACT! 6 For Dummies
  0-7645-2645-6
- iLife '04 All-in-One Desk Reference
  For Dummies
  0-7645-7347-0
- iPAQ For Dummies
  0-7645-6769-1
- Mac OS X Panther Timesaving
  Techniques For Dummies
  0-7645-5812-9
- Macs For Dummies
  0-7645-5656-8

- Microsoft Money 2004 For Dummies
  0-7645-4195-1
- Office 2003 All-in-One Desk Reference
  For Dummies
  0-7645-3883-7
- Outlook 2003 For Dummies
  0-7645-3759-8
- PCs For Dummies
  0-7645-4074-2
- TiVo For Dummies
  0-7645-6923-6
- Upgrading and Fixing PCs For Dummies
  0-7645-1665-5
- Windows XP Timesaving Techniques
  For Dummies
  0-7645-3748-2

OOD, HOME, GARDEN, HOBBIES, MUSIC & PETS

0-7645-5295-3

0-7645-5232-5

Also available:

- Bass Guitar For Dummies
  0-7645-2487-9
- Diabetes Cookbook For Dummies
  0-7645-5230-9
- Gardening For Dummies *
  0-7645-5130-2
- Guitar For Dummies
  0-7645-5106-X
- Holiday Decorating For Dummies
  0-7645-2570-0
- Home Improvement All-in-One
  For Dummies
  0-7645-5680-0

- Knitting For Dummies
  0-7645-5395-X
- Piano For Dummies
  0-7645-5105-1
- Puppies For Dummies
  0-7645-5255-4
- Scrapbooking For Dummies
  0-7645-7208-3
- Senior Dogs For Dummies
  0-7645-5818-8
- Singing For Dummies
  0-7645-2475-5
- 30-Minute Meals For Dummies
  0-7645-2589-1

NTERNET & DIGITAL MEDIA

0-7645-1664-7

0-7645-6924-4

Also available:

- 2005 Online Shopping Directory
  For Dummies
  0-7645-7495-7
- CD & DVD Recording For Dummies
  0-7645-5956-7
- eBay For Dummies
  0-7645-5654-1
- Fighting Spam For Dummies
  0-7645-5965-6
- Genealogy Online For Dummies
  0-7645-5964-8
- Google For Dummies
  0-7645-4420-9

- Home Recording For Musicians
  For Dummies
  0-7645-1634-5
- The Internet For Dummies
  0-7645-4173-0
- iPod & iTunes For Dummies
  0-7645-7772-7
- Preventing Identity Theft For Dummies
  0-7645-7336-5
- Pro Tools All-in-One Desk Reference
  For Dummies
  0-7645-5714-9
- Roxio Easy Media Creator For Dummies
  0-7645-7131-1

Separate Canadian edition also available
Separate U.K. edition also available

vailable wherever books are sold. For more information or to order direct: U.S. customers visit www.dummies.com or call 1-877-762-2974.
.K. customers visit www.wileyeurope.com or call 0800 243407. Canadian customers visit www.wiley.ca or call 1-800-567-4797.

SPORTS, FITNESS, PARENTING, RELIGION & SPIRITUALITY

0-7645-5146-9

0-7645-5418-2

Also available:
- Adoption For Dummies
  0-7645-5488-3
- Basketball For Dummies
  0-7645-5248-1
- The Bible For Dummies
  0-7645-5296-1
- Buddhism For Dummies
  0-7645-5359-3
- Catholicism For Dummies
  0-7645-5391-7
- Hockey For Dummies
  0-7645-5228-7

- Judaism For Dummies
  0-7645-5299-6
- Martial Arts For Dummies
  0-7645-5358-5
- Pilates For Dummies
  0-7645-5397-6
- Religion For Dummies
  0-7645-5264-3
- Teaching Kids to Read For Dummies
  0-7645-4043-2
- Weight Training For Dummies
  0-7645-5168-X
- Yoga For Dummies
  0-7645-5117-5

TRAVEL

0-7645-5438-7

0-7645-5453-0

Also available:
- Alaska For Dummies
  0-7645-1761-9
- Arizona For Dummies
  0-7645-6938-4
- Cancún and the Yucatán For Dummies
  0-7645-2437-2
- Cruise Vacations For Dummies
  0-7645-6941-4
- Europe For Dummies
  0-7645-5456-5
- Ireland For Dummies
  0-7645-5455-7

- Las Vegas For Dummies
  0-7645-5448-4
- London For Dummies
  0-7645-4277-X
- New York City For Dummies
  0-7645-6945-7
- Paris For Dummies
  0-7645-5494-8
- RV Vacations For Dummies
  0-7645-5443-3
- Walt Disney World & Orlando For Dummies
  0-7645-6943-0

GRAPHICS, DESIGN & WEB DEVELOPMENT

0-7645-4345-8

0-7645-5589-8

Also available:
- Adobe Acrobat 6 PDF For Dummies
  0-7645-3760-1
- Building a Web Site For Dummies
  0-7645-7144-3
- Dreamweaver MX 2004 For Dummies
  0-7645-4342-3
- FrontPage 2003 For Dummies
  0-7645-3882-9
- HTML 4 For Dummies
  0-7645-1995-6
- Illustrator CS For Dummies
  0-7645-4084-X

- Macromedia Flash MX 2004 For Dummies
  0-7645-4358-X
- Photoshop 7 All-in-One Desk
  Reference For Dummies
  0-7645-1667-1
- Photoshop CS Timesaving Techniques
  For Dummies
  0-7645-6782-9
- PHP 5 For Dummies
  0-7645-4166-8
- PowerPoint 2003 For Dummies
  0-7645-3908-6
- QuarkXPress 6 For Dummies
  0-7645-2593-X

NETWORKING, SECURITY, PROGRAMMING & DATABASES

0-7645-6852-3

0-7645-5784-X

Also available:
- A+ Certification For Dummies
  0-7645-4187-0
- Access 2003 All-in-One Desk
  Reference For Dummies
  0-7645-3988-4
- Beginning Programming For Dummies
  0-7645-4997-9
- C For Dummies
  0-7645-7068-4
- Firewalls For Dummies
  0-7645-4048-3
- Home Networking For Dummies
  0-7645-42796

- Network Security For Dummies
  0-7645-1679-5
- Networking For Dummies
  0-7645-1677-9
- TCP/IP For Dummies
  0-7645-1760-0
- VBA For Dummies
  0-7645-3989-2
- Wireless All In-One Desk Reference
  For Dummies
  0-7645-7496-5
- Wireless Home Networking For Dummies
  0-7645-3910-8

HEALTH & SELF-HELP

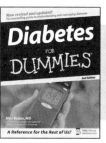

0-7645-6820-5 *†

0-7645-2566-2

Also available:
- Alzheimer's For Dummies
  0-7645-3899-3
- Asthma For Dummies
  0-7645-4233-8
- Controlling Cholesterol For Dummies
  0-7645-5440-9
- Depression For Dummies
  0-7645-3900-0
- Dieting For Dummies
  0-7645-4149-8
- Fertility For Dummies
  0-7645-2549-2

- Fibromyalgia For Dummies
  0-7645-5441-7
- Improving Your Memory For Dummies
  0-7645-5435-2
- Pregnancy For Dummies †
  0-7645-4483-7
- Quitting Smoking For Dummies
  0-7645-2629-4
- Relationships For Dummies
  0-7645-5384-4
- Thyroid For Dummies
  0-7645-5385-2

EDUCATION, HISTORY, REFERENCE & TEST PREPARATION

0-7645-5194-9

0-7645-4186-2

Also available:
- Algebra For Dummies
  0-7645-5325-9
- British History For Dummies
  0-7645-7021-8
- Calculus For Dummies
  0-7645-2498-4
- English Grammar For Dummies
  0-7645-5322-4
- Forensics For Dummies
  0-7645-5580-4
- The GMAT For Dummies
  0-7645-5251-1
- Inglés Para Dummies
  0-7645-5427-1

- Italian For Dummies
  0-7645-5196-5
- Latin For Dummies
  0-7645-5431-X
- Lewis & Clark For Dummies
  0-7645-2545-X
- Research Papers For Dummies
  0-7645-5426-3
- The SAT I For Dummies
  0-7645-7193-1
- Science Fair Projects For Dummies
  0-7645-5460-3
- U.S. History For Dummies
  0-7645-5249-X

Get smart @ dummies.com®

- **Find a full list of Dummies titles**
- **Look into loads of FREE on-site articles**
- **Sign up for FREE eTips e-mailed to you weekly**
- **See what other products carry the Dummies name**
- **Shop directly from the Dummies bookstore**
- **Enter to win new prizes every month!**

Separate Canadian edition also available
Separate U.K. edition also available

Available wherever books are sold. For more information or to order direct: U.S. customers visit www.dummies.com or call 1-877-762-2974.
U.K. customers visit www.wileyeurope.com or call 0800 243407. Canadian customers visit www.wiley.ca or call 1-800-567-4797.